Praise for City of the S

'[Parson] brilliantly conveys both the difficulty of working on the material and the excitement of the historical detective involved in the thrill of the chase'   William Dalrymple, *New Statesman*

'A wonderfully rich portrait of the people of Oxyrhynchos'
Sunday Times

'Parsons has entertainingly revived a noisy, gossiping world of migrant Greeks who lived through the decline of Rome and the rise of Christainity'   *The Times*

'A picture of life in the city in intimate detail, from the profound to the mundane'   *Herald*

'A learned and engrossing book'   *Daily Telegraph*

'Peter Parsons leads his readers on an adventure, peeling back the past and finding that the ancients were in many ways just like us'   *Good Book Guide*

'[A] captivating study'   *Catholic Herald*

'[Parsons] writes with tremendous verve and wit, and with memorable turns of phrase'   Mary Beard, *Times Literary Supplement*

Peter Parsons was lecturer in Papyrology at Oxford University from 1960 until 1989 and Regius Professor of Greek from 1989 until his retirement in 2003. He has been Fellow of the British Academy since 1977 and for many years he was head of the Oxyrhynchus Papyri Project. He has been fascinated by the decoding of ancient papyri for more than half a century. He lives in Oxford.

CITY OF THE
SHARP-NOSED FISH

Greek Papyri Beneath the Egyptian Sand
Reveal a Long-Lost World

PETER PARSONS

PHOENIX

A PHOENIX PAPERBACK

First published in Great Britain in 2007
by Weidenfeld & Nicolson
This paperback edition published in 2007
by Phoenix,
an imprint of Orion Books Ltd,
Orion House, 5 Upper Saint Martin's Lane,
London, WC2H 9EA

An Hachette Livre UK company

3 5 7 9 10 8 6 4 2

A CIP catalogue record for this book
is available from the British Library.

ISBN 978-0-7538-2233-3

Typeset by Input Data Services Ltd, Frome

Printed and bound in the UK by
CPI Mackays, Chatham ME5 8TD

The Orion Publishing Group's policy is to use papers that
are natural, renewable and recyclable products and
made from wood grown in sustainable forests. The logging
and manufacturing processes are expected to conform to
the environmental regulations of the country of origin.

www.orionbooks.co.uk

CONTENTS

ILLUSTRATIONS

Section One

1. *A Thousand Miles up the Nile*, 1890 edition (Smithsonian Institution Libraries, Washington, DC)
2. *The Hypaethral Temple at Philae* by David Roberts (Private Collection / Bridgeman Art Library, London)
3. The Egyptian Hall, Piccadilly (Mary Evans Picture Library)
4. The site of Oxyrhynchos: partial view by Denon, 1798
5. The site of Oxyrhynchos from the north-west, 1981 (photo by R.A. Coles)
6. Grenfell and Hunt (Egypt Exploration Society, London)
7. Excavation at Oxyrhynchos: digging the rubbish-mounds (Egypt Exploration Society, London)
8. Excavation at Oxyrhynchos: the workforce (Egypt Exploration Society, London)
9. The sacred oxyrhynchos fish (Michael C. Carlos Museum, Emory University, 1987.1)
10. The side-branch of the Nile at Oxyrhynchos, 1897 (Egypt Exploration Society, London)
11. 'Sayings of Our Lord', leaf from papyrus codex (P.Oxy.1 / Bodleian Library)
12. *A Reading from Homer* by Sir Lawrence Alma-Tadema (akg-images)

Section Two

13. Mummy portrait: 'The Nubian' (Ägyptisches Museum und Papyrussammlung, Staatliche Museen, Berlin. Photo by Georg Niedermeisser / bpk)
14. Mummy portrait: melancholy lady (British Museum EA 65346)
15. Mummy portrait: gilded youth (Ägyptisches Museum und Papyrussammlung, Staatliche Museen, Berlin. Photo by Georg Niedermeisser / bpk)

Section Three

TIMELINE

	THE WORLD OUTSIDE	EGYPT
c.2700 BC		Establishment of a centralised Egyptian state ('Old Kingdom') Capital at Memphis
c.1575–1087		Egyptian Empire at its height ('New Kingdom') Capital at Thebes
c.650		Greek merchants and mercenaries in Egypt Foundation of Naukratis as a Greek colony
550–530	Cyrus founds the Persian Empire	
525		Persians conquer Egypt
490, 480/79	Persian attacks on mainland Greece repelled	
334	Alexander III of Macedon ('the Great') attacks Persian Empire	
332/1		Alexander conquers Egypt Foundation of Alexandria Greek immigration
323	Death of Alexander	Alexander's general Ptolemy (I) becomes governor and then (305) King of Egypt
282–246		Ptolemy II Philadelphos Museum and Library of Alexandria
51		Cleopatra (VII)
30	Battle of Actium; suicide of Antony and Cleopatra	Egypt becomes a province of the Roman Empire
27 BC–AD 14	Augustus, the first Roman Emperor	

115–17		Jewish revolt in Egypt
130/1		The Emperor Hadrian tours Egypt His favourite, Antinoos, drowns in the Nile; foundation of Antinoopolis in his memory
c.165–c.180	Outbreaks of plague	Also in Egypt
172–175		Revolt of Boukoloi in Delta
199/200		The Emperor Septimius Severus and family visit Egypt Graeco-Egyptian cities allowed to set up town councils
212	The Emperor Caracalla grants Roman citizenship to all	Egyptian Greeks adopt the first name 'Aurelios' as sign of new status
215–6		Caracalla visits Egypt Massacre in Alexandria
226–651	Neo-Persian Empire	
244–9	The Emperor Philip the Arabian	General reform of the Egyptian administration
249–51	The Emperor Decius	Christians required to sign certificates of sacrifice
c.250–72/3	Palmyrene hegemony	
253–68	The Emperor Gallienus	Lollianos the public grammatikos
270–2		Egypt conquered by the Palmyrenes (Queen Zenobia), reconquered by the Emperor Aurelian
284–305	The Emperor Diocletian	General reform of Egypt, closer integration with the wider Empire
303–13	General persecution of Christians	
313	The Emperor Constantine issues his edict of toleration	
324	Constantine founds a new imperial capital at Constantinople	
391	The Emperor Theodosius I prohibits pagan cults and closes temples	Destruction of Great Serapeum of Alexandria
395	Final division of Roman Empire into East and West	

TIMELINE

619–28		Egypt under Persian rule
622	Hegira of the Prophet Muhammad	
639–42		Arab conquest of Egypt; Egypt a province of the Caliphate
968–1171		Fatimid Dynasty Egypt effectively independent Great flowering of Muslim culture Foundation of Cairo 969
1250–1805		Rule of the Mamluks (a military oligarchy of ex-slaves) in Egypt
1453	Ottoman Turks capture Constantinople (Istanbul)	
1517		Ottoman Turks conquer Egypt Egypt a province of the Ottoman Empire
1798–9		Napoleon's expedition to Egypt First systematic survey of Egyptian antiquities
1801		French forces in Egypt capitulate to the British Rosetta stone obtained for the British Museum
1805–1953		Regime of Muhammad Ali and his descendants
1822	Champollion publishes his decipherment of Egyptian hieroglyphic script	
1878	Cleopatra's Needle reaches London	
1882	Foundation of the Egypt Exploration Fund	British occupation of Egypt
1896/7–1906/7		Grenfell and Hunt excavate el-Behnesa (ancient Oxyrhynchos)

ROMAN EMPERORS

Roman emperors from Augustus to Constantine. Would-be emperors recognised for a time in Egypt are in italic. Brackets indicate emperors who ruled jointly.

Augustus	27 BC– AD 14		Pupienus	238
Tiberius	14–37		Balbinus	238
Caligula	37–41		Gordian III	238–44
Claudius	41–54		Philip the Arabian	244–9
Nero	54–68		Decius	249–51
Galba	68–9		Gallus	251–3
Otho	69		Aemilian	253
Vitellius	69		Valerian	253–60
Vespasian	69–79		Gallienus	253–68
Titus	79–81		*Macrianus*	*260–1*
Domitian	81–96		*Quietus*	*260–1*
Nerva	96–8		Claudius II	268–70
Trajan	98–117		Quintillus	270
Hadrian	117–38		Aurelian	270–5
Antoninus Pius	138–61		Vaballathus	270–2
Marcus Aurelius	161–80		Tacitus	275–6
Lucius Verus	161–9		Florianus	276
Avidius Cassius	*175*		Probus	276–82
Commodus	180–92		Carus	282–3
Pertinax	192–3		Carinus	283–5
Didius Julianus	193		Numerian	283–4
Septimius Severus	193–211		Diocletian	284–305
Pescennius Niger	*193–4*		Maximian	285–310
Caracalla	211–17		Constantius I	293–306
Geta	211		Galerius	293–311
Macrinus	217–18		*L. Domitius Domitianus*	*?296–7*
Elagabalus	218–22		*Aurelius Achilleus*	*?297–8*
Alexander Severus	222–35		Maximin	305–13
Maximin	235–8		Severus II	305–7
Gordian I and II	238		Maxentius	306–12
			Licinius	308–24
			Constantine I	306–37

For details see Dietmar Kienast, *Römische Kaisertabelle* (2nd edn, Darmstadt 1996).

EGYPTIAN MONTHS AND YEARS

Thôth (Sebastos)	29 August–27 September
Phaôphi	28 September–27 October
Hathyr	28 October–26 November
Choiak	27 November–26 December
Tybi	27 December–25 January
Mecheir	26 January–24 February
Phamenôth	25 February–26 March
Pharmouthi	27 March–25 April
Pachôn	26 April–25 May
Payni	26 May–24 June
Epeiph	25 June–24 July
Mesorê	25 July–23 August
Five 'additional days'	24–28 August

The Egyptian year (as reformed to suit the Julian calendar) consisted of twelve months of 30 days each, plus five 'additional days' at the end. In leap years there were six 'additional days', so that Thôth 1 = 30 August, and all Julian dates were pushed forward one day until the Julian intercalary day 29 February brought them back into step. Phamenôth 5 always = 1 March.

'Year 1' of a king or emperor's reign lasted from his accession until the end of the current Egyptian year. 'Year 2' began on the next Thôth 1.

NOTE ON SOURCES

This book draws its material largely from published Greek papyri. The principal relevant publication is the series *The Oxyrhynchus Papyri*, vols. I–LXX (London 1898–2006). Documents published there are referred to simply by volume and item-number, for example '42.3052' = *The Oxyrhynchus Papyri*, vol. XLII, no. 3052. Within any one text, line-numbers are indicated in Arabic numerals (42.3074.2 = vol. XLII, no. 3074, line 2) and column-numbers (where necessary) in Roman numerals (2.237 vii 20 = vol. II, no. 237, column 7, line 20).

For a key to other publications of papyri, see *Bibliography*, p. 217.

The translations of documents and literary sources quoted in this book are my own except where otherwise indicated.

Within translated documents, italic type in square brackets indicates words restored by editors in spaces where the papyrus is damaged, and italic type in angle brackets indicates words inserted by editors to correct an omission by the original scribe.

In transliterations of Greek words, ê and ô represent the Greek long vowels eta and omega. In spelling the names of ancient people and places, I have been inconsistent: most Greek names appear with their Greek termination, for example Isidoros not Isidorus, but names widely familiar in their Latin form retain that form, thus Herodotus (not Herodotos), Strabo (not Strabôn).

GLOSSARY

agora	the marketplace
amphodon	'quarter', administrative subdivision of a city
archidikastês	Roman official, 'Chief Justice'
aroura	basic unit of land-area (0.68 acres)
artaba	basic measure of capacity (standard *artaba* = about 8½ gallons or 1 bushel)
attikê	'Attic drachma', Greek name for *denarius*
basilikos grammateus	'royal scribe', deputy to the *strategos*
boulê	town council
choinix	measure of capacity (40 or 48 choinikes make 1 *artaba*)
chômatikon	tax for maintenance of dikes
chôra	'the country', i.e. Egypt excluding Alexandria
chous	liquid measure of variable content (for wine, perhaps 3 pints)
comarch	head of administration in each village
conventus (Latin)	travelling assizes conducted by the Prefect
dekaprôtoi	ten-man commission which took over the work of the *sitologoi*
denarius (Latin)	standard Roman silver coin, equivalent to a *tetradrachm*
dioikêtês	Roman head of the financial administration
drachma	unit of money and weight; as currency, normally circulating in the form of 4-drachma pieces (*tetradrachms*)
ephebe	boy who (from age fourteen) qualifies to belong to the *gymnasium*
epistratêgos	Roman governor of one of the three or four main divisions of Egypt
eutheniarch	city official in charge of food supply
exêgêtês	city official (literally 'interpreter')
Fayûm (Arabic)	fertile and heavily populated depression between the Nile and the Western Desert (ancient name 'Arsinoite Nome')
fellahin (Arabic)	traditional name for Egyptian peasants

grammatikos	teacher of literature
gymnasiarch	city official in charge of the *gymnasium*
gymnasium	club, gym and perhaps school for town elite
hierophant	'revealer of the holy', a kind of priest
idios logos	'privy purse', Roman official in charge of imperial property
kotyle	liquid measure of variable content (for wine, perhaps half a pint)
liturgy	temporary compulsory administrative duty owed to state
logistês	from the fourth century AD, the main administrator of a *nome*
mêtropolis	capital city of a *nome*
mina	unit of money and weight (100 *drachmas*)
naubion	measure of capacity (27 cubic cubits) used to quantify earth to be moved in building up dikes and dredging canals
nome	'county', one of the forty-odd regional divisions which represent the basic administrative units of Egypt
obol	unit of money (1 *tetradrachm* = 24 obols, but often for accounting purposes 28 or 29 obols)
ostrakon	piece of broken pot used as writing material
paidagôgos	slave who escorts a boy to and from school
paktôn	a light (wicker) boat
polis	'city', notionally self-governing, on the classical Greek model
Prefect	the imperial viceroy of Egypt
prytanis	'mayor', president of the town council (*boulê*)
rationalis (Latin)	'accountant', a high Roman official
rhêtôr	'speaker', teacher of rhetoric
saqia (Arabic)	water-wheel
shaduf (Arabic)	counterweighted device for lifting water
sitologos	official in charge of collecting and transporting the tax-grain
sophist	intellectual (often itinerant) who specialised in public declamation
stratêgos	governor of a *nome*
syndikos	(in the fourth century AD) imperial official involved in the admininstration of the city (Latin *defensor civitatis*)
systatês	official in charge of record-keeping and liturgical nominations in one of the quarters of the city
talent	unit of money and weight = 6000 drachmas
tetradrachm	'silver' (but in fact billon) coin of 4 drachmas

GLOSSARY

Thebaid	'Upper Egypt', the southern part of the country with its capital at Thebes
toparch	official in charge of a *toparchy*
toparchy	administrative subdivision of a *nome*

PREFACE

This book began, in a way, fifty-five years ago, when as a schoolboy I became fascinated with the strange symbols of the ancient Greek alphabet, and discovered that, with some grammar and a dictionary, it was possible to make sense of the high poetry encoded in these symbols. When I went on to follow the traditional classical course at Oxford, I found that the corpus of Greek texts was not in fact static. Works long lost were being reconstructed, in fragments, from papyri – above all, by the austere genius of the legendary papyrologist Edgar Lobel, from the great collection of papyri excavated at the ancient city of Oxyrhynchos in Egypt. In 1958, after my final examinations, I approached the then Professor of Greek, E. R. Dodds, for advice: if I was to undertake postgraduate work, what areas might be most profitable? He replied (in those unregimented days) that anything was possible; but that in the Oxford context two areas particularly needed research and the teaching that might follow from it, Papyrology and Greek Religion. I thought, rightly, that Greek religion would require more subtlety and imagination than I possessed; papyrology, on the other hand, depended in the most concrete way on the process of decoding from which I had started.

I had enthusiasm but no knowledge, and so I went to learn the elements of the trade. First, in Oxford, I had the good fortune to be taught by the Revd Dr John Barns. He was a genial and eccentric figure, who straightened papyri by sitting on them and halfway through our sessions would produce a bottle of Guinness and drink it ('Sorry I haven't got one for you, old man'). He was also a scholar of exceptional learning (he knew Egyptian as well as Greek) and broad interests, and under his supervision my vision widened from the familiar literary texts to a whole new world of everyday documents. For the sake of the documents, I moved on to the University of Michigan at Ann Arbor, to study with Professor Herbert C. Youtie, the world leader in the field. To him and his wife Louise (also a papyrologist) I owe a year of kindness (including the gift of ear-muffs against the bitter Michigan winter) and a paradigm of scholarship conducted in the spirit of international amity and collaboration. Youtie understood the documentary language as few others, and his intuitive gift enabled him to decipher the most illegible script and also to detect errors in the decipherments of others: I remember how he would read through newly published texts, questing like a bloodhound, and then a sudden 'Hah' showed that he had found a mistake and imagined the correction required. He made himself the arbiter of the subject, but without any arrogance: 'We all stand on one another's shoulders', he would say.

When I returned to Oxford in 1960 I found myself teaching documentary papyrology and deciphering unpublished papyri from the Oxyrhynchos collection. This research was by then (as it remains) a team effort, under the direction of Eric Turner, Professor of Papyrology at University College London, whose organising genius gave the enterprise a more formal shape, along with institutional premises (in the Ashmolean Museum, Oxford) and the funds (from the British Academy) to appoint a curator of the rehoused collection and to carry through the first systematic cataloguing. In Oxford I had the privilege of working alongside two colleagues of extraordinary accomplishment, John Rea and Revel Coles. The Egypt Exploration Society, which had funded the original excavation, continued (and continues) to publish our results in yearly volumes of *The Oxyrhynchus Papyri*.

The pleasures of the project have been threefold. First, there is the pleasure of the chase: open a box of unpublished papyri, and you never know what you will find — high poetry and vulgar farce, sales and loans, wills and contracts, tax returns and government orders, private letters, shopping lists and household accounts. Then, there is the pleasure of comprehension: as you decipher the ink, still black after two thousand years, you begin to make words out of letters and then sentences out of words; the eye looks for shapes, and the mind looks for sense, and the two in alliance will (all being well) turn a string of symbols into intelligible text. Thirdly, your new text finds its place within larger structures. A fragment of Greek Comedy may add a new scene to a play already known from other fragments; an edict of the governor of Egypt may join other documents to hint at reform and politics; the lease of a vineyard will contribute evidence about price-inflation and consumer preference. Throughout the process, the researcher becomes aware of a unity. Every fragment of every kind in every box belongs in one historical and geographical context - the reading, writing and working citizens of Oxyrhynchos, the City of the Sharp-nosed Fish.

The work of publishing the papyri reached its centenary in 1998. I wrote a piece about it in *TLS* of 29 May 1998, and on this basis Toby Mundy commissioned the present book. His encouragement got it going; but progress was slow. As a step on the way I contributed the material for four programmes on BBC Radio 4, broadcast in May 2002, with readings by Michael Kustow: it was a great pleasure to work with the producer, Amanda Hargreaves of BBC Scotland. Still progress was slow, and it has taken all the bracing diplomacy of my long-suffering editor, Benjamin Buchan, master of the carrot and the stick, to bring the book to a conclusion. I am most grateful to all the midwives who have helped to induce delivery.

This was to be a book in which I shared my enthusiasm with the general reader. Its purpose is simply to illustrate some aspects of life in Oxyrhynchos, a Greek city in Egypt under Roman rule, from the original documents. Professional colleagues will find it sadly lacking in many aspects. It cuts corners, when it comes to technical problems; the translations of documents (my own) often choose one alternative, when other scholars have understood the text differently. It is Greek-centred, since it draws entirely on Greek documents, and male-centred, since such was the society it describes. It focuses on the initial period of Roman rule (from the first to the mid-fourth century AD), though it brings in earlier and later evidence for phenomena which represent continuing features of the landscape, but within that period overemphasises continuity against change. There will be many simple mistakes, and many failures to incorporate the latest scholarship. There would be many more but for the expert friends who so kindly read portions of the book in typescript: Revel Coles, Nick Gonis and David Thomas.

Readers who look for something less anecdotal will find an up-to-date survey, by a cohort of professionals, in the symposium *Oxyrhynchus: a City and its Texts*, edited by A. K. Bowman and others (London, forthcoming, 2007); more basic information, and images of the papyri themselves, on the web site *Oxyrhynchus Online*. Alan Bowman, *Egypt after the Pharaohs* (2nd edn, London, 1996), and Roger S. Bagnall, *Egypt in Late Antiquity* (Princeton, 1993), provide magisterial overviews of Greek Egypt; Richard Alston, *The City in Roman and Byzantine Egypt* (London and New York, 2002) offers rich resources of fact and argument. Even the most banal documents can, in expert hands, contribute powerfully to social and economic history; see for example Dominic Rathbone,

Economic Rationalism and Rural Society in Third-century AD Egypt (Cambridge, 1991), and Jane Rowlandson, *Landowners and Tenants in Roman Egypt* (Oxford, 1996).

Barbara Macleod encouraged the writing of this book, even in her last illness, and it is dedicated to her memory. Her friends found in her an unfailing pleasure of intelligence and vitality, affectionate empathy and practical unshowy kindness: a brave heart and a gentle hand.

Peter Parsons
Oxford
September 2006

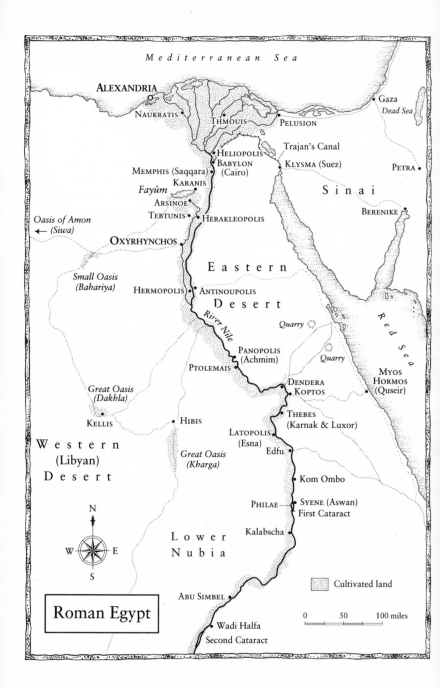

Mediterranean Sea

ALEXANDRIA

NAUKRATIS

THMOUIS

Gaza
Dead Sea

PELUSION

PETRA

Trajan's Canal

HELIOPOLIS
KLYSMA (Suez)

MEMPHIS (Saqqara)
BABYLON
(Cairo)

KARANIS

Sinai

Fayûm
ARSINOE

BERENIKE

TEBTUNIS

Oasis of Amon
(Siwa)

HERAKLEOPOLIS

OXYRHYNCHOS

Eastern

Small Oasis
(Bahariya)

HERMOPOLIS
ANTINOUPOLIS

Desert

River Nile

Quarry

Red Sea

PANOPOLIS
(Achmim)

Quarry

PTOLEMAIS

Great Oasis
(Dakhla)

DENDERA
KOPTOS

MYOS
HORMOS
(Quseir)

KELLIS

HIBIS

THEBES
(Karnak & Luxor)

LATOPOLIS
(Esna)

Western
(Libyan)
Desert

Great Oasis
(Kharga)

Edfu

Kom Ombo

PHILAE
SYENE (Aswan)
First Cataract

Kalabscha

N

W   E

S

Lower
Nubia

Cultivated land

ABU SIMBEL

0   50   100 miles

Roman Egypt

Wadi Halfa
Second Cataract

PROLOGUE

The Spanish-American War looked nearly over, the Dreyfus case had taken another turn, the Prince of Wales's knee had been treated with 'the X rays', Rugby and Marlborough had drawn at Lord's. *The Times* of 29 July 1898 noted these facts; it noted also, under 'Books of the Week', the publication of *The Oxyrhynchus Papyri*, Part One. From this austere grey volume, the reviewer singled out 'The Sayings of Jesus', one leaf from a totally unknown Gospel; and a tattered poem in which Sappho prays for her brother's safe return – a poem not seen by human eyes since the fall of Rome. These papyri had turned up a year earlier, at a Greek site in Egypt, not from houses or offices, but from the sand-covered rubbish-dumps which circled the city. Two young excavators from Oxford, B. P. Grenfell and A. S. Hunt, had found, mixed with debris in accumulations 30 feet deep, the entire life of a town encapsulated in its waste paper.

CHAPTER I

EXCAVATING EGYPT

• • • •

Twenty years earlier, on 13 September 1878, *The Times* had reported on a more public event. Egypt had come to town, in monolithic form. Originally, the monument, 180 tons of red granite, had stood in Egyptian Heliopolis, a dedication by Pharaoh Tuthmosis III (*c.*1475 BC); then in the new Greek capital of Alexandria, set up by the Roman conquerors of Egypt. In Alexandria it remained until 1819, when the Turkish viceroy of Egypt, Muhammad Ali, presented it to the British nation, a reward for their services in the Napoleonic Wars. There it continued to remain, half-buried in sand, for the British government had no mind to fund its transport. Finally, in 1877, the eminent surgeon Erasmus Wilson put up the money: £10,000, a small fortune in Victorian terms. The engineer John Dixon undertook transport and installation. He built a wrought-iron cylindrical pontoon, 92 feet long and 15 feet in diameter, to encase the obelisk, and in this it was towed out to sea for the voyage to London. A stormy voyage: the cylinder capsized in the Bay of Biscay and floated free until a Glasgow steamer salvaged it. Eventually, in January 1878, the obelisk moored near the Houses of Parliament. In September it was duly installed on the Victoria Embankment, to be known, then and now, as Cleopatra's Needle. A plaque on the plinth commends the 'patriotic zeal' of Wilson. It was a noble and indeed imperial gesture: just so the emperors and popes of Rome had adorned their capital with obelisks.

The history of the Needle – a history of institutional indifference and private initiative – parallels the history of British Egyptology in the nineteenth century.

For the eighteenth century, Egypt had existed largely in the imagination, and mostly an imagination fed by Greek and Latin sources. The Egypt of Plato, fountain of age-old wisdom, subsisted in the mysteries of adepts and Hermetics and freemasons; so it is that *The Magic Flute* combines masonic ritual and Egyptian décor. The Egypt of the Romans could be seen in the wall-paintings of the grand villas of Pompeii, the buried town rediscovered in 1748, and from there egyptianising motifs spread to the north. Wandering objects, mummies and scarabs, came into the hands of antiquarians; powdered mummy still featured in medical textbooks as a powerful drug, expensively imported from Egypt (cynics doubted whether these were ancient mummies, or the cheaper substitute of executed criminals, the bodies treated with spices and bitumen and then baked to friability).

At the same time there were also real travellers: Egypt attracted noblemen, antiquarians and pillagers from all over Europe, English among them. There was a curiosity to see, and curiosities to collect. Already in 1711 the essayist Joseph Addison had satirised the country squire, who sums up his journey thus: 'having read the Controversies of some great Men concerning the Antiquities of *Egypt*, I made a voyage to *Grand Cairo*, on purpose to take the Measure of a Pyramid; and as soon as I had set myself right in that Particular, returned to my Native Country with great Satisfaction'.[1] The cultured and persistent Lord Charlemont made the journey in 1747, only to attract the scorn of Dr Johnson: 'What did Lord Charlemont learn in his travels, except that there was a snake in one of the pyramids of Egypt?'

The door was ajar; it took Napoleon to kick it in. When he landed in Egypt in July 1798, he brought an army of soldiers and a platoon (167 persons) of scholars and artists. While the army took over the country from the decaying military that controlled it, nominally as a province of the Turkish Sultan, the savants systematically surveyed and drew the monuments. In its political intention, to attack by the back-door the British Empire in India, the expedition failed; naval defeat cut off the invaders from home, Napoleon left Egypt in August 1799 to organise his *coup d'état*, his troops were eventually defeated and repatriated in 1801, and Egypt returned to the authority of the Sultan and his viceroy. Culturally, however, it was a watershed. The splendid volumes of the *Description de l'Egypte*, published between 1809 and 1826, laid the foundations of scientific Egyptology.

The British won the war, but in Egypt, at least, the French continued to dominate. An enterprising Albanian tobacco-merchant, Muhammad

Ali, made himself so powerful that the Sultan was compelled to appoint him viceroy in 1805. He and his descendants ruled, as khedives and then as kings, until 1953. Theirs was a regime of sporadic westernisation, basically on the French model. Characteristically, when France was given its own obelisk in 1829, the authorities took only four years to remove it to Paris and erect it in the Place de la Concorde. Thus it was a French engineer who built the Suez Canal (opened in 1869), French bankers who, along with their British rivals, lent money to the bankrupt khedives, and France, along with Britain, that in 1876 established a condominium over Egypt to guarantee repayment of those loans. The British government continued to fret, even after 1875, when it bought the controlling interest in the all-important canal. The heavy presence of the colonial powers created a nationalist opposition, and the khedives came to rely on those powers to protect themselves. In the event, it was the British army that defeated the rebellion at the battle of Tel el-Kebir (1882). In the event a series of British 'residents and consuls-general' governed the country from 1883, and even after the end of the British 'protectorate' in 1922, the British remained heavily involved in the government.

On the intellectual side, too, it had been the French who made the running. Whatever the turns of politics, the exploration of ancient Egypt remained largely their preserve for the century after Napoleon. It was a Frenchman who deciphered the hieroglyphic script and a Frenchman who initiated and organised the systematic excavation of material remains.

'Hieroglyphs' was their Greek name, but the Greeks had preserved no real knowledge of their function. 'Horapollo', an author or pseudo-author of the fourth century AD, had left an account which combined a few nuggets of truth with the false premise that each little picture could be explained symbolically – a premise that appealed to mystics, but sent all too many later decipherers in the wrong direction. The key was buried until 1799, when Napoleon's men, digging foundations for a fort, unearthed it; as the 'Rosetta Stone' it passed to the British Museum, one of the spoils of war. The Stone contains three sections, one in Greek and two in Egyptian (one in the more formal hieroglyphs, one in the more cursive demotic script). Assuming that all three sections present the same text, the intelligible Greek would give a clue to the unintelligible Egyptian. The English doctor and physicist Thomas Young (inventor of the wave theory of light) took up the problem in 1814 and showed how the Greek royal name Ptolemaios was spelt out in Egyptian hieroglyphs. But the real breakthrough came in France, on 29 September 1822, when Jean-François Champollion read his *Lettre à M. Dacier* to the savants of the Academy of Inscriptions. Champollion was able to show that the hieroglyphic script was predominantly phonetic, most signs representing a letter or syllable, and that the language it transmitted was (as had been suspected) the same as the language of contemporary Egyptian Christians, now called Coptic. At last the code was broken, and from 1822 the world would read with increasing fluency the inscriptions and the papyri of Egypt, even as opportunism and then archaeology recovered them.

Such recovery was in full swing. In parallel with the struggle for political influence went the jostles of cultural imperialism. There were the great museums of the colonial powers to fill: the British Museum, the Louvre, the Aegyptisches Museum in Berlin. Napoleon's expedition had opened Egypt; the regime of Muhammad Ali followed suit, and in the first part of the nineteenth century the country was prey to plunderers of every kind – dealers, noblemen on their travels, tomb-robbers native and foreign. It was an age of freebooting. The Italian adventurer Belzoni used a battering ram to enter the tomb of one pharaoh; in 1836 the English soldier Colonel R. H. Howard Vyse penetrated new chambers in the Great Pyramid and its smaller neighbours – in part by the use of dynamite. Diplomats collected antiquities and organised digs – the French consul-general, Drovetti, the British consul-general, Henry Salt, the Swedish-Norwegian Giovanni d'Anastasi. Many objects and papyri thus discovered were sold to the museums of the West – Drovetti's collections to Turin, Anastasi's in part to Leiden, Salt's and more of Anastasi's to the British Museum. There curators studied and catalogued them without thought of excavating themselves.

All this haphazard energy and treasure-hunting left monuments damaged and archaeological finds without context. That made all the more vital the two great scholarly surveys of the period. The expedition of Champollion and Rosellini was cut short by Champollion's early death in 1832; but the results, *Monumenti dell'Egitto e della Nubia*, were published by Rosellini in Florence between 1832 and 1840. The expedition of Carl Richard Lepsius, sent in 1842 by the King of Prussia to record the monuments of Egypt, produced a report in thirteen volumes, published in 1849, which remains a standard work of reference.

The tide began to turn in 1850, when there arrived in Egypt a young assistant curator from the Louvre, Auguste Mariette. Finally, in 1858, the Khedive was induced to appoint Mariette as Director of Excavations. With Mariette began systematic archaeology in Egypt; it was Mariette who conceived the Cairo Museum, so that Egyptian antiquities should have an Egyptian home. Mariette alone had the right to excavate, and the export of antiquities was made illegal. Illicit digging and trading of course continued, and the French monopoly was resented, but it was a first step away from the epoch of plunder.

Britain, meanwhile, conceived no such grand projects. Ancient Egypt was not yet an enterprise, although it was, from time to time, a fashion. Thus, war or no war, the French Egyptomania inspired by Napoleon spread across the Channel. 'Everything now must be Egyptian,' wrote the poet Robert Southey in 1807, 'the ladies wear crocodile ornaments, and you sit upon a sphinx in a room hung round with mummies, and with long black lean-armed long-nosed hieroglyphical men, who are enough to make the children afraid to go to bed. The very shopboards must be metamorphosed into the mode, and painted in Egyptian letters, which, as the Egyptians had no letters, you will doubtless conceive must be curious. They are simply the common characters, deprived of all beauty and all proportion by having all the strokes of equal thickness, so that those who should be thin look as if they had elephantiasis.' Five years later, in Maria Edgeworth's novel *The Absentee*, Mr Soho the interior decorator needs to warn his socially aspiring patron, Lady Clonbrony, against hieroglyphic wallpaper, as yesterday's choice – 'one sees it everywhere – quite antediluvian – gone to the hotels even . . .'[2] Interest continued in Egyptian art and Egyptian scenery. Scholar-artists of the 1820s and 1830s produced facsimiles (many never published) of Egyptian reliefs and wall-paintings, a valuable record of much that has since vanished; the most famous, John Gardner Wilkinson, used his own drawings to illustrate his *Manners and Customs of the Ancient Egyptians* (1837). A little later, the watercolourist David Roberts made his trips to Egypt (1838) and the Holy Land (1839); his paintings became familiar to a wide audience when published as hand-coloured lithographs in the 1840s. The general public could go to exhibitions and freak-shows at the Egyptian Hall, built in Piccadilly in 1812 on the model (so it was alleged) of the Temple of Dendera. When they flocked to the Great Exhibition of 1851, they found a visual history of art and architecture beginning with the Egyptian Court.

The learned world meanwhile continued its researches. No university had a post in Egyptology, but at the British Museum the pioneer Samuel Birch reorganised and catalogued the Egyptian collections, some 10,000 items. In 1838 he produced the first part of his *Sketch of a Hieroglyphical Dictionary*, which already exploited and extended the work of Champollion. In the wider world of letters, papers to the Royal Society of Literature included Egyptological subjects; among the attenders was the Prussian ambassador, Baron von Bunsen, then writing his five-volume work, *Egypt's Place in Universal History* (the English translation published in 1848–67). Birch did much to publicise the texts and monuments now being deciphered: so in his selection of Egyptian literature, *Archaic Classics* (1877), and his *Ancient History from the Monuments. Egypt from the Earliest Times to B.C. 300* (1883). Yet he never went to Egypt; his contribution was as cataloguer, decipherer and publicist. Apart from Colonel Howard Vyse, no Englishman had been involved in exploring the monuments of Egypt on the ground; and the idea of systematic excavation would come as a novelty. In all this there were two material factors: under Mariette's regime no foreign excavation seemed possible; and under his new law, no object excavated in Egypt could be exported – a prime disincentive to an aspiring museum.

With the Needle, Egypt again made the news. Its arrival coincided with a new and active interest in the monuments of pharaonic civilisation, and more. Politically, Egypt – the essential link between England and India, after the opening of the Suez Canal in 1869 – remained a focus of attention. Romantically, Egypt still connoted grandeur in ruins; every reader of Palgrave's *Golden Treasury* knew Shelley's sonnet on the fallen colossus – 'My name is Ozymandias, king of kings: Look on my works, ye mighty, and despair!' But Egypt fitted too with other late Victorian preoccupations. Egypt belonged also to the classical world: the topsy-turvy Egypt described by the Greek historian Herodotus, the Egypt of antique mysteries described by the Greek philosopher Plato. It belonged no less to the Christian world, as the home of famous martyrs, heretics and patriarchs, and also to the scriptural world which lay behind Christianity – this was the land of Joseph and the Jewish captivity, of Mary and Joseph's flight into Egypt. Mesopotamia had yielded, from clay tablets excavated at Nineveh and published in 1876, copies of Babylonian creation-myths that bore an extraordinary similarity to the Book of Genesis: what might Egypt contribute to confirm (or undermine) the historicity of the Bible?

The time was ripe for an initiative. In 1881 Mariette died, and his successor as Director of Antiquities to the Egyptian government, Gaston Maspéro, had more liberal notions. If a British expedition could be mounted, he would grant the required permission. But how to fund a British expedition? The French, German and Italian governments had financed missions, noted Sir Erasmus Wilson, but no such thing could be expected of the British government; for the honour of England 'it is earnestly to be desired that private enterprise should do something towards vindicating our rational aim to a place among the scholars and Archaeologists of Europe'.[3]

In the event, it took the happy collaboration of a publicist, Amelia Edwards, and a scholar, Reginald Stuart Poole of the British Museum.

Poole's primary interest lay in numismatics. As Keeper of Coins in the Museum since 1870, he had organised and participated in the cataloguing of the vast collection, especially the ancient Greek coins. Nonetheless he had Egyptian interests, having lived in Egypt between the ages of ten and seventeen, under the guardianship of his uncle, the arabist Edward William Lane. His enthusiasm made a contrast with the attitude of the Museum's veteran Egyptologist, Samuel Birch, who had no time for a project that he thought unlikely to benefit his collections. In the background, perhaps, were divided priorities: philologists put the emphasis on conserving and interpreting older finds, archaeologists on new digging and new discoveries. The division is serious and continuing. 'Candour', wrote the great philologist Sir Alan Gardiner in 1961, 'obliges us to add that there has been, and still is, far too much excavation, especially when left unpublished or published badly . . .'[4]

Amelia Edwards had made a most successful career as novelist, journalist, traveller and travel-writer. Her novel of bigamy, *Barbara's History* (1864), had established her public; *Lord Brackenbury* (1880) would reach fifteen editions. Her *Untrodden Peaks and Unfrequented Valleys* (1873) introduced the Dolomites to a new readership. In the autumn of 1873, escaping from a rainy holiday in France, she set out for Egypt and travelled by houseboat the full length of the country, as far south as the great rock-cut temple of Abu Simbel. On her return she described her experiences in *A Thousand Miles up the Nile*, which became a bestseller. It fuelled the popular enthusiasm for Egypt. It lamented also the neglect, decay and pillaging of Egyptian monuments:

The wall-paintings which we had the happiness of admiring in all their beauty and freshness, are already much injured. Such is the fate of every Egyptian monument, great or small. The tourist carves it all over with names and dates, and in some instances with caricatures. The student of Egyptology, by taking wet paper 'squeezes', sponges away every vestige of the original colour. The 'collector' buys and carries off everything of value that he can get; and the Arab steals for him. The work of destruction, meanwhile, goes on apace. There is no one to prevent it; there is no one to discourage it. Every day, more inscriptions are mutilated – more paintings and sculptures are defaced . . . When science leads the way, is it wonderful that ignorance should follow?[5]

Not only was there much to see; there was much to rescue before it was too late.

Consultations began, and sponsors were sought. The Archbishop of Canterbury and the Chief Rabbi expressed support; so, among others, did the poet Robert Browning and Sir Henry Layard, the discoverer of Nineveh. Finally, in April 1882, there emerged a new society, whose Joint Honorary Secretaries were Poole and Amelia Edwards: the Egypt Exploration Fund, then and now (as the Egypt Exploration Society) the chief organiser of British Archaeology in Egypt. A leaflet publicised its aims and invited subscribers: 'A Society has been formed for the purpose of cooperating with Professor Maspéro, Director of Museums and Excavations in Egypt, in his work of exploration. The Society under-takes to conduct excavations especially on sites of biblical and classical interest, without infringing the Egyptian law, by which objects found are claimed for the Boolak [Cairo] Museum.' The immediate object was to raise funds for an archaeological expedition. The site in mind lay in the Nile Delta, the site of the biblical Land of Goshen.

Funds gathered and permissions obtained, the new Fund had one last striking difficulty: to find an excavator, so little experience had the British. Its first season was indeed conducted by the French Egyptologist Naville, after an interval during which Arabi's forces were defeated at the battle of Tel el-Kebir. He carried out his commission by digging what he identified as the biblical city of Pithom, one of the two 'treasure cities' which (according to the Book of Exodus) the enslaved Children of Israel built for Pharaoh. For a second season, he asked for a young British scholar to train. The choice fell on W. M. Flinders Petrie. Before too long Petrie went his own way, the EEF another, both enterprises heavily dependent on the subscriptions of individual enthusiasts. The world was changing. A modification of the Egyptian law allowed new finds to be divided between the excavator and the Cairo Museum. That encouraged both archaeologists and their subscribers. From now on there would be no shortage of British excavators, and excavators with professional training, as Egyptology took root in the universities. In 1892 Petrie himself was appointed Professor of Egyptology at University College London, the chair funded by a legacy from Amelia Edwards, anxious to the end for the subject she had done so much to promote. This was the very first post in this subject in the United Kingdom, but by no means the last.

Most Egyptologists had a special interest in pharaonic Egypt, but the original idea of 'classical and biblical sites' was not forgotten. Indeed, chance finds of Greek papyri from Egypt continued to show what serious excavation might achieve. On 1 July 1897 the EEF set up a special branch, the Graeco-Roman Research Account, 'for the discovery and publication of the remains of classical antiquity and early Christianity in Egypt'. It was this mission that attracted two young scholars from Oxford, B. P. Grenfell and A. S. Hunt, and it was Grenfell and Hunt who rediscovered, in the unpromising mounds round the village of el-Behnesa, the City of the Sharp-nosed Fish.

CHAPTER 2

A WEALTH OF GARBAGE

• • • •

The modern tourist who visits the village of el-Behnesa, a hundred miles south of Cairo and ten miles west of the Nile, will find very little left of the ancient town. Nothing shows to the eye, except one standing column. The walls, the baths, the theatre, the colonnades and porticoes of what its inhabitants referred to as the Glorious and Most Glorious City have perished or been recycled. Ancient Oxyrhynchos has a long history, traceable from the high days of the Egyptian New Kingdom through successive conquests Greek and Roman. In early medieval days it boasted a bishop, thirty churches and (according to report) 10,000 monks and 20,000 nuns, and the remains of the Christian cemetery show the size and wealth of the population. The Arab conquest of Egypt in AD 642 did not end it. Arabic documents from the site illustrate the new order, which (with a change of supremacy) was not so much unlike the old. The city remained important; in AD 917 it was producing gold brocade curtains for the Palace of the Caliphs in Baghdad.[1] Why it declined we do not know. But it seems clear that, at least from the thirteenth century, during the military regime of the Mamluks, the city began to dwindle into a village.

Certainly, by 1798, there was nothing to impress. The savants and artists of Napoleon's expedition to Egypt surveyed and depicted its antiquities in splendid detail, but from ancient Oxyrhynchos they recorded nothing, just one ancient column set off by the palm trees and a minaret of the modern village. The explanation is simple: nothing remained on the surface. It took another century of experience to show what might lie below the surface of such a site, and especially within the low hills which represented the rubbish-dumps of ancient settlements.

Accidental finds made by farmers digging out the fertile earth (*sebbakh*) which remained, and by the trial excavations of foreign archaeologists, showed that the dry climate and drifting sands of southern Egypt could preserve contemporary written records whose material, a 'paper' manufactured from the papyrus reed, would have perished on the wetter sites of classical Greece or Italy; and that many such documents belonged, not to the older Egypt of the pharaohs, but to the millennium when, between Alexander the Great and the Arab conquest, Egypt was colonised and governed by Greek immigrants and their descendants. In that period, first as an independent kingdom and then (after the death of Cleopatra) as a Roman province and then (when the capital moved to Constantinople) as a province of the Byzantine Empire, Egypt went about its usual business, but in Greek and sometimes in Latin, under the control of a ruling class who saw themselves as part of the Hellenic diaspora.

The written rubbish that they left behind included two categories of text which had special importance for Victorian scholars: fragments of classical Greek literature, especially of works otherwise lost in the great destruction of the Middle Ages; and fragments of early Christian literature, especially of works eventually purged from the orthodox canon. Accidental finds from Egypt had reached the antiquities market: so the British Museum acquired the only surviving copies of three Greek classics then known only from quotations in ancient sources – the *Athenian Constitution* by Aristotle (1889), the *Mimiambs* of Herodas (1889) and the *Odes* of Bacchylides (1896). The Egyptian sands were now supplying what the watery sites of Greece and Italy had destroyed: books and papers that had been in the hands of the contemporaries of Callimachus and Plutarch and St Athanasius.

Accident prompted a new initiative: systematic excavation with the recovery of papyri directly in mind. In London the Egypt Exploration Fund took note, and agreed in 1896 to devote 'some fixed share of their energies and income to the recovery of classical papyri and the prosecution of Greek archaeology in Egypt'. The excavators were B. P. Grenfell and A. S. Hunt. The site they chose was this village of el-Behnesa, which covered in part an ancient town known to have been populous and prosperous and eventually an important Christian centre – likely therefore to yield texts and especially biblical texts – a town whose ancient name was Oxyrhynchos, 'City of the Sharp-nosed Fish'.

Grenfell and Hunt

Grenfell and Hunt were then in their late twenties. To us they seem, names, background and all, typical of their time. Bernard Pyne Grenfell (1870–1926) was the son of a master at King Edward's Birmingham, educated at Clifton College; Arthur Surridge Hunt (1871–1934), son of a solicitor, educated at Eastbourne College. Both were thought less than robust, and exempted from the Victorian routine of team games, except for a little cricket. Both won scholarships (1888) to The Queen's College, Oxford, where they became friends (they were off mountaineering in the Tyrol in the summer vacation of 1889). Both did well in the regular classical course, and both won graduate scholarships to keep them going. They were going to be scholars: but in what? By 1895 the die was cast: they were in Egypt, digging for papyri in the ancient villages of the Fayûm. They were to spend the rest of their lives pioneering a new branch of Classics: papyrology. It was not easy. Tony Harrison's play *Trackers of Oxyrhynchus* (first performed in 1988) makes true-life drama of the stress and excitement of discovery. Grenfell, the more mercurial, suffered a third nervous breakdown in 1920, which ended his working life. Hunt went on until 1934, his last years clouded by the early death of his only son. But their partnership had achieved extraordinary things, in bringing back to life Oxyrhynchos and its many voices.

El-Behnesa was chosen for the season of 1896/7 ('season' means winter to spring, when the temperature was moderate and local workmen could spare time from their fields). The choice depended partly on the city's reputation as a great Christian centre (the 10,000 monks and 20,000 nuns), which held out the prospect of interesting relics of early Christian literature. Certainly the site itself did not at first promise much. About half the area was occupied by the Arab village (not much populated, since the easy route down from the desert exposed it to Bedouin raids). 'With regard to the other half,' wrote Grenfell, 'a thousand years' use as a quarry for limestone and bricks had clearly reduced the buildings and houses to utter ruin. In many parts of the site which had not been used as a depository for rubbish ... lines of limestone chips or banks of sand marked the positions of buildings which had been dug out; but of the walls themselves scarcely anything was left, except part of the town wall enclosing the north-west of the site, the buildings having been cleared away down to their foundations, or to within a few courses of them.' There was little hope, then, of finding papyri still in the remains of ancient houses. Various mounds might have concealed buildings, but proved in fact to be tips of ancient rubbish. For three weeks the excavators explored the Graeco-Roman cemetery, with little to show.

Then, on 11 January 1897, they dug a low mound. Very soon there came to the surface a papyrus page with unknown *Logia*, or 'Sayings of Jesus' (it turned out later to be the apocryphal *Gospel of Thomas*), then a leaf from St Matthew's Gospel. The papyrus-hunters were in business. The mounds proved rich beyond the wildest expectation. 'The flow of papyri soon became a torrent it was difficult to keep pace with.' Three months' digging yielded enough papyri to fill 280 boxes. The *Review of Reviews* compared the sudden treasure of Oxyrhynchos to the discovery of gold in the Klondyke.[2] Grenfell described his workforce: 'As the papyrus digging was comparatively light work, I had more boys than men diggers, the former being not only easier to manage and more trustworthy, but quite as keen about the work as the men, which is remarkable seeing that all their earnings go to their parents. But I should think that nearly every boy in the district who could walk wanted to be taken on to the work ... One of the smartest workers of all was also the smallest, a little chap about eight years old, who had a wonderful eye for the right kind of soil for finding papyri ...'[3] This 'little chap', Sabr' Said, enjoyed his fifteen minutes of fame: the London *Daily Graphic* for 21 July 1897 printed a sketch of him, alongside views of his village and photographs of the excavators, with the caption 'The Boy who found the *Logia*'.

Almost every item of this huge hoard was of Roman or Byzantine date. For the moment the excavators had other priorities. 'Our desire to discover a collection of Ptolemaic texts, for which the Fayûm offered the best field, and the necessity for pressing on excavations in that district, owing to the rapid extension of the area of cultivation round and even over the ancient sites, and the constant plundering of the natives, led us to postpone further work at Oxyrhynchus until the Fayûm was exhausted.'[4] For some years, therefore, they diverted their attention to Tebtunis and el-Hibeh. But in February 1903 they were back at el-Behnesa. 'When we were here before,' wrote Grenfell, 'we avoided digging a certain mound which adjoins the modern Mohammedan cemetery and has a Sheikh's tomb of peculiar sanctity and several others on top. One side of this mound however has near the surface a rich papyrus-yielding layer (2–4th century A.D.) and lower down a 1st century B.C. layer. A remarkable feature of the papyri from the upper levels especially, is the great number of literary fragments – classical, theological, and even some Latin which is very unusual. We have already obtained several pieces of the first importance, and there is still a considerable piece of ground to be covered, though the top of the mound we shall have, unfortunately, to leave alone.'[5]

The tomb of the Sheikh was restored and repainted after the dig, but not before it had generated its own legend – that Grenfell was struck blind for disturbing the site, and had his sight restored only when the Sheikh reflected that the poor villagers were benefitting from the wages paid by the excavators.[6] Grenfell supervised the digging, Hunt dealt with the finds: 'Looking after 100 men fishing up papyri in a high wind with a mixture of sand and cinders driving in their faces (this is one of the windiest places in Egypt) isn't exactly easy. Hunt has been very busy sorting and flattening out the papyri, but so far is a long way in arrears, and the larger lots there will not be time to examine in this country.'[7]

They returned to el-Behnesa again for the winters of 1903/4, 1904/5, 1905/6 and 1906/7. Progress was unpredictable, and some of the most spectacular finds came late. On 13 January 1905, 'shortly before sunset, we reached, at about 6 feet from the surface, a place where in the third century AD a basketful of broken literary papyrus rolls had been thrown away. In the fading light it was impossible to extricate the whole find that evening; but a strong guard was posted on the spot during the night, and the remainder was safely removed in the following forenoon. Before being condemned to the rubbish heap, the papyri had, as usual, been torn up; but amid hundreds of smaller fragments there were a couple of cores of rolls, containing ten or twelve columns, other pieces containing five or six, and many more one or two columns.' This find could be pieced together into twelve rolls. Apart from the usual classics (Thucydides, Plato, Isocrates), there were a number of major works which had gone missing in the Middle Ages – the *Paeans* of Pindar, Euripides' *Hypsipyle*, an anonymous History of Greece. Three days later, the excavators had moved to a different mound, where they found a second hoard of literary items: eight feet down, Greek lyric poets; 25 feet down, a mass of other texts. There were songs by Sappho and Alcaeus and Ibycus, dithyrambs and paeans by Pindar, dithyrambs and drinking songs by his rival Bacchylides, learned elegies and learnedly offensive satires by Callimachus, sermons in verse by the Cynic

Cercidas – all lost treasures of the classical inheritance. The dig stopped short, to avoid disturbing the tomb of a local saint, Sheikh Ali El Gamman.

The sixth season was interrupted in December 1906, when Grenfell suffered a nervous breakdown. However, he was back at the dig by the beginning of February 1907. This was, and was intended to be, the last season. 'We have now dug everything that we wish to excavate here, and do not contemplate any further work at this site, which has been practically exhausted.'[8] The six seasons had yielded, at a cost of some £4000, 700 boxes of papyri, which might be estimated at 500,000 pieces and scraps, along with a miscellany of small daily objects which linked the papyri yet more closely with those who wrote and read them – coins, tokens, dice, pens, keys (iron and bronze), combs, rings, lamps, amulets, tweezers, bracelets, socks, slippers, marbles of particoloured glass, dolls of papyrus or rags, stone heads of Venus and Horus, statuettes in bronze or terracotta, a birdtrap, a set of moulds for counterfeiting coins, 'a knife-handle representing an ape carrying a lantern', 'an ivory panel from a casket with a hare running', and 'some loaves of Roman bread, in appearance much resembling Hot Cross buns'.

The dig was over; the task of publishing the papyri continued. This task was to occupy Grenfell and Hunt for the rest of their working lives, and their successors up to the present day.

During the dig, they spent the winters in Egypt. We see them in photographs, moustaches neatly trimmed, cloth caps on, sitting outside their tent. Thirty foremen and a hundred workmen (in those days the wages came to £30 a week for the whole force) attacked the mounds. They found papyri, mixed with earth and other rubbish, heaped 30 feet deep. The finds were collected in baskets, then boxed and shipped back to Oxford – one roll in an old biscuit tin ('Huntley and Palmer's Best'), most of the finds in tin boxes which workmen made up on site from old kerosene containers. It was a lonely life, and even potentially dangerous: a shopping list of Hunt's includes medicines, fish-hooks, *The Old Curiosity Shop* and a revolver with forty cartridges. 'Good luck with the gravedigging,' wrote Grenfell's brother.

Grenfell described the work, which required trenching each mound in rising steps:

> The method of digging a mound on a large scale is extremely simple. The workmen are divided into groups of 4 or 6, half men, half boys,

and in the beginning are arranged in a line along the bottom of one side of a mound, each group having a space two metres broad and about 3 metres long assigned to it. At Oxyrhynchus the level at which damp has destroyed all papyrus is in the flat ground within a few inches of the surface, and in a mound this damp level tends to rise somewhat, though of course not nearly as quickly as the mound rises itself. When one trench has been dug down to the damp level, one proceeds to excavate another immediately above it, and throw the earth into the trench which has been finished, and so on right through the mound until one reaches the crest, when one begins again from the other side. The particular mixture of earth mixed with straw and bits of wood in which papyrus is found, and is to the papyrus digger what quartz is to the gold-seeker, sometimes runs in clearly marked strata between other layers of cinders, bricks or all kinds of debris containing no papyrus, but in many of the mounds at Oxyrhynchus papyri are found continuously down to a depth of five or even eight metres ... The clouds of dust and sand, which are quite inevitable when one is digging in very loose dry soil on the edge of the desert, give you an idea of the difficulties under which the excavator for papyri has to work. It is really marvellous how the men manage to keep their eyes open through it all.[9]

The method was simple, but the practicalities were formidable. There were two of them to supervise the work and preserve the finds. The workforce normally numbered 100 men and boys. Once it reached 200, a number beyond which Grenfell could not cope. They were glad of the work, but at the end of February they began to drift away, since the spring planting called them back to their fields. On top of wages, a special payment was made for each papyrus found; there was a danger of plunder, so that rich finds needed to be guarded overnight, and of private leakage to dealers. Of the season begun in December 1904 Grenfell and Hunt reported, 'In spite of the general rise of prices in Egypt, which is carrying the rate of wages upward with it, nearly all our old hands were anxious to work on the former terms; but we found it advisable to increase somewhat the scale of bakhshish, especially as the dealers are at length turning their attention to Behnesa, and papyri continue to command extravagant prices in the market.'[10] On top of all this came the need to account in detail for money spent, and the perennial shortage of funds.

Summers they spent in Oxford. Here there were more comforts (we find Grenfell ordering '500 Best Egyptian Cigarettes' from a dealer in London – the cost, in 1896, £1 7s 6d), but no less work. The papyri offered quite new problems: the problem of understanding strange fragmentary poets whom no one in the West had read for fifteen centuries; the problem of understanding late technical Greek from this unknown Hellenic outpost. Sixteen substantial volumes appeared, full of new information and new insights, all set out briskly and economically and without any parade of learning. Each editor revised what the other wrote, and the result was published in joint names. It was an ideal partnership: Grenfell impetuous and extrovert, Hunt shy and cautious; one contributing ideas and intuitions, the other control and critical judgment.

Despite Grenfell's words, the site was not exhausted when they left. Italian expeditions excavated there in 1910 and 1913/14 (Pistelli), and again in 1927–34 (Breccia); papyri from these digs are housed in the Istituto Vitelli in Florence. In between, Sir Flinders Petrie surveyed the ground in 1922. By that time much top-soil had been removed for fertiliser – Petrie estimated that 100–150 tons left each day by rail, and more by river. Petrie identified the stage, seating and portico of a substantial theatre, 120 metres in diameter (as large as the Theatre of Epidaurus) and capable, he thought, of holding 11,000 spectators; parts of two colonnaded streets, at right angles to one another; and the cemetery north of the town. Most of that stone has since disappeared. Much more recently, a Kuwaiti dig investigated the Islamic town (1985–7), and a joint force, Egyptian and Catalan, under Professor Padró, has surveyed the necropolis to the north-west and located fragments of public buildings from the Roman period.[11]

A Second Renaissance

The literature of ancient Greece and Rome had never completely died out. Handcopying, in the Latin West and the Greek East, preserved a small selection of works, and what survived until the Renaissance made its way into print and a guaranteed immortality. What did survive provided evidence of what did not. At the Renaissance, scholars rediscovered in libraries 7 remaining tragedies of Aeschylus, 7 of Sophocles,

19 of Euripides: ancient sources showed that originally there had been 70 or 80 of Aeschylus, 120 of Sophocles, 90 of Euripides – a survival rate of 10 to 20 per cent. If Shakespeare had suffered the same losses, we should know him, at best, by 8 plays out of 37. A whole series of famous names, whose works had been available in every library of the Roman Empire, came down simply as names, with a few quotations to exemplify their genius. Such, for example, were the lyric poets, once household names – Sappho, Alcaeus, Anacreon, Simonides.

By the eighteenth century, it seemed, there was little left to find in the libraries. As for the books of the ancients themselves, they were unlikely to be recovered by excavation, since in damp soil they rot away. Then came hints of what might be possible. Diggers chanced, near Naples, on a Roman villa which had belonged to the ancient town of Herculaneum and been buried in ash, like the town, by the eruption of Vesuvius in AD 79. The excavations, begun in the 1750s, brought to light the only ancient library ever found in situ, one or more rooms of book-rolls carbonised by the heat. The work of deciphering these finds went slowly; the papyrus was brittle, the surface had turned as black as the ink, the rolls at least on the outside were stuck shut and could be unrolled only by cutting them up and peeling off layers one by one. Nonetheless, they caused international excitement; the Prince Regent sent his chaplain, the Reverend John Hayter, to help with the work.

It was a false spring. Decipherment made it increasingly clear that this was a philosophical library, probably indeed the library of a specific philosopher. Philodemos of Gadara had come to Rome c.75 BC and obtained the patronage of a Roman noble family, the Pisones; it may well be that the family owned the Herculanean villa in which he housed his books – many works of Epicurean philosophy and many of his own works (some both in draft and in fair copy) in this tradition. Lyric poets there were none, however suitable for seaside reading. There will have been some disappointment. In September 1819 the poet Wordsworth fell to comparing the autumn birdsong with his own now elderly Muse. His thoughts turned to the fresh inspiration of the Greek poets; most of their work was lost, but perhaps scholarship might recover more:

> O ye that patiently explore
> The wreck of Herculanean lore,
>   What rapture, could ye seize
> Some Theban fragment, or unroll

One precious tender-hearted scroll
Of pure Simonides.[12]

What he had in mind were the lost works (three-quarters of the whole) of the Theban poet Pindar, and the entire works of Simonides, the great international star of his day, famous for his avarice, his glamorous clients and his talent for pathos.

Conditions at Herculaneum were very special. The volcanic debris had sealed off the papyri from the corrupting moisture. Dryness was all. As it turned out, there was at least one other area of the Greek and Roman world that offered similar protection. In central and southern Egypt it rarely rains; the perishable will survive for millennia under the protecting sand. It was in Egypt that a Danish scholar, Niels Iversen Schow (1754–1830), bought a roll of original papyrus written in Greek. According to legend, he was offered fifty rolls, but bought only one (whereupon the locals burned the rest in order to enjoy the smell). This he presented to Cardinal Stefano Borgia. The roll, now known as the Charta Borgiana, did not preserve lyric poetry: when published (in 1788) it turned out to contain a document, a list of 181 men who, over a five-day period in February AD 193, the 33rd year of the (recently murdered) Emperor Commodus, carried out forced labour on the embankments at Tebtunis.[13] The find opened a window on the daily life of Greek Egypt, but it raised little excitement with contemporary scholars, who had more interest in literature than in life.

Egypt, for long cut off, was about to re-enter the European consciousness. Napoleon's campaign there (1798–9) took also a team of scholars, who produced the remarkable collection of drawings and reports published as the *Description de l'Égypte*. Among their finds was the Rosetta Stone, which was to provide the key to deciphering the hieroglyphic script. The expedition, though politically unsuccessful, opened another door. Egyptomania swept Europe; travellers began to visit the country more frequently; and serious Egyptology began, in 1822, with Champollion's decipherment of the script.

At this stage, excavation did not focus on papyri. But the informal diggings of local peasants made finds which then appeared on the antiquities market. So it was that in 1821 Sir William John Bankes (1786–1855), an indefatigable explorer of Egypt and Nubia (he brought back the obelisk which still adorns the family seat at Kingston Lacy), bought, at Elephantine, a roll of *Iliad* XXIV, which in 1879 entered the British

Museum.[14] This was a rare survival of the ancient Greek book, and the painter Alma-Tadema took care to depict it in ancient hands in *A Reading from Homer* (1885). Later, in 1847, the antiquarian Joseph Arden acquired at Thebes a substantial papyrus roll which had contained several speeches by the orator Hyperides (389–322 BC). That was a famous name (second only to Demosthenes in the ancient canon) without the famous works, all of which (except a few quotations) had perished in the Middle Ages.

This discovery made an immediate sensation in London. In spring 1851 Arden introduced his purchase at a conversazione in the house of Lord Londesborough. Afterwards the papyrus itself was put on show in the rooms of the Royal Society of Literature. In 1853 came the publication, Greek text and facsimile of the whole papyrus. The list of subscribers included 'The Prince Albert KG (Chancellor of Cambridge University)' and the Chancellor of the Exchequer, W. E. Gladstone. Foreign subscribers were headed by 'The King of Prussia KG' and his ambassador in London, Baron von Bunsen, who was himself publishing a five-volume work called *Egypt's Place in Universal History*.

This fashionable interest in classical scholarship was hardly surprising in a world whose elite had received a classical education. Once archaeology began in earnest, Egyptologists like Sir Flinders Petrie would raise funds for their excavations by popular lectures, exhibitions of finds, appeals to institutions and individuals. Grenfell and Hunt did the same, for the budget of the Egypt Exploration Fund, which financed their dig, was often on a knife edge. They lectured, in the UK and the US; they provided suitable press releases; they recognised and encouraged the particular interests of the educated public. Early Christian texts had particular resonance. They took steps to produce (1897) one of their most spectacular finds, the *Logia* or *Sayings of Jesus*, as a separate pamphlet (two shillings with collotype plates, a cheaper version at sixpence) which sold more than 30,000 copies.[15] New texts of classical Greek appealed not only to classical scholars, but to the classically educated. Even *Punch*, the leading comic journal of the time, took note. The publication, in 1908, of the long-lost *Paeans* of Pindar was a scholarly event. But a larger audience remembered Pindar as the most difficult of set texts. Mr Punch drew an inky schoolboy, eying a stout volume entitled *The Oxyrhynchus Papyri*, vol. V: 'Pindar,' says the boy, 'more Pindar – as if there weren't enough of the wretched man already.'

Even high society might take note, if the text were suggestive enough.

Ronald Firbank, eying Mayfair from his seat at the Café Royal, where he was drafting on blue postcards his novel *Vainglory* (1915), visualised a fashionable dinner at Mrs Henedge's, at which Professor Inglepin would read the new fragment of Sappho. The professor, it seems, had been surveying, by donkey, the ruins of 'Crocodileopolis Arsinoe', when he had come upon this precious papyrus. After dinner he declaims the immortal words in Greek. An embarrassed guest asks for a translation. '"In plain English," the Professor said, with some reluctance, "it means: *Could not* [he wagged a finger] *Could not, for the fury of her feet!*"'[16] A fragment, apparently, of one line and no context: the novelist's eye catches perfectly the encounter of social and academic snobbery.

Literature and Life

Grenfell and Hunt had been drawn to Oxyrhynchos in search of early Christian texts and pagan literature. One product was a minor Renaissance in the study of Greek literature; the Egyptian connection opened a door on the well-stocked libraries of the high Empire. The sand yielded works long lost – Pindar's *Paeans to Apollo*, the only known comedy of Sophocles, a Euripidean drama of recognition and rescue. It yielded fragments of authors who had survived only as great names and small quotations: the songs of Sappho, the invectives of Hipponax, the lyric epic of Stesichorus, the sitcoms of Menander, Callimachus' postmodern elegies. It yielded whole genres of which nothing had been known – the comic novel, father (or son?) of Petronius' *Satyricon*; the tabloid biography, in which the life of Euripides was recreated from his work, his enemies and a large pinch of credulity; the pagan martyrologies, true trials of patriotic Alexandrians face to face with the coarse Roman oppressor.

Wordsworth had desired Pindar and Simonides. Both were found, and, bit by bit, as Grenfell and Hunt and their successors sorted through the 500,000 fragments, published. The new literature, now accessible for the first time since the fall of Rome, has things as memorable as the old. At last we can follow Stesichorus' Herakles on his journey across Ocean, in the golden cup of the sun, to kill (one head at a time) the triple monster Geryon, or join Menander's sensitive soldier Thrasymachos as he mooches lovelorn in the rain. We glimpse lost splendours: Alcman celebrates a Spartan beauty, 'her look more melting than sleep or death'; Pindar visualizes the mythical Temple of Delphi, 'bronze the walls and bronze the pillars below, and on the pediment sang six Sirens of gold'. At the same time, the new texts have tested the categories and structures of scholarship, the *fable convenue* which nineteenth-century positivists based on the assumption that the texts then surviving were typical and to be explained simply in relation to one another. New texts, randomly preserved, show up the aesthetic prejudices and unquestioned categories that lie below the would-be scientific surface.

Literature accounted for perhaps 10 per cent of the rubbish; its publication and exploitation fell in the familiar area of Classical Philology. The remainder belongs to a field then hardly explored, the life and society of the Greeks in Egypt. From the 1870s on, papyrological finds (purchased and excavated) offered a detailed, documented view of Egypt as Greek kingdom and Roman province in a way unmatched for any other part of the Mediterranean world. It was an opportunity, though not one that appealed to traditional classicists: 'If I were to occupy myself with papyrus documents,' mused the great Cobet, Professor of Greek at the University of Leiden, in 1841, 'αὐτίκα τεθναίην' ('may I drop dead on the spot').[17] But true students of antiquity in all its aspects saw the possibilities: according to the great Mommsen, the twentieth century would be the century of papyri as the nineteenth was of inscriptions. Grenfell and Hunt took a lead. Their publications pay the same attention to documentary as to literary texts and show the same concern to elucidate their detail. They did not attempt a synthesis, as their great German colleagues Mitteis and Wilcken did, but they applied themselves to the language of the people and the structures of the administration with the same pragmatic lucidity they brought to Pindar and Callimachus.

Publicists too seized not only on the *Sayings of Jesus* but on the human voices preserved over two millennia in the private letters. The letter of the boy Theon, first published in *The Oxyrhynchus Papyri* vol. I and often referred to by Grenfell in his lectures, fitted admirably: 'If you don't take me with you to Alexandria, I won't eat I won't drink so there.'[18] In a novel of 1913, *A Wife out of Egypt* by Norma Lorimer, a love-sick archaeologist shows this letter to the heroine. 'How deliciously human!' she says. 'Human nature never changes,' he said, 'only customs.'[19]

Deciphering the Past

Excavation requires publication. Grenfell and Hunt dug the site of Oxyrhynchos over six years; the papyri they found have occupied scholars of six generations. Volume I of *The Oxyrhynchus Papyri* came out in 1898; volume LXXII is due out in 2007; at least forty more volumes are planned.

With hindsight, the achievement of Grenfell and Hunt is all the more astounding. They pioneered a new subject; they left a written legacy of extraordinary quality. At the same time, they had to cope single-handed with the sheer physical problems of organising an immense collection. There was the jigsaw puzzle work of reuniting fragments and reassembling archives which lay dispersed among shelves of boxes. Even the work of conservation fell to them. Papyrus is flexible and durable, but if it gets too dry it may crack or crumble. Dried-out pieces need to be 'relaxed' before the decipherer can straighten out folds or creases. Specialist conservators developed scientific prescriptions for this process. Hunt, on the other hand, remained resolutely down-to-earth:

I use no boards, blotting paper, leaden weights, relaxing boxes, etc: my implements are:

1. Any table of convenient size, the surface of which will not be spoilt by damp;
2. a couple of smooth cloths (worn out face-towels are convenient in size and texture);
3. three small brushes, one soft, one medium, one hard;
4. a rather blunt pen-knife;
5. good sized sheets of paper . . .

The cloths are dipped in cold water and then wrung out, so that they are left fairly moist. They are then spread out on the table, and the papyri to be flattened or unrolled (after surface dirt has been brushed off so far as possible) are placed between them.

After a few minutes the flattening or unrolling process can be started, and is proceeded with as the papyrus absorbs moisture enough to become soft. It should not be allowed to get really wet.

For smoothing the papyrus, there is nothing like the human thumb and fingers . . .[20]

The same no-nonsense spirit informed the storage of the papyri. Within each box, each layer had (and has) its own paper folder, marked up with its inventory-number. For the folders they needed a large quantity of good-quality paper, and for that they turned to a publication which cost nothing, arrived weekly and soon outlived its readability – the *Oxford University Gazette*, whose double sheets fitted neatly into the original tin boxes.

Hunt continued to work on the collection until 1936. The project remained a largely private business between the editors and the Egypt Exploration Society, which published the volumes. Edgar Lobel (1889–1982) continued the tradition. In a career of seventy years he trawled the collection for the Greek poets who interested him, and to his austere genius – the sharp eye, the learning without parade, the cautious precision – classical scholars owe many more missing links patiently reconstructed from hundreds of fragments – songs of Sappho and Alcaeus, ballads by Anacreon, cantatas by Alcman and Pindar, mythological epic by Hesiod, tragedies of Aeschylus, allusive elegy and avant-garde epic by Callimachus and his contemporaries.

In the meantime, scholarship began to take more institutional forms. Sir Eric Turner (1911–83) searched the papyri above all for fragments of the New Comedy of Menander, theatrical hits of the fourth century BC and bestsellers well into Roman times, yet lost without trace, or so it had seemed, in the turmoil of the Middle Ages. At the same time, he had the vision and enterprise to set up a more formal organisation. The project became a Project, 'The Oxyrhynchus Papyri Project', under the auspices of the British Academy and later of the Arts and Humanities Research Council. These learned bodies have funded a curator for the collection, and it was possible in the 1960s to produce a preliminary catalogue – a catalogue that is still being refined. The cataloguers too came to know the collection in detail, and to pick out neglected treasures literary and also documentary; for documentary work was receiving a new impetus as historians of the Roman Empire shifted their interest from the capital and its high politics to the provinces and their social and economic structures. Grenfell and Hunt had already published the records of the town council of Oxyrhynchos; John Rea and Revel Coles were now to assemble and publish other archives central to the city's history – the papers of its corn dole in the late third century AD (vol. XL, 1972), and the papers of a new official, the city curator, who faced tumultuous times in the early fourth century (vol. LIV, 1987).

The work of decipherment and publication continues and will continue: a labour of love as well as a labour of organisation. There is always the excitement of the chase. Open a box of unpublished papyri, and you never know what you may find. One scrap can easily be identified as Homer, but the next may come from one of those Greek authors whose works perished in the Middle Ages; next to them in the box lie a shopping list, a tax-receipt and remains of a private letter. Your new papyrus may offer you unknown Greek poetry; it may offer unique evidence for the inflation of donkey-prices at the height of the Roman Empire.

The decipherer faces several problems. To 'read' is to create sense from written signs: the reader therefore must be intimately familiar with the signs he sees and the language they represent. The papyrologist, then, must acquire an expertise in signs (palaeography) and in words (philology); on both sides, he or she has to get inside the skin of an ancient Greek.

The script itself is not straightforward. A book (a text of Homer, for example) was normally written in separate capital letters, with the aim of beauty and legibility: ΜΗΝΙΝΑΕΙΔΕΘΕΑ. A document – whether a bureaucrat's circular or a sale of donkey – gets written in what we would call 'handwriting', a cursive version of the capitals which aims for speed. The less often you lift your pen from the papyrus, the faster you write; and so letter shapes change to suit the law of least effort – E (four strokes) to ε (two strokes) to ℓ (one stroke and a link to the next letter). The skilled scribe can write half a dozen letters in one stroke: thus the Greek for 'in the year' (the normal way of beginning a date) can be written formally as ΕΤΟΥϹ and informally as 〰. At worst, the letters turn into a wavy line; like a doctor's signature, they can be read easily only by those who know what to expect. This cursive can be complicated by abbreviations – words shortened to their first few letters, common words represented by conventional symbols (thus L represents ΕΤΟΥϹ).

Ancient Greek writing does not divide one word from another. Tousthisseemstoofferaspecialdifficultyinreadingandunderstanding. Of course, it is a matter of habit, but treacherous for those not habituated. One document published by Grenfell and Hunt refers to the hire of a mouse-catcher 'to catch mice ENTOKA': that might be one word, 'pregnant', or two words, 'in [the village of] Toka'.[21] In another, a private letter, we read: 'Write to me how you are, since I was going to come back and put it off until I knew whether Izzy is in love or not.'[22] 'Love' does not play much part in the private correspondence of the Oxy-rhynchites, who save their words for more practical issues. The Greek says EI ('if') ERAISAS. You can take this as two words, ERA ('he loves') ISAS ('Izzy', short for Isidore), as Grenfell and Hunt did. But you could also take it as one word, ERAISAS, 'you have got better'. Of course the second is right, though less romantic – 'Write me how you are, since I was going to come back and put it off until I knew whether you are better or not.' The eyes see letters, which are ambiguous; the brain resolves the ambiguity in context.

The difficulty increases if the papyrus is damaged. Some discarded papers had been torn up by their owners, other have fallen apart with time; a once handsome book survives only in a dozen lines broken, worm-eaten, pitted with holes, the ink scuffed and the fibres stripped. If letters are completely lost, the decipherer will try to guess them from the overall context. **B**RN*TT**E*HA*I*TH**UE*TI** (each asterisk represents a letter lost) will eventually yield sense, and indeed turn out to be a quotation. There the modern scholar has a short cut not available to the heroic age of Grenfell and Hunt: two separate databases, available online, of which one, the *Thesaurus Linguae Graecae*, contains the whole of classical Greek literature and more, the other, the *Duke Databank of Documentary Papyri*, aims to include text of all published documents. In both you can search for a sequence of letters, which may identify your passage if it is already known, or provide suggestive parallels when the text is entirely new.

Damage does not always destroy the ink completely. Sometimes we have all the ink, but faded or abraded; sometimes just bits of letters, ambiguous in themselves; sometimes nothing but specks and the pos-sible track of the pen. Any such traces may be difficult to distinguish from background dirt and stains. Science again has come to the rescue in recent years. A binocular microscope can articulate ambiguous ink. Infra-red light can bring up dim traces; ultra-violet shows up the metal-based inks used from late antiquity. The photographer's lights, even the colour xerox, pick up ink that the eye has ignored. Most recently we have digital scans, which can be manipulated on screen; and more advanced multispectral imaging, a technique (originally developed for the NASA space programme) which can combine images taken at dif-ferent wavelengths or trawl the wavelengths until the optimum image is obtained – ideal for the desperate cases where faded or abraded ink, or muddy or carbonised papyrus, impede decipherment.

Science helps, but in the end it comes back to eye and mind. Consider the scrap shown above, 2 inches by 4.5 inches.[23] The neat script suggests book, not document; the name Theseus near the end suggests mythology; the visible words look as if they were in metre, and specifically the metre of tragedy. That is the genre. One extraordinary word, 'licking out', recurs in an odd line quoted from the tragedian Euripides. Therefore our scrap may belong to a tragedy of Euripides. Since the words do not come from an extant work, it will be one of the seventy or so lost plays, probably from one of the two plays devoted to the story of Theseus. This is the context. Now words can be pulled out and fitted in. 'Columns' – 'spectator' – 'curved' – 'cleaning out' – 'Theseus' –

'taking off' – 'club' and 'right hand': a watcher watches as Theseus, stripped down and a club in his right hand, faces a monster with curving horns and a tongue that cleans out its nostrils – the famous bull of Marathon, or even the Minotaur itself. So in thirteen broken lines we begin to recover the narrative of an epic battle from a Greek tragedy lost since the Roman Empire. It is a fragment; the faith is that there will be other fragments, so that, jigsaw fashion, the lost play will come together. Even Professor Inglepin's lone line of Sappho might eventually find a home. It is this patient manipulation that, beginning with Grenfell and Hunt, has resurrected some of the casualties of time.

The rubbish-dumps of the Sharp-nosed Fish proved extraordinarily fruitful. Ever since the *Logia*, published in 1897, individual literary and biblical texts have been coming back from the dead to make the headlines. From the same dumps comes a humbler sensation: documents public and private of every kind, a vast unselected sampling of life. Here it is not individual pieces that stand out; it is the paper mountain as a whole, an extraordinary phenomenon in 1897, when the only contemporary records of the Roman world were those inscribed on stone, and still an extraordinary resource as more and more gets deciphered, published and interpreted in context. This material documents in detail an epoch almost unknown a century ago, a whole millennium of Hellenic civilisation in the shadow of the pyramids – the world of the Egyptian Greeks.

CHAPTER 3

EGYPTIAN GREEKS

• • • •

To the Greeks of the third century BC, Egypt was the new-found land, a California of opportunity. 'Egypt has everything in the world,' says a character in the Greek satirist Herodas: 'money, wrestling, power, peace, glory, shows, philosophers, gold, youths, the sanctuary of the brother gods, a good king, the Museum, wine, all the good things your man might desire, and as for women . . .'[1]

Egypt had played a special part in Greek culture and in the Greek imagination since their beginning. In imagination the exotic pre-dominated: Herodotus the anthropologist described a strange civil-isation which reversed all norms; Plato the philosopher depicted a haunt of gurus and antique wisdom; everyone knew about the flooding of the Nile and the worship of animals. And the material reality was not a matter of conjecture. Minoans or their cousins left wall-paintings in the Nile Delta; the poet Sappho's brother traded there and got entangled with an unsuitable woman (so his sister thought). By 600 BC Greeks had settled in their own city of Naukratis; later, Ionians and Carians inhabited special quarters of the northern capital, Memphis. There were the merchants, and the mercenaries, all Greeks seeking their fortune outside their barren homeland. So it was under the late pharaohs, and so when Egypt succumbed to the Persian Empire and remained, apart from revolts encouraged by the Greeks, a Persian province until Alex-ander the Great.

Herodotus had seen a pattern in Mediterranean history: successive aggressions between East and West. The Persian Empire, expanding from its base in Iran, had finally attacked Greece itself, and was turned back in the great patriotic wars of 490 and 480 BC. The retaliation had to wait for the rise of a new unified power in northern Greece, the kingdom of Macedon. In 334 its young king, Alexander, set out to defeat Persia. In 332, having conquered Asia Minor and Palestine, he crossed the desert of Sinai (three days' march without water) and entered Egypt. The Persian governor surrendered without a fight. Alexander marched to Memphis, the old capital, sacrificed to the sacred bull and assumed the traditional titles of Pharaoh. Returning downriver, he founded a new city, on the Mediterranean coast, which was to become the most famous and enduring of the cities he named from himself. To the west lay the Libyan Desert, and in it the oasis of Siwa, famous for the temple and oracle of the ram-headed god Ammon, whom Greeks identified with Zeus. Alexander and a small escort set out over the desert, surviving a sandstorm (two talking snakes guided him, wrote an admiring historian). He had an audience with the god, who acknowledged him as his own son. So Alexander became, like Herakles, a child of Zeus, half-divine, and coins show him with Ammon's horns. Then, in April 330, the hero was off and away, with new worlds to conquer: Babylonia, Persia and beyond, Afghanistan, India as far as the Indus. There he turned back. He reached Babylon, where, in 323 BC, he died at the age of 33, leaving an empire of West and East to his unborn son Alexander IV and his idiot half-brother Philip III.

Egypt meanwhile had retained a Macedonian garrison and a Greek governor with local knowledge, Kleomenes of Naukratis, while native Egyptian officials ran the basic administration. The new rulers took pains not to alienate the local elites. A surviving placard, issued by garrison-general Peukestas, says in block capitals 'KEEP OUT. THIS HOUSE BELONGS TO A PRIEST' – a warning to marauding Greek soldiers.[2] On Alexander's death, his marshals parcelled out the real power. The most far-sighted of them, Ptolemy the son of Lagos, obtained Egypt, notionally as governor for the legitimate King, Philip III. That did not last. Philip III was murdered in 317 (by Alexander the Great's elderly mother), Alexander IV in 310. There was a vacuum to fill, and by 304 all the marshals had declared themselves kings, in a Greek Empire now split into three realms: Macedonia and Greece, Asia Minor and Mesopotamia (the Seleucid Empire), Egypt and its dependencies. Ptolemy founded a dynasty of Ptolemies which ruled Egypt for three centuries, down to the death of Cleopatra (VII) in 30 BC.

From Greek Kingdom to Roman Province

Ptolemy I had made his way as a general (indeed his name means 'warlike'), and he was over sixty when he claimed the title, only one degree below god, of King. He was also a canny strategist. He hijacked the mummified body of Alexander the Great and installed it in pomp, first in Memphis, then in the new capital of Alexandria: this was a claim to inherit the world-conqueror's charisma. He played an active part in the politics of the new Greek kingdoms; and in one way the move of the capital was a move towards Greece, for Alexandria (known officially as 'Alexandria next to Egypt', as if it were detached from the rest of the country) stood on the Mediterranean coast, 150 miles from Memphis and 600 miles from Thebes. Yet he and his successors played also to the Egyptian audience. Alexandria, though a Greek city, displayed Egyptian sculpture, as recent underwater archaeology has shown.[3] Hieroglyphic inscriptions showed Ptolemy with all the traditional titles and accoutrements of Pharaoh. At some stage there emerged a deity both Greek and Egyptian, Serapis: his image had elements of the Greek god of the underworld, Pluto, and of the Egyptian Osiris, whose manifestation was the sacred bull of Memphis. Ptolemy took advice from Egyptian notables; at the same time he grecised the upper levels of administration, and a flow of immigrants provided him with soldiers, bureaucrats and intellectuals. He gave Greek Egypt its shape. When he died and was deified, he received the founder's title, 'Soter' (Saviour).

Egypt was a good choice: compact, defensible, organised and prosperous. Contemporaries were impressed above all by its wealth. When Ptolemy I took over from Kleomenes (whom he killed not long after), he inherited a treasury of 8000 talents and, more importantly, the machinery to collect much more. For two thousand years or more Egypt had been a centralised despotism; the land and its fruits belonged to Pharaoh, and from capital to village a hierarchy of officials enforced his rights. The arable land of the Nile valley was of limited area, but continuous and fertilised each year by the Nile's sediment. It supported a population estimated at seven million, who cultivated the land and manned a flourishing production of vegetable oil and linen. By comparison the resources of the Greek mainland, broken, mountainous and politically divided, with a population of perhaps two million, were negligible. Egypt was rich (and the Greeks took steps to make it richer, introducing new breeds of sheep, new varieties of fruit-tree, a wheat which grew and ripened in three months), and richly exploited. The state set taxes on land and trade (a sixth of the produce, for example, from all vineyards and orchards) and maintained monopolies or government control on essential products and exports – oil, salt, beer, linen, papyrus. The bureaucrats oversaw the system. The actual business of collecting a tax was outsourced to private individuals, who bid for the contract (so providing a secure return to the state) and hoped to raise more than they bid from the taxpayers, subject always to the rules issued by the treasury and the monthly accounting that it enforced. The royal income was huge, and part of it went to recruiting a reliable army. 'King Ptolemy is the best pay-master for a free man,' says a veteran in a mini-drama by the court poet Theocritus:[4] these soldiers kept order at home and maintained a wider empire which came to include Libya, Cyprus, Samos and parts of Palestine.

Ptolemy I left this substantial state to his son Ptolemy II (285–246), who proceeded to enjoy it. Foreign wars were still fought, with varying success. But the folk-memory of historians dwelt on other aspects. The glamour of monarchy, and the glamour of Alexandria, were at their height. Ptolemy II was remembered for his marriage and his mistresses. He married his full sister Arsinoe II: a normal pharaonic practice, in Greek morality a perversion. Court poets referred delicately to Zeus, the monarch of the gods, who married his sister Hera. The satirist Sotades commented less tactfully, 'you stick your prick in an unholy hole,' and left the city, only to be caught, put in a lead case and dropped into the sea. When Arsinoe died, she was deified, with the title 'brother-loving'. The mistresses meanwhile pleasured and profited. The most famous, Bilistiche, entered a chariot in the Olympic Games, the prerogative of the super-rich, and she too became a god on her death, worshipped as Aphrodite Bilistiche.

Yet king and court, in the way of Renaissance princes, counted intellectual interests too among their pleasures. The Alexandrian Library became the greatest collection of books in the new Hellenistic world; it collated and consolidated the fragile, scattered manuscripts that represented five centuries of the Greek literary inheritance. The Museum of Alexandria, not a museum in our sense but an Institute for Advanced Study, attracted and supported scholars from old and new Greece. Between these institutions, and the private patronage of a lavish court, medicine and mathematics, poetry and scholarship enjoyed a golden age. The new monarchy drew prestige from its connection with classical culture; classical culture was reinvented for the new environment, as scholar-poets like Callimachus founded a new poetry on the interpretation of the old. For the Egyptian Greeks, scholarly study of the past reinforced their Hellenic roots, while new aesthetics and new discoveries extended their creative frontiers, just as Alexander's conquests had extended their physical empire.

Some of the immigrants certainly made their fortune on the new frontier. Alongside the poets and scholars and scholar-poets, attracted by royal favour and the fame of the Library and Museum, there were fixers and entrepreneurs like Zeno the Carian, who ran the prime minister's estates at Philadelphia (we have his private papers). Such was Medeios son of Lampon, a doctor who left Olynthos in northern Greece, learned to cure the bite of the Libyan asp and made such a figure at the Ptolemaic court that he became a priest of the dynastic cult.[5] As Alexandria asserted itself as the grandest centre of the Greek diaspora, its leading figures took care to cultivate their prestige in the Old Country: Ptolemaic princesses ran chariot-teams in the Olympic Games; Medeios celebrated his success with a dedication (complete with verses by the fashionable poet Poseidippos) at the greatest sanctuary of Apollo the healer, Delphi.

Later Ptolemies had to contend with the weaknesses which underlay the glamour: foreign wars, Egyptian nationalism, court intrigue, family feuds and (intervening more and more) Rome, the superpower from the West. The infancy of Ptolemy V (210–180 BC) saw Egyptian revolts and the loss of Ptolemaic possessions in Palestine and Asia Minor. Ptolemy VI (180–145), at war with his brother Ptolemy VIII (nicknamed 'Fat-gut'), faced conquest by the Seleucid Antiochus IV, until Rome intervened. Rome indeed would gather in the fragmented empire of the Greeks: first Macedonia and Greece (146 BC), then the remains of the Seleucid kingdom (64 BC). Egypt lasted longest, but when Ptolemy XII (nicknamed 'Fluteplayer') was expelled by the Alexandrians (58 BC), it was the Roman governor of Syria who restored him, for a bribe of 10,000 talents – the Egyptian monarchy still possessed considerable resources. The Ptolemies were on notice. The Fluteplayer's successor, his daughter Cleopatra (VII), played for a time a successful part in Roman politics, but in the end on the wrong side. With the defeat of her lover Mark Antony, and the suicide of Cleopatra herself (30 BC), Egypt fell to the victorious Octavian, soon to be renamed Augustus, the first Emperor of Rome.

In this new Roman Empire, Egypt remained the jewel in the crown: rich, fertile, and difficult to attack. It provided the city of Rome with a third of its corn. It would have provided any would-be emperor with a grand base, but the prefects who now governed it were hand-picked by Rome for loyalty. Episodes apart (incursions from the south and west, a brief conquest by the economic imperialists of Palmyra), it did not slip from Rome's grasp, and from Rome it passed eventually to the new Eastern capital, Constantinople, as it passed also to a new religion, Christianity. In the seventh century, when for a decade (AD 619–28) another oriental aggression submitted it to a resurgent Persian state, the Greek Empire struck back, successfully as it seemed. But the East had a much more formidable force preparing. In AD 627 the Byzantine Emperor Heraclius had received a letter from Muhammad the Apostle of God, requiring him to submit to Islam. He replied with polite nothings. Thirteen years later the Caliph Omar sent four thousand Arab horsemen to invade Egypt. On 8 November 641, Alexandria capitulated. Egypt belonged to Islam, and so it has remained ever since as province, kingdom and republic.

Egypt and its Greeks

This book is concerned with the Egypt of the Greeks: the Greek immigrants and their descendants who, for the millennium from Alexander to the Arab conquest, dominated Egypt as a progressively more assimilated colonial class, first under the Macedonian kings of the Ptolemaic dynasty, then under the absentee authority of the Roman and Byzantine emperors. To some extent the Greeks remade Egypt; to a much larger extent, it remade them. From the pharaohs they inherited an absolute monarchy, a centralised economy, a complex religious system attuned to local conditions. They adopted and adapted, from the necessary standpoint of an immigrant minority – perhaps 300,000 Hellenes, in their sense of Hellenic, among seven million Egyptians. The monarch in principle owned the land; his serfs, or the owners to whom he gave it, cultivated the fields. On the monarch's divinity depended the crucial event of the year, the Nile flood: too much water, or too little, and the whole harvest might fail. To the monarch taxes were owed, and the information on which tax-assessments were based: each village, each district, each county, each province had its scribes and secretaries, who passed information up the hierarchy and instructions down. Land, houses, cattle, people were all registered; the state exacted its dues in kind and in money and in labour – the administrative services on which the system depended, whether bureaucratic (the literate are not so numerous) or physical, for without the maintenance of dikes and canals the water could not be distributed, and without water there would be famine.

Life in Egypt depended on conditions common to most of Europe and the Near East before the industrial revolution: even the privileged must reckon with unreliable harvests, slow and expensive transport, primitive medicine partly supplemented by magic. But to other Hellenes Egypt must still have seemed an extraordinary place. Its literary reputation already put it in topsy-turvy land; in the true tradition of orientalism, it offered a native population uncertainly distributed between gurus and kaffirs. Greek kings and their Roman successors showed different faces to Egyptians and to Greeks. They commissioned temples in the Egyptian manner, on whose walls they appeared kilted, crowned and conquering in traditional style. At the same time they imposed their own cult and culture at the highest level.

Up and down the Nile valley Greek immigrants settled and dominated the main towns. They and their descendants maintained a Hellenic identity, through language and education. The first arrivals spoke their original dialects, the next generation adopted 'the common tongue', the neutral Greek of the diaspora everywhere. That Greek developed with time in the direction of Modern Greek, but schooling (for those who had any) tried to hold the classical line; educated Hellenes could define themselves by an education which taught classical grammar and prescribed classical texts, Homer first and above all. Egyptian Greeks distinguished themselves from Egyptians: 'What do you think me?' wrote one. 'A barbarian or an inhuman Egyptian?'[6] To the outsider the distinction might not be so clear. In the late first century AD, the belletrist Plutarch looked out on the world from his library at Chaironea, in the rural heart of Old Greece. In Egypt, he wrote, 'in our own time', the people of Kynopolis and the people of Oxyrhynchos massacred one another, because the Kynopolites had eaten the sacred fish of Oxyrhynchos, and the Oxyrhynchites had eaten the sacred dog of Kynopolis.[7] This typological anecdote serves to illustrate the absurdity of animal-worship and the savagery of such worshippers. That is all we hear in

Greek literature of Oxyrhynchos, 'City of the Sharp-nosed Fish'. What we know of it, from its surviving archives, shows that its citizens studied Homer at school and a few even read Plutarch for pleasure. But outsiders focused their snobbery on the Egyptian ambience rather than the Hellenic inheritance.

It is true that the Egyptian Greeks went native in some respects. The less educated (some of course may be Egyptians to whom Greek was a second language) spoke with Egyptian accents, unable to distinguish L from R, D from T. Their Greek speech had adopted a few Egyptian words: months, measures, crops. Some elements of Egyptian law and custom took root, even occasionally marriage between brother and sister. Above all, Greek-speakers took over much of the local religion. Two long-established habits of mind came into play. One was particularist: the belief that divinities had their particular places of influence, and so (as private letters often say) the traveller will pray to the god of whatever place he visits. The other habit sought universals, to identify any foreign god with one of the Greek gods, so that (for Herodotus) Egyptian Neith was another name for Greek Athena. Egyptian Greeks, therefore, could pray for fertility at the temple of Athena-Thoeris, which united in one the grey-eyed goddess of the Acropolis with the pregnant hippopotamus of Egyptian tradition. Serapis, whose cult spread from Egypt all over the Roman Empire, combined traits of Pluto and Osiris, and his images might reflect the bearded Homeric image normal to Greeks or the formal mummified figure familiar to Egyptians.

Gods, of course, provided benefits, and a magician could invoke familiar Greek names and strange powerful Egyptian names side by side. Even death could be tackled. Greeks in Egypt took up the practice of mummification. A few even took to the grave a book of revelation (the recently identified papyrus of the Greek magus Empedocles may be one of them), to serve like the Book of the Dead traditional in Egyptian tombs. Two surviving linen shrouds show young men, in Greek or Roman dress, being introduced to a mummified Osiris by Anubis, the jackal-headed god of the dead. Anubis is painted in profile, in accordance with Egyptian tradition, while the young men appear full-face and in Greek pose; one of them holds a book-roll.[8] Nor did they despise the much-despised cult of sacred animals. Several statuettes show the worshipper adoring the sharp-nosed fish. Among the rubbish of Oxyrhynchos is a pair of crocodile eyes, drawn, coloured and cut out on papyrus, clearly intended to adorn the outside of a mummified crocodile, another holy creature.

Mummification demanded money. The process was expensive; so too the armour of the dead – a full case of carved wood, a full case or a partial suit (mask, pectoral, leg-guards, boots) made in papier-mâché and then covered with gesso and painted and gilded. At some times and places the mask was replaced by a portrait, painted on wood in coloured wax – a portrait, it seems, painted in life and inserted in the mummy-case after death. These are virtually the only examples of portrait-painting to survive from the classical world; and their apparent realism opens the door on vanished personalities – the coiffed and bejewelled lady with the melancholy eyes, the jowly bruiser whose tight curls assert his energy, the almond-eyed youth whom early death left in perpetual adolescence.[9] The process aimed to secure survival in the next world; instead, because Egypt is so dry (almost no rainfall south of Cairo), it has secured the sitter two thousand years of life in this world.

Papyrus: the Writing in the Sand

Dry sand preserves the things which Greece and Italy rarely offer the archaeologist. Wood, textiles, even paper can survive – so long as they lie higher than the ground-water – for millennia. Greeks and Egyptians alike used a variety of materials on which to write: stone for perpetuity, potsherds ('ostraca') for economy, wooden tablets as notebooks to be scrubbed and reused, papyrus for longer texts like books and registers or for the shorter texts of everyday life. Something depended on avail-ability. In the valley, papyrus was in good supply, except to the poor. Out in the desert, for example at the quarries down by the Red Sea, where the workforce (free, slave and convict) laboured under military guard, the soldiers used mainly ostraca, being so many camel-days from civilisation.

Egypt was the main, perhaps the only, supplier of papyrus paper to the Mediterranean world. The papyrus reed (*cyperus papyrus*) itself grew plentifully in the marshes of the Nile; its triangular stems reached a height of ten feet or more, and sportsmen hunted wildfowl in its thickets. Manufacture (to judge from the one description that survives) followed a traditional and as usual labour-intensive process.[10] The reeds were harvested, their skin removed, their pithy interior cut into lengths and then sliced lengthwise into thin strips. On a flat surface you placed one layer of strips, each touching the next; on top, but crossways, a second layer of contiguous strips. You then compressed this double layer, with the result that the sappy pith amalgamated, strip with strip and layer with layer, to produce a flexible, homogeneous sheet. One side might then be smoothed to produce a better writing surface. The pith consists of fibres, usually with a few thicker fibres projecting and a few darker fibres visible against the lighter ones. The sheet, being double, would have the fibres running east–west on the front, but north–south on the back. Given the choice, you wrote on the front, in parallel with the fibres; if you tried to write on the back, across the fibres, your pen might be impeded by projecting strands. Sheets once made were pasted up into rolls, each sheet overlapping the one to its right, in such a way that all the fibres ran east-west on one side of the roll (the good side), and north-south on the back. A complete roll would be used for a book or a long document; for a smaller item a suitable piece could be cut off. The longer texts were written column by column along the length of the roll. You read them by rolling out the roll with your right hand and rolling it in with your left, so that the columns passed before your eyes like the frames on a videotape.

Writing had a long history in Egypt, and high prestige. Priests and bureaucrats required it for their calling in the pharaonic kingdom, and mastered a complex script in its various forms – the stately Hieroglyphic, the more fluid Hieratic, the hasty cursive Demotic used for more ordinary documents. In the centralised administration, literacy opened the way to power. 'Consider the tanner,' says an Egyptian school-text, 'he stinks to high heaven, he falls into the pit and is drowned. But the scribe, he is at the head of everybody's work.'[11] No wonder that Egyptian civil servants show themselves, in their statues, worshipping the baboon-god Thoth, patron of writing.

To our way of thinking, the very nature of the script – some 800 separate signs in Middle Egyptian – restricts literacy (a Chinese would not agree), whereas the simplicity of the Greek alphabet makes it much easier; and in the end the old Egyptian scripts died out, to be replaced in the third and fourth centuries AD by an adaptation of the Greek alphabet, Coptic. Certainly, as we see it, the Greeks in Egypt made much use of the written record: commerce and administration were amply documented, and the reading-culture of the educated encouraged the copying of books for public and private libraries. As we see it: but we see the Egyptian Greeks quite differently from the Greeks elsewhere, through that same climatic accident which allows written papyrus to survive under the sand in huge quantities. We do not know what Plutarch's neighbours left on their windowsills or dropped into their garbage; but we can investigate the house in Egyptian Karanis, where excavators found a private letter propped on the doorstep (it is a letter from Antonis, serving in the Roman navy, to his mother at home), or the rubbish tips of Egyptian Oxyrhynchos, where discarded books and documents mingle with other waste in mounds 30 feet deep, 700 years of a city in a time-capsule of refuse.

Books and documents on papyrus were a familiar part of the furniture of the Greek and Roman world. In most areas, they are lost to the archaeological record, except where chance or climate intervened. We do have papyri from outside Egypt, occasionally preserved in the arid conditions of the Dead Sea or northern Mesopotamia. We do have papyri which survived by a paradoxical accident. Normally, fire destroys such material; exceptionally, it hardens and preserves it. From classical Greece only one papyrus book survives; it had been thrown onto a funeral pyre, and charring apparently made it waterproof.[12] From classical Italy a whole library survives, the library of a villa at Herculaneum, baked and buried by the ash and mud from Vesuvius when it erupted in AD 79. The Byzantine province of Arabia had its capital at Petra, the rose-red city; archaeologists recently found the archives of a nearby church, carbonised and thus insulated when the building burned down. Such scattered finds have special importance and excitement in the glimpses they give of the written culture at different corners of the Hellenic world. But the finds from Greek Egypt are on quite another scale and offer a much more comprehensive view: 500,000 pieces and scraps in Greek alone, which paint a picture of Greek Egypt in a concrete detail and with an everyday realism unparalleled elsewhere in the Mediterranean world.

Not that all Egypt is the same. Lower Egypt, the northern part, fan-shaped and fertile, is the creation of the Nile, a delta through which seven branches of the river flowed to seven mouths. Its reedy marshes sheltered brigands and sometime freedom-fighters, its fields of silt provided wide areas of cultivation (twice as much as the rest of the country), but the watery ground does not preserve papyrus: we have archives from Boubastis, the city of the lion-goddess, but only because the archive-building burned down. Alexandria remains a glamorous name; but the written record is negligible, since the sea air and the damp soil compound the wear and tear of history. In Upper Egypt, from Memphis southwards to the Nubian border, habitation stretches in a ribbon along the river. The valley averages some 14 miles in width, delimited by cliffs and escarpments. Rainfall is very rare: the valley takes water from the Nile. Beyond the cliffs lies desert, with only the occasional oasis. In the valley, on higher ground, beyond the reach of the annual flood, fragile writings on papyrus or on wood can survive for millennia, their ink (soot mixed with gum) almost as fresh as the day they were written.

Cities and Races

From Memphis, the old Egyptian capital, to Thebes, the later seat of the pharaonic empire, Greek immigrants settled in towns to which in many cases they gave Greek names: Philadelphia, Arsinoe, Herakleopolis, Hermopolis, Panopolis and the rest. We get, from the papyrus documentation, a clear view of this society, though in various ways a one-sided view. There are accidents of excavation: not all sites have been dug with the same thoroughness. There is an inequity of survival: the earlier the material, the closer to the ground and to the ground-water, so that a typical rubbish-dump will preserve more salvage from the Roman Empire than from the Ptolemaic kingdom which preceded it, just because the bottom of the heap crumbles first. The writing culture depends on social conditions as much as it illuminates them. Among Greek speakers, the second and third centuries AD leave us the largest output of books and documents; the fifth century AD for some reason represents a marked decline. As for Egyptian-speakers, we hear much less of them. That is in part because their papyri have been less studied by Egyptologists than those of the high pharaonic kingdom; in part because our material comes predominantly from towns, while the peasant-farmers (modern *fellahin*) lived and laboured in the villages of the countryside; in part no doubt because peasant life depended much more on the institutions of pre-literacy – verbal agreements, subsistence farming and an economy of barter.

Despite this imbalance of evidence, we can see something of race relations, at least at the literate level. Greek myth and tradition had presented one stereotype of the Egyptians as typical 'orientals' – cruel, perverse, depraved and treacherous. In the early days of the Ptolemaic kingdom, Theocritus published a short comedy of Alexandrian manners (once again a realistic comedy) in which two immigrants from Sicily praise the King's attention to law and order: no more danger of being mugged by a native, 'sidling up to you in Egyptian fashion'.[13] As the Ptolemaic kingdom collapsed, Horace presented the last Cleopatra (his master's rival's mistress) as 'crazy drunk',[14] a Macedonian princess turned into another debauched oriental.

Within the country, of course, there were social and economic frictions. Intellectually, some attempts were made to bridge the divide. Manetho, High Priest at Heliopolis in the third century BC, narrated Egyptian history in Greek; Apollonides, High Priest of Memphis in the first century AD, expounded Egyptian law in Greek under the Egyptian title *Semenouthi*. Some made it their business to translate Egyptian texts into Greek: the prophetic dream of the Pharaoh Nectanebo, the romance of Tefnut the lioness, daughter of Ra, goddess of justice, the apocalyptic *Oracle of the Potter*, which foretells the expulsion of evil foreigners from Egypt. All these have religious or prophetic force, and that perhaps explains their appeal to a Greek public, however dire the prophecy (the *Oracle* looks forward to the day when Alexandria, city of the Greeks, 'shall become a place where fishermen dry their nets'). All depend on translators who understood both languages. Only later, in the fourth century AD, when the old Egyptian scripts were history, do we find the charlatan Horapollo interpreting the 'meaning' of hieroglyphs for Greek readers – a few facts buried deep in pure fantasy. The secondary fascination with the age-old magic and mystery of Egyptian beliefs did not call up a class of serious interpreters like the pioneer Sanscritists of British India in the eighteenth and nineteenth centuries.

At the level of the everyday, of course, life depended on living together. Yet cultural assimilation had its limits. Certainly more Egyptians learned Greek than Greeks learned Egyptian. Individuals of Egyptian birth might take Greek names, Graeco-Egyptian families might adopt double-barrelled names, one element from each language, but that did not exclude a predictable strain of low-level contempt. 'Please send me a policeman with a warrant against Lastas,' wrote one Oxyrhynchite Greek. 'He has afforded me considerable violence. Don't forget! You know how the Egyptians are.'[15]

The Roman conquerors indeed established a formal hierarchy: at the top, the grandees sent from Rome to occupy the highest offices of government; next, the citizens of those cities (Alexandria, Naukratis, Ptolemais, later Antinoopolis) which had maintained the basic institutions of a classical city-state; then the ruling classes of the local capitals, who could prove their privileged ancestry by reference to a register established under Augustus; then the mass of the population. From the Roman point of view, many Greek-speakers counted among 'Egyptians'; and in practical terms the edict of AD 212, in which the Emperor Caracalla granted Roman citizenship to all the people of the Empire, made little difference, except that many now adopted the Emperor's first name, Aurelius, and appealed to Roman law and procedure when it seemed advantageous. It was the same emperor who referred with contempt to the 'rural Egyptians'; such people, whose looks and bearing and lifestyle showed how alien they were to 'urban residence', should be expelled from Alexandria.[16]

Alexandria naturally took pride of place. Magnificent it was; its Arab conquerors were warned not to go out by moonlight, since the sheen of its marble might blind a man. It was also unmanageably huge and volatile, a magnet for the starving and the fugitive. One prefect, early in Roman rule, needed his bodyguard to save him from lynching. Its aristocracy was no less fractious. It waged a long struggle with the city's substantial Jewish community, and with the Roman governors and their imperial masters. As the patriotic struggle continued, there circulated more and more glamorised accounts of Hellenic martyrdom, in which heroic Greeks face down brutal Romans. Romans might command power, but Greeks commanded culture.[17]

From Alexandria Roman authority ruled the kingdom of the pharaohs. At the head, the Prefect himself, governor and commander-in-chief. Below him, other high officials sent from Rome: the Chief Justice, who handled courts and archives; the Privy Purse, who administered the private domains of the Emperor; the High Priest, who controlled the temples, their large estates and their influential hereditary priesthood. Below them came three (perhaps four) more Roman officers, the *epistrategoi*, each with some administrative responsibility for one of the sub-provinces into which Egypt was divided. Below that, the pharaonic system, as adapted by the Ptolemies, remained in place, a descending hierarchy of counties (*nomes*), districts, villages. From flea-bitten homestead to the viceregal palace, the chain took information upwards and commandments downwards.

Commands and information lived in mutual dependence. The state required revenue, in cash and in corn. For that it needed labour, from its peasant-farmers and from its local officials. Both sides of the system depended on full and elaborate record-keeping – land-registers, tax-accounting, regular data from the census. In principle, the state disposed of all the mechanisms necessary to enforce its demands: courts, police, soldiery, and a culture of threat. Yet it could not go too far. If officials were pressed too hard, they would resign their property rather than serve. If peasants despaired (particularly in a year of bad flood), they might leave their land and retreat to the desert with bandits and hermits. In such circumstances the government might be forced to issue an amnesty, or to promise reform. Despotism and the command economy had no sure weapon against passive resistance.

Plentiful papyus, the writing habit, proliferating bureaucracy: as the citizen carved out a living between the vagaries of nature and the demands of the state, he left a paper trail. At the lowest level, of course, life goes on without writing, and we can only guess at its events. But once it enters the written medium, it enters history; and it is the pleasure of Greek Egypt that the accident of climate has preserved, through the papyri, the lives and the voices of ordinary people with rare vividness. Among the cities strung out along the Nile, one site stands out for the concentrated richness of its written rubbish: Oxyrhynchos. This book sets out to picture Oxyrhynchos and its people in the high days of the imperial province, between the coming of the Romans and the establishment of Christianity. We begin with a snapshot of the city on a peak of civic pride, shortly after it had adopted a new and more resounding title, 'the Glorious and Most Glorious City of the Sharp-nosed Fish'.

CHAPTER 4

'GLORIOUS AND MOST GLORIOUS CITY'

•　　•　　•　　•

It is the fifth year of the Emperor Caesar Lucius Domitius Aurelianus, Conqueror of the Goths, Conqueror of the Carpi, Greatest, Pious, Fortunate, Unvanquished, Augustus, Restorer of the World: AD 273. The Emperor has regained his eastern provinces from the Queen of Palmyra, and now campaigns on the northern frontier of the Empire. His viceroy governs Egypt from its seaside capital, Alexandria. Up-country and up-Nile, half-hellenised towns compete in urban splendour. On one of them the fans begin to converge for the sporting event of the year. The Worldwide Capitoline Games are to be hosted by Oxyrhynchos, the Glorious and Most Glorious (it is a new title) City of the Sharp-nosed Fish.[1]

There is a road, the military road which follows the western bank of the Nile before turning a little inland to pass through Takona and Oxyrhynchos (the other bank would be quicker, if you are heading for the sights of Thebes or the garrison at Koptos).[2] But of course the stations on the road, which provide lodging and food (bread, meat and wine for men, barley and chaff and water for their beasts),[3] are reserved for government officials. It would be easiest by boat, up-Nile from the new capital, Alexandria, to the old capital, Memphis, turning off into the ship-canal for the Fayûm and then at Ptolemais Hormou onto the natural side-branch of the Nile later known as Joseph's Canal: 250 miles, against the current, which take ten uncomfortable days. A traveller's diary ends most days on a note of relief: 'we took a bath'.[4] Sailing by night, or in a storm, is not advised.[5] The last stage, at least, is plain sailing: Joseph's

Canal, which the Oxyrhynchites called 'the Tomis river' or simply 'our river', provides a north–south route, parallel to the Nile or 'great river', past Herakleopolis Magna and then the Oxyrhynchite villages of Artapatou, Senekeleu and Paimis, to the harbour of Oxyrhynchos.[6] *Oxyrhynchos* means 'sharp-nosed'; the city takes its name from the fish it worships.[7]

The traveller disembarks at one of the quays (north and south), not far from the Small Nilometer, where the rise and fall of the annual flood could be checked.[8] On the bank, the city shelters within its town-wall: some three miles of wall, with five gates, protecting perhaps 20,000 inhabitants in an area of less than one square mile, which they share with thirty temples, three or four public baths, a theatre, a gymnasium, a race-course, a town-hall and a military command-centre.[9]

This is an old city. Fifteen centuries earlier the Pharaoh Ramesses III had funded its temple of Seth the destroyer of Osiris, then its patron deity. The Greek settlers renamed the city for its sacred fish, and now the pharaonic town is overlaid with the Hellenic accoutrements of civic pride. Since about AD 200 it has possessed some kind of independence, with its own town council. It has taken a title – first 'The Glorious City of the Oxyrhynchites', then 'The Glorious and Most Glorious City of the Oxyrhynchites'. A Roman would find some aspects familiar: main streets crossing at right-angles, four triumphal pillars at the junction, porticoes and colonnades; Roman names for Roman institutions – the *campus* for exercise, the *circus* for horse-racing, the *praetorium* as military command, a *Capitol* with its hint of Roman worship. Other features less so: houses of two or three storeys, not blocks of tenements; temples approached in the Egyptian way by a processional avenue.

Enter, through the East Gate. A walk about reveals, around the main avenues and squares, a complex of narrow streets and lanes – you do well to watch out for donkeys driven at speed.[10] The streets have names, but there are no street signs; a traveller who has to deliver a letter (the public post is reserved for official correspondence) gets his own 'sign' in a descriptive address – 'At the camp . . .', 'In the Temenouthis quarter, in the lane opposite the well'.[11] Within the walls, the Mayor and the town council administer a close-knit community, divided into parishes (*amphoda*), each of some 200 houses, whose names in themselves show the historical structure of the town. There are ethnic quarters (Jews, Cretans, Lycians), occupational quarters (goose-herds, shepherds), quarters named for their main building – Gymnasium Square, Serapis Square,

Theatre Square, Thoereion Square; others recall a familiar local feature, a myrobalanos tree, a grasshopper, a burial of sacred Ibis birds.[12] Houses and public buildings crowd together. When the town council's inspectors survey the East Stoa (north to south), they pass the houses of Demetrios and Sarapion, the place of Athenodoros and the place of Didymos the fruiterer (perhaps the pitches of street-vendors), the house of Euporion the retired seller of condiments, the Temple of Hadrian; then, opposite the Street of the Hot Baths, a vetch-seller's and a beer-shop; then, opposite temples of Demeter and Dionysus, a butcher's. When they take the parallel route down the West Stoa, they note the surgery of Doctor Dioskoros, a stable, the school of the teacher Dionysios, the Temple of Fortune, the Temple of Achilles; a record office, a market, a town-crier's stand, and the house of Thonis the girdle-maker.[13]

Temples and Baths

The tourist, once disembarked, will make for the city centre, the square at the Temple of Serapis.[14] An avenue approaches the temple, a wall surrounds it (a sack-maker trading at its side-door); its ceremonial gateway, in the Egyptian style, carries a great image of the patron god.[15] Priests and personnel (lamp-lighters and the like) come and go. Believers arrive to worship (they take a sacred palm-branch from the attendant under the gateway),[16] and to consult the oracle. In the evening, private parties can be held there.[17] Outside, bankers keep their counters, and traders set up their stalls. At the Serapeum Market you can find fine bread and coarse bread, butchers' meat, fruit, olives and dates, beans, marrows, cucumbers and other vegetables, wood and rushes, dung and cowpats, tinwork and pottery, salt, spices and natron, wool and yarn, shoes and clothes and garlands. A board of overseers sets the tariff, collects a daily rent per stall and puts in its accounts monthly and yearly.[18] The same officers account for a monthly levy on each brothel.

An older cult occupies a complex no less grand, that of Athena Thoeris, the Most Great Goddess,[19] 'our ancestral temple' as one distinguished citizen calls it (he dedicates there the gold crowns given him by a grateful city).[20] The buildings are large enough to need seven night-watchmen (and another one outside), and a nearby crossroads is adorned with four triumphal columns in the grand style.[21] Its gold statue of the goddess had caused a municipal scandal, when some of the gold went missing. The case went to the highest authority, the Prefect, and two successive prefects handled its ramifications (in the end the overseers of the project and the gymnasiarchs and others had to repay a substantial sum).[22] Athena, the Greek goddess of wisdom, here merges with the Egyptian goddess Ta-weret, patron of fertility and childbirth, whose statues show her part hippopotamus and part lion.

The temple is served by a variety of priests and priestesses, and maintained by special craftsmen.[23] It too offers a venue for religious feasts: 'The god invites you to a dinner to be held in the Thoereion tomorrow from the 9th hour.'[24] One guest wrote to the goddess: 'I was dining yesterday with my friends in your most happy precinct. Falling asleep . . .' – he had no doubt an oracular dream.[25] Elsewhere in the city, at least two other shrines show how important Thoeris is. One of them seems to serve as base for a company of town-criers, for an advertisement says: 'If anyone has found a pair of child's tunics, colour nut-brown . . . let him give them to the company of criers in the Thoereion of the Proclamations, receiving 16 drachmas and 2 drachmas for the goddess.'[26] Other temples and shrines house other gods and goddesses. Egyptian and Greek deities range side by side, Isis and Osiris next to Apollo, Demeter, Hera, Hermes, Kore, Nemesis and Zeus. A temple of Dionysus stands near the great Thoereion.[27]

The visitor may stop for a drink, even in the Capitol, where the Mayor has been leasing out spare space (Aurelios Horion had bid for it, with a view to opening a tavern, the premises to be returned at the end of the lease 'clean of excrement and filth' and complete with all its doors and keys).[28] Then he can work out at the gymnasium, or wash off at the baths, or check the programme for the theatre.

The gymnasium is cultural centre and country club in one. You can go for a stroll, or sit under its arcades; you can wrestle or play ball.[29] The president (*gymnasiarch*) can be expected to provide oil for a rub-down, and refreshments as well; as a reward, a local poet salutes his generosity – not just for the flowing oil, not just for the gifts of holy Demeter, 'which any rich man could provide', but as one expert in the craft of the Muses. The refreshments may be substantial: 'for the gymnasium, 82 cakes.'[30] There are staff to look after the visitor: cloak-room attendants, masseurs.[31] Behind the services, benefactors or the city council pay to heat the bath and refurbish it and replace its windows.[32]

Baths are not just for the traveller. They represent an important part of the citizen's life. One set of accounts shows 'bath' almost every day, at a normal cost of one obol, all on a par with the essential shopping: 'oil, water-melon, vegetables, lunch, bath'; 'oil, cabbage, melon, bath'; 'oil, beetroot, bath, eggs' . . .[33] 'Going to the baths,' says a petitioner, 'I locked the street-door of my house' – but came back to find much of his wardrobe stolen.[34] By now, the city has several such establishments: the hot baths (which gave their name to a lane off the Eastern Stoa, and indeed to a whole district),[35] or the imperial, or the sacred, or the baths of Antoninus and Trajan at the Gymnasium.

The city has invested heavily in these amenities, once it set its sights on providing the essentials of *confort moderne*; it even took over the private baths of Arrios Apolinarios.[36] Already in AD 128 the Prefect himself had approved the city's plan 'to adorn their fatherland' by constructing a bath with moneys already collected and possible future donations.[37] Twenty years later, a generous gymnasiarch was giving money for just such a purpose.[38] By the year of the Games, the running costs and maintenance represent a substantial charge. Heating (perhaps by burning chaff, since wood is always in short supply) has to be paid for.[39] At a later stage, the guild of glass-makers supplies 6000 pounds of glass for work on the hot baths and the walks. Seven talents of tin are required for soldering lead pipes in the imperial bath. Bronzesmiths also contributed.[40] And then there are staffing costs: the changing-room with its boxes for clothes is leased out, and the lessees recover their rent in fees; but the bath-man and the water-pourers received a monthly salary on the Mayor's instructions.[41]

Water, of course, comes from 'our river', running higher or lower according to the season. There is no question of springs, or of an aqueduct, which would have led only to the waterless desert beyond the valley. Normal households draw river-water as it filters into their wells. But the city needs more elaborate arrangements to deliver the piped supply required for the baths and for any public fountains. There will be a water-tower, or more than one, from which the flow is distributed by gravity. To fill this reservoir, water must be raised mechanically from the river, and raised by simple continuous labour. The city of Arsinoe, some way to the north, had developed a comprehensive system quite early. It used three devices to fill its water-tower (*castellum*, a Latin name for what was perhaps a Roman borrowing), which distributed water (for a charge) to baths, public fountains, a brewery and a synagogue. There was the screw-pump named after Archimedes. There was the *saqia*, a vertical wheel of pots turned by a horizontal wheel moved round by oxen. Most basically, there was the *shaduf*, a long boom with a bucket tied to one end and a counterweight to the other, balanced on a horizontal support (the bucket is pulled down to fill with water, and the counterweight helps to raise it again). The Arsinoite system required two saqia, manned by six ox-drivers; and 16 shaduf, with one and a half workers to each, working from dawn to dusk and sometimes through the night. The incidental costs are high: wood and nails to repair the wheels, pots for the wheels and rope to tie them on, fodder for the oxen, lamps for the night shift – and then pipes and spouts for the public fountains and provision for cleaning them out. Nile water is thought healthy, by outsiders, in part because it is so thick with silt.[42]

Oxyrhynchos has a less ambitious system, but even that is not fool-proof. Ten years before the Games, in AD 264, the Mayor had received a despairing letter from a town councillor, Aurelios Didymos, who had been awarded the contract for drawing up water for the hot baths: 'I attached the greatest importance, difficult as it was and beyond my means, especially because of the peculiar conditions of the past year, to carrying out the duties of this service, so that through the relevant months I did not fail, being pressed to serve, nor indeed for providing for the present month though it falls outside the contract. But I believe you too realise the slowness of the river's rising, for which reason fodder for the beasts is in short supply . . .' For that reason, 'I declare that I have given up.'[43] The water, that is, is raised by a wheel, and the wheel is powered by oxen; no fodder, no bath.

After his bath, the tourist can move on. At the edge of the city, near the walls, stands the theatre, all in stone and by now at least a century old, with seating for more than 11,000 and on a scale to match the theatres of much more famous cities.[44] Its stagefront is set off by columns of red granite, bases and capitals of marble; before every fourth column stands a colossal marble statue. It serves as a public space: official diaries show officials and magistrates appearing there, civic accounts mention them offering sacrifices on public holidays.[45] The city pays for its upkeep, and its security guards; at night, one guard is stationed outside and three inside.[46] In the square outside, craftsmen craft and watchers watch. Gaios the tinsmith works there, and Senthonis uses him as an accommodation address to receive a business letter and goods arriving by water – a jar of honey and a pillow-case full of dates ('Wash the case and send it back to me, so that I know you've got the dates').[47] Taor was to turn up there, her brother wrote, 'and find out about the stone bowl on the boat and pass the word to everyone there, Philokyros and Zosimos, to keep an eye out for it, in case Agathinos himself decides to grab the bowl'.[48] But the theatre is also a theatre, a main venue no doubt for the Worldwide Games as for other shows, festivals and competitions, when the organisers might pay professional participants – a town-crier, an athletics-organiser, umpires; wrestlers, boxers, ball-players; machinists and water-sprinklers; pipers, mime-artists, Homeric reciters.[49] A venue also for classic drama, at least for revivals of the tragedies of Euripides and the comedies of Menander: some surviving copies distinguish the characters not by name but as '1', '2' and '3' – these were used by actors allotted the lead, second and third roles in the production.[50] A generous gymnasiarch has given money to subsidise the tickets, as for other civic amenities.[51]

Houses and Gardens

Round about the public buildings cluster private houses great and small, mostly of two or three storeys. The town, of course, stands on raised ground, above the level of the Nile's annual flood. The limits of the site, and the need to spare valuable farmland, make it necessary to build upwards rather than sideways.[52] 'Towers' constitute an important enough part of the structure to describe the house – many have two, at least one luxury residence possesses three.[53] The outer walls, twice as thick as those within, keep out sun and intruders; an inner court often provides light (and some shade) for the rooms inside. Most houses are of brick – Egypt provides mud in plenty. Some are substantial: the house of Dionysios, son of Sarapion, near the Serapeum includes a two-storey 'tower', a gate-house, a balcony, a light-well, a store-room and, attached to the tower, a yard with a stone well, plus a vacant lot – a total area of 150 square yards.[54] Others cram themselves onto a cabbage patch. One house and yard, 'formerly a vacant lot', covers an area of less than 60 square feet.[55] An architect's drawing shows how to use space: a gate-house gives onto an inner court which includes the door to the cellar (down steps) and stairs up to the first floor, and an inner room. The gate-house seems to measure 5 x 7 feet (35 square feet), the inner room is 9 feet wide; the whole site totals 225 square feet. Even with the room or rooms on the first floor, plus perhaps a gallery or sleeping platform, this is a bijou residence, not much more than two up and two down.[56]

The rich can afford bigger houses, sometimes even stone houses. There is a stone house in the Quarter of the Gooseherds, belonging to two aristocratic sisters, citizens of Alexandria and citizens of Rome; it is their next-door neighbour, the rich landowner Claudia Isidora, who can afford to buy it at a high price.[57] Stone is costly, and it has to be transported. So Antonia Asklepias agrees with a pair of stone-cutters that they will provide for her house, the stone to come from 'the northern quarry'; seven different sizes, according to function, all of them 'camel stone', i.e. of a weight to be transported by camel over a distance (assuming that the quarries lie in the escarpment) of some three miles; the cutters to cut out the stones, 'with no ornamentation falling on us'; they will be paid per stone, and in addition each man each day a loaf of bread and something to eat with it.[58]

Here and there gardens intervene.[59] Pammenes' Garden, out by one of the city gates,[60] gives its name to a whole quarter. The Garden of Diktynos, within the walls, has an orchard with plants and irrigation and a rentable value of 2400 drachmas a year (Lollianos, the town's public schoolmaster, hopes to obtain it in lieu of his unpaid salary).[61] Otherwise, outside the main avenues, habitation and workshops, a camel-stable[62] and a cookshop[63] huddle close together, secured by walls, doors and massive locks (keys are large enough to serve as offensive weapons). Wood is scarce, so doors are precious (you take care to specify that any tenant should return your house with all its doors and shutters). There are the usual inconveniences of close quarters: you need legal possession of your entrances and exits;[64] you need to make sure that your neighbour's gutter does not discharge onto your house.[65] In any case, thieving neighbours could always climb in;[66] brick walls could not resist a battering-ram.[67]

Sales and leases describe the property in detail. Well-appointed houses even boast a private bath-house.[68] None mentions a lavatory, whether from modesty or more likely because the concept does not exist. Household furniture can include pots and even close-stools. These have to be emptied, perhaps on the dung-hills which build up in streets and the refuse-tips which accumulate round the periphery. There everything could be dumped, including unwanted (normally female) babies – an imported habit, it seems, for Greek writers report with surprise that Egyptians 'rear all their offspring'. The more pragmatic Greeks see the difficulty of feeding too many mouths, especially the females, who will only repay their costs by a good marriage. Such babies can be picked up by anyone interested, who then owns them as slaves or to sell on; wetnurses are hired to get them through the infant stage.[69] Round and about the visitor can expect the familiar smell of waste, animal and human. House-leases commonly specify that the rooms should be returned 'cleansed of excrements and every kind of filth'.[70] In an affectionate if mispelled letter Kallirhoe writes to an absent friend: 'I make obeisance on your behalf every day before the Lord God Serapis. From the day you left we miss your turds, wishing to see you.'[71]

Twenty minutes at a leisurely pace take you across the city, from 'our river' to the West Gate. Outside, on lower ground, and stretching to the north, are the cemeteries: here gravestones in Greek style, there tombs in Egyptian style. Here lies Akousilaos son of Dios, who left money to his slaves and freedmen so that, once a year, on his birthday, they could party at his tomb. Here lies Sintheus daughter of Diogenes, who willed that her body be prepared and buried 'in an Egyptian burial'.[72] The road continues through the fields, to the cliffs which bound the valley, and up the escarpment to 'the mountain', the desert plateau. Down this path come raiding Bedouin; only a dozen years before, the Goniotai, a tribe from the Libyan border, had descended on the rich and peaceful valley.[73] Up the road go those who have business in the desert and – more than a hundred dry miles away – in the Small Oasis, where underground water sustains a flourishing entrepot closely tied to Oxyrhynchos in trade and in administration: camel-dealers, fugitive peasants, caravans of donkeys, and the mummified bodies, carefully labelled, of those who can afford a resting place in the Valley of the Golden Mummies, closer to the setting sun.[74] More ambitious pilgrims can rest here before undertaking the caravan route, twelve days at least by camel, which leads to the Oasis of Siwa, where the oracular god Ammon had blessed Alexander the Great.

Games or no games, the Oxyrhynchites get on with their lives, from dawn to the lighting of the lamps,[75] day by day and hour by flexible hour (since, as in the rest of the Empire, their hour is a twelfth of the daylight, shorter in winter than in summer). They describe themselves, in the verbal self-portraits which documents carry as a guarantee of identification. 'Aged about 50, middle height, honey-coloured, long face, scar on the left foot'[76] – but there is no standard type: skin white or dark or honey, faces long or broad or round, noses straight or sharp or slightly snub, sight sometimes short or squinting or impaired by cataract, moles often on the face or neck, scars very frequently on face, arms, legs, anywhere left exposed by a tunic. They have names, some of Greek origin, some of Egyptian; most of them carry the first name 'Aurelios', a reminder of the Emperor to whom they owed their Roman citizenship.

Elites and Tax-payers

The city has its elites. At the top of the pyramid stand the magistrates and the town council; the city is to some extent self-governing. Some magistrates are real grandees. Thus Aurelios Euporos, otherwise called Agathos Daimon, who holds triple office as recorder, interpreter (*exêgêtês*) and town councillor, has served as superintendent of the food supply, superintendent of the *ephebes*, and (again) interpreter of Alexandria itself: nobility doing the honours in the backwoods, where no doubt he owned country estates.[77]

Higher officials keep official diaries, which list their activities and include summaries of cases heard before them. Among magistrates, the exegete at least follows suit. Euporos' successor takes on a delicate case delegated by the top military official of the province, the *Corrector Aegypti*, Claudius Firmus.[78] The exegete takes his seat 'in the public street' outside his house, to make himself accessible to petitioners. Aurelia Didyme, a citizen and an image-bearer in the temple of the Hippopotamus-goddess Thoeris, hands in her petition, and her advocate states her case: both parents of her nephew Aurelios Pekysis, otherwise called Chairemon, have died 'of some feverish illness'; Didyme now seeks the appointment of a guardian, who would safeguard the boy and administer his property, and proposes her brother, another image-bearer of Thoeris, as the nearest male relative. The Corrector has approved, but left it to the local exegete, who in such cases could act as recorder, to make the appointment. So, 'Here is the child, who is very young, and the person approved on my client's request by his Excellency the Corrector to act as guardian of the child by reason of kinship and because he himself is in religious service: we ask that the appointment be made.' Life-expectancy is short; widows and orphans abound. The Prefect himself may intervene to appoint a guardian[79] or to protect those whose inheritance – 'land, livestock and slaves' – have been stolen during their minority.[80]

The administration devolves on the Mayor (*prytanis*) and the town council. They take responsibility for meeting the government's demand for money, supplies and 'liturgists' – the well-to-do citizens who are nominated to administrative functions and pay out of their own pockets if they fail to meet targets. The council's minutes strike a note of drama as it wrestles with day-to-day problems. The city must provide a gold crown to celebrate the Emperor's latest victory: how much to pay the goldsmiths? Nominations are due for city offices: the Mayor nominates Neilos as overseer. 'The councillors said: "Good faithful Neilos! Neilos always does the right thing! Strength to him!"'[81] The state requires a levy of flax, but the flax-merchants are asking higher prices; the local governor needs men to escort a levy of livestock downriver, but who will serve? The Mayor suggests an arrangement, to general enthusiasm: 'The councillors said, "Invaluable Mayor! Preserve yourself for us! You do your office well!"' The Mayor emphasises, understandably, that it is time to appoint his successor: 'I am sick and coughing from my lungs.'[82]

The structure rests on a hereditary class-system. Those who claim citizenship, and among them those who claim membership of the Gymnasium, have to prove ancestral right. So Aurelios Patermouthis, aged fourteen, 'no identifying marks, resident in the quarter of Pammenes' Garden', is presented by his brother to be recognised and enrolled in the gymnasial class. The document testifies that their great-grandfather's grandfather had been enrolled in the fifth year of the Deified Vespasian, their great-great-grandfather in the fourth year of the Deified Trajan, their great-grandfather in the fourteenth year of the Deified Hadrian ... So the privileged status goes back five generations and two hundred years, during which the family has moved house at least four times.[83]

Citizens have privileges: in the year of the Games, 3000 of them are drawing a monthly bread ration from city funds.[84] The gymnasial class provides councillors and magistrates. The price is responsibility for the functioning of city and state. The city needs public transport; Euporos son of Hermeinos is nominated to provide a quarter of a donkey.[85] But then again, if you provide a donkey, you qualify for free rations.[86] The city needs food, and here the local governor (*stratégos*) intervenes with maximum formality: Aurelios Theodoros swears by the Imperial Genius to sell fine oil every day, at his establishment in the market, 'so that there shall be no subversion of the supply'.[87] Soldiers need food: when the Palmyrene invaders appear, the district must contribute enough barley to feed a hundred horses for three days;[88] for 'the most noble soldiers' of the imperial army, the gymnasiarch goes from village to village, rounding up pigs, which their owners must bring to the city to be weighed – any delay to be punished by the Prefect.[89] Threats grease the wheels of administration. When the state needs grain in a hurry, the Prefect appoints a local worthy, Septimios Eudaimon, to expedite matters: 'As you know the peril to yourself involved in this service, take care to make all the public donkeys serve the lading, so that the boats being sent to transport the grain shall not be delayed.'[90]

At the private level, of course, citizens richer and poorer pursue their normal business. Land is the basic investment. Aurelios Herakleides son of Pindaros leases from Aurelios Severos, gymnasiarch and councillor, land to be sown with wheat or barley or any other crop, the owner to pay the taxes and retain ownership of the crop until the rent is paid.[91] Aurelios Serenos alias Sarapion rents land under green fodder from the heirs of Vibius Publius (a veteran, honourably discharged, once on the staff of the Prefect himself)[92] and bids publicly to purchase land from the state administration[93] – all part of a long profitable career in house-property, agricultural land and vineyards.[94] Inheritance accumulates and disperses property: Aurelios Thonis claims for himself and his half-brothers the property of his sister Saraeus, who has died childless and intestate – the lawyer has drawn up the application in solemn Latin, with a signature in Greek, though in fact Thonis is illiterate and someone else signs for him.[95] (For fifty years now all citizens of Oxyrhynchos have been citizens of Rome, and may invoke the language and procedure of Roman law. Roman law provides privileges for the parents of three or more children, and Julius Theon alias Zoilos goes so far as to claim that his property is beyond the law, in virtue of his fecundity.)[96] Investment produces income, in money or produce; wheat serves as currency as well as commodity, wheat cheques can be drawn on wheat accounts, and wheat trading can be organised three hundred miles away, at Pelusium on the easternmost mouth of the Nile.[97]

But there is no business without taxes, and taxes have to be paid even for the year of the Games. 'Paid at the granary of Iseion Tryphonos, for the produce of the past 5th year of our Lord Aurelianus Augustus, by Isos son of Hermeias, through Artemidoros the farmer, of wheat artabas twenty-two, that makes 22 art. wh. [Signature of receiving official]: I Aurelios Heras, dekaprotos, have signed for the twenty-two artabas of wheat, that makes 22 art. wh.'[98] Death does not exempt you: 'Paid by bank-transfer to the collectors of the Imperial Anabolikon, account of the heirs of Sarapas, through his wife, drachmas fifty-six, makes dr. 56. Year 5, Phamenoth 19. I, Aurelios Antonios, have signed for them.'[99]

The rentiers, the entrepreneurs, the traders need services. Far down the ladder, Eudaimon makes his living minding the cloakroom in a public building, probably one of the public baths. For that he pays rent to the city (535 drachmas a month), and duly receives a receipt from the Mayor.[100] It looks like a family business. Some fifteen years earlier the city had invited bids for the right to run two cloakrooms in the hot baths attached to the Gymnasium.[101] The lessee, just dead, was called Eudaimon; his son now bids to take over; it may well be that our Eudaimon was the son's son, named as often after his grandfather and continuing the family firm. Baths are business, and the clothes-thief a commonplace figure. The cloakroom concession is worth bidding for, the investment then recouped from fees charged to individual bathers. The rent stated has increased from 17 drachmas a month to 535 drachmas a month; these are different buildings and circumstances, but it looks like a thirty-fold inflation. This sort of cost affects many citizens; and it is one of the items included when the Emperor Diocletian tries, thirty years later, to check inflation (with predictable lack of success) by fixing the cost of goods and services throughout the Empire: 'To the attendant, for each customer being towelled down, 2 denarii.'[102] The younger Eudaimon will hope to do good business, as the Games bring in the tourists.

Glories and Crises

The city's fortunes have varied. *Polis* ('city' or 'city-state') is an evocative word to Greeks. Classical Greece, that cultural exemplar, had consisted of independent *poleis*; the rise of the monarchies could be seen as the end of true civilisation. The true polis possesses democratic institutions, its own magistrates and its own town council. Egypt too possesses poleis in this full sense, notably the old Greek foundation of Naukratis and the newer Greek foundation of Ptolemais. The old Egyptian towns, on the other hand, received the title of polis without the full political organisation, and even Alexandria had lost its council at an early stage. It was only in about AD 200 that the imperial government permitted them a last symbol of cityhood, a town council (*boulê*). This organ of self-government was to prove a mixed blessing. It exercises authority over the city's administration and finances; at the same time it (and its individual members) assume responsibility for fulfilling the financial and other demands of the central government – taxes, requisitions, unpaid compulsory service in the local administration (so-called *liturgies*).

Oxyrhynchos has certainly registered ups and downs in the wake of its new-found civic status. In AD 235 many houses in the city are empty.[103] At some time between 232 and 247 the Oxyrhynchites officially bewail their own ruin. In 246 a deputation protests to the prefect about new taxation. In 258 the Mayor dwells on their straitened circumstances.[104] Some of this may be traditional fare; there was never a middle class that did not feel overtaxed. But there may have been objective factors, external (for this is the time of the first great crisis of the Roman Empire) and internal: in 246 grain is so short that the government resorts to compulsory purchase; the burden of liturgies is such that the government concedes a reduction.[105] In 253, Egypt is ravaged by plague.[106]

Yet there are signs, at least in the second half of the century, of pride and prosperity. In 249 public buildings are under repair.[107] Around 255 the city appoints a public schoolmaster, thus imitating the cultural institutions of much greater cities.[108] From 265 it sets up a corn-dole, a free ration issued to selected citizens, again on the model of Rome.[109] Towards 269 it takes the title 'Glorious', a few years later 'Glorious and Most Glorious'. By 283 it is constructing a new street. In 284–6 it is important enough for the Prefect to hold assizes there.[110] Within this rise, the holding of the Worldwide Capitoline Games in 273 represents another assertion of civic magnificence.

The Games touch the city's life in various ways. Its citizens too have the opportunity to compete, and gain glory, even vicariously. The gymnasiarch, titular head of the gymnasium and representative of its social functions, intends to take part in the chariot race – not in person (it is a dangerous business, and perhaps also beneath his dignity). He therefore hires a professional, Aurelios Demetrios son of Diophanes from the neighbouring town of Hermopolis, who contracts 'of his own free will and choice to act as charioteer for you with your horses at the sacred Capitoline games to be auspiciously celebrated in the said city of the Oxyrhynchites, properly and faithfully . . .'[111]

Victors join the World Association of the Artists of Dionysos, whose members enjoy high prestige and practical advantages. Such is Aurelios Apollodidymos son of Ploution, citizen of Oxyrhynchos, recently admitted to membership. The town council, through the great Aurelios Euporos, now Mayor, informs the keepers of tax-records that, 'bowing down before the imperial decree', they have confirmed Apollodidymos' rights; and 'since we judged it appropriate to report this explicitly to you, so that you recognise the exemption owed him by law and make the necessary annotation on his file, this letter is sent to you, dear colleagues.'

His actual application survives in all its grandeur.[112] It begins by quoting, one by one, the emperors who have confirmed and extended the privileges of the World Association – Claudius, Hadrian, Septimius Severus and Caracalla, Alexander Severus. Those privileges included protection of property, front seats on public occasions, exemption from military service, exemption from public offices, exemption from duty on goods imported for personal use, freedom from jury-service and from acting as guarantor and from being forced to billet strangers ... Apollodidymos serves also as secretary to the Association, and transmits its decree on his own behalf: the Association confirms his election as member, the proper fee having been paid, and its three directors sign and seal. One director turns out to be a trumpeter of international celebrity, citizen of Pergamum and Rhodes, 'victor at the Capitolia in Rome, three times victor at the Pythian Games, ten times at the Olympic Games, twelve times at the Actian Games, thirteen times at the Asclepian Games, Remarkable ...'

So it was, in AD 273, that the citizens of an Egyptian market-town played host to the world and its celebrities, on the occasion of the First Sacred Triumphal Worldwide Five-yearly Capitoline Festival of Drama, Athletics and Horseriding being held in the Glorious and Most Glorious City of the Oxyrhynchites.

CHAPTER 5

LORD AND GOD

• • • •

'He set Egypt apart,' says the historian Tacitus, looking back to the achievements of Augustus, the first Roman Emperor. Egypt was a prize. The future Emperor, then a warlord in pursuit of autocracy, took it from his rival Mark Antony and Antony's wife Cleopatra, the last of the Ptolemies. Egypt became a province, but a province of a special kind. It retained its own separate currency; it retained its own system of dating, by regnal years and not by Roman consuls. No senator could visit it without special permission; anyone leaving it might need a permit from the Prefect if he was to pass harbour control in Alexandria.[1] That is a tribute to its strategic importance. It could provide an impregnable base for a rival emperor. It did provide the city of Rome, during a third of the year, with the corn supply which prevented food riots at home.

The Emperor was pharaoh: lord, and god. On Egyptian temples, he stands carved in traditional Egyptian regalia. On him depended the rising of the Nile and the fertility of the kingdom. To Hellenes he presented himself as godlike in life and deified after death. Towns like Oxyrhynchos had their *Kaisareion*, the shrine of Caesar, or *Sebasteion*, the shrine of Sebastos (the Greek for Augustus). Living emperors needed the support of other gods, and their subjects interceded for them. Thus in AD 163–4 the 'sacred virgin' Taarthoonis was elected by her fellow priests to organise the procession for the Good Fortune of their Lords the Emperors. Some time later, and further out in the country, another priestess (name unknown to the urban grandee who gave the order) was to provide for the general well-being – 'Markos Aurelios Apollonios, hierophant, to the priestess who carries the basket at Nesmimis, greetings. Please go off to Sinkepha, to the temple of Demeter, and carry out the customary sacrifices for our Lords the Emperors and their victory and the rise of the Nile and the growth of the crops and the temperateness of the climate. I pray for your health.'[2]

A new Emperor required public rejoicing. When the news reached the Prefect, he wrote to the strategoi with instructions to celebrate. So, on 25 August AD 117, his Excellency Rammius Martialis wrote to (among others) the governor of the Oxyrhynchite: 'Know that, for the salvation of the entire human race, Imperator Caesar Traianus Hadrianus Optimus Augustus Germanicus Dacicus Parthicus has taken over the leadership from his divine father. So, praying to all the gods that his continuing presence be preserved to us for all time, we shall wear garlands for 10 days. Make this public to the districts in your charge.'[3] Martialis was quick off the mark; the new Emperor, Hadrian, had been proclaimed by the army only a fortnight earlier, at Antioch in Syria, and neither he nor his prefect waited for the Senate in Rome to confirm him in office.

When the news came from Rome, it arrived later (depending on the wind), 20 or 25 days to Alexandria, 30 days to Oxyrhynchos, 50 days to reach the old pharaonic capital, Thebes, in the deep south.[4] Thus Nero dated his reign from 13 October AD 54, but it was only on 17 November that someone at Oxyrhynchos (the strategos?) was drafting, rather incoherently, the announcement that 'Caesar the manifest god has gone to the ancestors to whom he is owed, and he who was both expected and hoped for by the world has been appointed Emperor – Nero Caesar, the world's good fortune and the origin of all good things, has been appointed. Therefore we must all acknowledge our gratitude to the gods by wearing garlands and offering sacrifices.'[5]

When the succession was disputed, the Prefect might face a perilous gamble. In AD 68, after the murder of Nero, his prefect Tiberius Julius Alexander acknowledged the accession of Galba; a long edict seeks popular support for the new regime by reforming the 'new and unjust exactions' and 'very recent outrages' of the old.[6] However, there seemed no hope of stability in this 'year of the four emperors', and it was the legionaries under Alexander's control who proclaimed the veteran general Vespasian, then commander in Judaea, as Emperor – a successful gamble, for Vespasian won and founded a dynasty. By contrast, in the dangerous days after the murder of Caracalla, the Prefect Valerius Datus paid with his life for having served faithfully (so says the historian Dio) – but perhaps also for being late to proclaim the new emperor Macrinus.[7]

This is not to say that information arrived by official channels only.

On 7 March AD 285, the chicken-man Ammonios received an order:
'From Melas, secretary, to Ammonios the chicken-man, greetings. Give
Ammon the guard, for domestic supplies, ten eggs, total 10 eggs. Year 1
of Diokles, Phamenoth 11.'[8] The date refers to the new Emperor, whose
name appears elsewhere as Diokletianos. Secular and Christian historians
say that Diokles was indeed his name before his accession; it was this
form that native Egyptians transposed into their own language, but no
Greek or Latin document, private or official, uses it. No doubt the
extended and Latinised version rang more congruously in the imperial
titulature. This Emperor had proclaimed himself on 20 November 284, at
Nikomedia in Bithynia. It would be nearly a year before his predecessor,
Carinus, was defeated and killed, but in nearby Egypt the new claimant
seems to have been acknowledged already by 10 February 285.[9] Had
Diocletian originally announced his real name? We do not know. Yet
it seems likely that any official announcement would have used the
romanised form; the Oxyrhynchite poet who celebrated the new ruler
certainly took care to use it, even though it fitted badly to his metre.[10]
How then did Secretary Melas know the original form? Perhaps by a
route particularly powerful in a world without mass-media: the grape-
vine.

Imperial Visits

Most emperors were absent deities. Some, however, did visit Egypt. In
the heyday of the imperial peace, Hadrian made a leisurely tour (AD
130–1). In harder times, soldier-emperors came to confirm their victory
over rivals and to reorganise this important province – Septimius
Severus in 199/200, Diocletian in 297 and 302. For the inhabitants, there
was a price to pay for being visited by the master of the world. The
imperial presence, like an Elizabethan progress, came expensive. There
were special levies to defray the cost; places en route had to provide food
and entertainment. A year before Hadrian arrived, some Oxyrhynchite
villages were put under contribution. 'To Asklepiades, governor, from
Horion, village-secretary of Tholthis and Mouchinaryo in the lower
district. List of the items prepared at present, up to the twentieth of the
present month Choiak, against the presence of the greatest Imperator
Caesar Traianus Hadrianus Augustus in my village-area: barley, 200

artabas; fodder, 3000 bundles; sucking pigs, 372; wood [—]; piglets, 8; sheep, 200; radish oil, 3 measures; chaff, 7 baskets; whole lentils, 3 artabas.'[11] Diocletian was accompanied by a large military escort as he travelled up-Nile; the prospect generated a volley of correspondence, as the governor of the Panopolite nome organised and pressurised ('not once but twice and many times have I sent you written notice ...') 'receivers' and 'superintendants' of every necessity – meat, sour wine, lentils and other vegetables, bread from 'the other large bakery near the theatre' (which had to be refurbished and staffed), bedding for the troops and bedding for the imperial residence.[12]

Hadrian, a peripatetic intellectual, did the sights, and wrote his own account of the trip, which lasted some eight months. The court sailed upriver. At Thebes it halted to view the famous Colossi of Memnon, two huge seated statues of a monarch (in fact the Pharaoh Amenophis III) whom the Greeks identified as Memnon, King of Ethiopia, a hero of the Trojan War until killed by Achilles. One of the pair, mutilated by an earthquake, gave out a sound at sunrise ('like the note of a broken harp,' said a credulous tourist): thus, it was believed, Memnon greeted his mother Eos, the goddess of dawn.

On the first day of Hadrian's visit the statue remained mute, but on the second it duly performed for the Emperor and the Empress Sabina. A royal lady-in-waiting, Balbilla, granddaughter and step-daughter of prefects of Egypt, celebrated the occasion in verse. Her poems, composed in the long-obsolete dialect of Sappho, the first and greatest of poetesses, can still be seen on Memnon's left leg: 'Egyptian Memnon, I learned, when warmed by the sun's ray, utters from his Theban stone. And when he saw Hadrian, the universal king, even before dawn he greeted him as he could. Then, when the Sun, driving on his white horses through heaven, maintained in shadow the second measure of the hours, Memnon let out again a clear voice as of smitten bronze; then in greeting he let out even a third sound.'[13] Ordinary visitors were lucky if Memnon sang once; the ruler of the world elicited three performances.

Not long before this, on 30 October AD 130, the Emperor's young lover, Antinoos, fell into the Nile and drowned. The emperor founded a city, Antinoopolis, in his memory, near the place of his drowning, with the full Hellenic complement of splendid buildings and privileged citizenry. The accident (or sacrifice or suicide) created a modern legend, a Greek tragedy of beauty cut short, in parallel with the ancient Egyptian legend of Osiris dead and resurrected; sculptors represent Antinoos both as Greek ephebe and as Egyptian divinity. Hadrian and Antinoos were long remembered. Oxyrhynchos instituted a Temple of Hadrian, and Baths of Hadrian, and a religious calendar found there notes sacrifices for the deification of Antinoos and 'on the day on which the deified Hadrian entered the city'.[14] Poets who were read there, and indeed poets who wrote there, recall the event in all its pathos and glamour – not just contemporary poets, who might have hoped for preferment, but poets a century and a half later. Certain themes recur: Antinoos' lion-hunt with Hadrian, the red lotus named after him (sprung from the lion's blood), his drowning and assumption into heaven, as a star in the constellation Aquila – Antinoos lost to Hadrian as other boys (Narkissos, Hyakinthos, Adonis) to the gods who loved them. The Egyptian Greeks had acquired a myth all their own.[15]

At the end of the century came a second and more businesslike visitation. Hadrian's adopted son, Antoninus Pius, and Pius' adopted son, Marcus Aurelius, had continued the peaceful succession of emperors. Marcus' own son, Commodus, proved less successful. After his murder in 192, and that of the virtuous Pertinax three months later, various contenders sprang up at Rome and in the provinces. Pescennius Niger, the governor of Syria, was duly recognised in nearby Egypt, for a time; but fate favoured Septimius Severus, an African who held an important command on the Danube frontier, and the viceroy of Egypt changed sides just before Niger's final defeat.[16] The new Emperor had wars to fight on the eastern frontier, against the Parthian Empire. After the second of these he took the opportunity to spend a year in Egypt (AD 199–200), with his son Antoninus (later nicknamed Caracalla), residing in Alexandria and then travelling up Nile.

The Emperor was the judge of final appeal, and individuals seized their opportunity; papyri preserve a whole series of imperial verdicts delivered during the stay in Alexandria. On at least one occasion, the whole community approached the throne. The occasion was recorded, in Latin, in the imperial diary. An informal extract, translated into Greek but still dated in Roman style, turns up at Oxyrhynchos. 'In the consulship of Severus and Victorinus, 7th day before the Ides of March, in Alexandria. Caesar took his seat in the court with his friends and those invited to the council, and gave orders to call in the envoys of the Egyptians who were presenting their common requests. After other matter: Dionysios having made a request about the pig-breeders, because the farmers were already engaged in harvesting, Caesar said . . .': whatever the problem (pigs must be fed, but fodder is short at this season?), the master of the world would pass judgment on crops and swine.[17] Individuals submitted their own cases, in person or by petition, and received decisions by letter or by short answers ('rescripts') posted on the walls of the Gymnasium of Alexandria.[18]

Many cases referred to the public services (liturgies) which the state imposed on individuals qualified by income and education to carry them out: it was a way to man the administration without cost to the treasury. One rich Oxyrhynchite, Horion, who had also held high office in Alexandria, begged permission to set up two foundations, citing the loyalty shown by Oxyrhynchos to the Empire, notably in helping to suppress the Jewish revolt of 115–17. One foundation was to provide prizes for the annual athletic competition at Oxyrhynchos; the other to provide financial help for inhabitants of the Oxyrhynchite villages in which Horion and his sons owned estates, since the villagers were exhausted by the pressure of the yearly liturgies and so likely 'to become as good as dead from the standpoint of the treasury and to leave your land uncultivated'.[19] The Emperors agreed. Indeed, they took more general action. The classic Greek polis had a town council (*boulê*) to discuss its affairs. This had never been allowed to the hellenised towns of Egypt, nor for centuries to the city of Alexandria. The imperial grant added an ornament of civic pride. It also reinforced the structures of financial responsibility – in future the councillors as a body, and their property, would have to guarantee the payment of taxes and levies in their town and the area under its control.[20]

Young Antoninus, otherwise Caracalla, returned, now sole Emperor, in December 215. Amid clouds of incense and festive music, the citizens garlanded with flowers and carrying torches, he made a formal entry into Alexandria, there to visit the tomb of Alexander, his hero, and the Temple of Serapis, a favourite deity.[21] When he left, in March 216, the city commemorated him in marble as 'lover of Serapis' and 'ruler of the world' – the latter epithet had been used of the world-conquering Alexander, of the heavenly bodies on whom depend the destinies of mankind, and (by St Paul) of the sinister princes of the world's darkness.[22] In actual fact, his stay had been bloody. The Alexandrians had no respect for dignity; they had lampooned the Emperor's morals (he had killed his brother) and his stature – how ridiculous for so short a man to emulate Alexander and Achilles. The Emperor revenged himself with a massacre of the city's young men; dead and dying were heaped

1. A Victorian public discovers the land of the pharaohs:
Amelia Edwards' *A Thousand Miles up the Nile* (1876)
became a best-seller.

2. A Victorian artist in Egypt: David Roberts, *The Hypaethral Temple at Philae, call the Bed of Pharaoh* (1843).

3. Egyptomania: the Egyptian Hall, Piccadilly, built in 1812 on the model (allegedly) of the ancient Temple of Dendera.

Part of the site of Oxyrhynchos in 1798, sketch by Denon. The top of a Roman
umn projects above the accumulated debris.

The site of Oxyrhynchos from the north-west in 1981. In the foreground is the base
a Roman column (the 'Phocas Pillar'), possibly the same pillar that Denon drew,
w cleared to ground level but robbed of its upper part.

6. The cloth-capped excavators: B.P. Grenfell (on the right) and A.S. Hunt (on the le
photographed in the Fayûm, c.1900.

7. Excavating Oxyrhynchos: a view of a rubbish-mound, with Grenfell outlined
against the sky. On the right, at the top, is the tomb of the Sheikh Abu Teir.

3. Excavating Oxyrhynchos: the stepwise trenching of a mound, as described by Grenfell (see pages 17–18). The workforce is half men, half boys. Men with mattocks loosen the ground; the others stand by with baskets to remove soil or papyri.

9. Bronze figurine, *c*.500 BC. A worshipper kneels before the sacred oxyrhynchos fish (sharp-nosed and wearing the crown of the goddess Hathor, cow-horns framing the disk of the sun).

10. View of the Bahr Yusuf ('Joseph's Canal') in 1897, the side-branch of the Nile that Oxyrhynchites called 'Our River'.

11. *Oxyrhynchus Papyri*, vol. I, no. 1, the *Logia* or *Sayings of Jesus*, the most sensational find from Grenfell and Hunt's first season, and one of the earliest surviving Christian books. The text is now known to be part of the lost apocryphal *Gospel of Thomas*. Original size: 15 x 9.7cm.

12. Detail from Sir Lawrence Alma-Tadema's painting,
A Reading from Homer (1885). The idealised classical bard
holds a book-roll modelled on the 'Bankes Homer', a papyrus
that had been recently acquired by the British Museum.

in mass graves, and the sea grew red with blood.[23] Not only the citizens suffered. At some stage (and here the grandeurs of the state visit came to touch the masses of the countryside) he ordered the expulsion from Alexandria of 'the Egyptians and especially the rustic Egyptians' – 'not the pig-merchants and river boatmen and those who bring down reeds to fire the baths, but the rest, throw them out, since they disturb the city by their number without being useful'.[24]

Damnatio Memoriae

The Emperor, however absent, was omnipresent. His image looked out from coins; his bust was carried in festive processions;[25] his portrait (whether as classical hero or as Egyptian Pharaoh) stood as statue or relief in temples everywhere. The chronological frame of existence depended on him: all events were dated by the years of his reign, months might be named from him or a predecessor, even certain days were designated 'imperial days'. In principle, emperors were good emperors, displaying the imperial virtues of justice, mercy and liberality. Good emperors were remembered, bad emperors must be forgotten; and some indeed were officially consigned to oblivion, denied the immortality which memory would have given them, by the process of 'condemnation of memory'. So the Senate decreed for Nero, and (on the suggestions of their successors) for Caligula and Domitian; so it decreed, with diminishing autonomy, for many of the military emperors and their unsuccessful rivals in the third century AD (some, notably Commodus and Alexander Severus, were first condemned and then rehabilitated).

There was no easy way of air-brushing the fallen out of history, as happened to Soviet leaders when they fell from power. The names and images of the late great obtruded everywhere. It needed serious organisation to erase them totally. Yet it could be attempted. On 4 February 211 the Emperor Septimius Severus died, or rather became a god, at York, where he was on campaign. He had two sons, Bassianus and Geta. Bassianus, the elder, had been renamed Antoninus, in tribute to the good Emperor Marcus Aurelius Antoninus, whose son his own father now claimed to be; history remembers him by his nickname, Caracalla, from the Gallic burnous that he chose to wear. The sons had been emperors with their father, and they were duly proclaimed as joint successors. Together they conveyed their father's ashes to Rome.

But two emperors proved one too many. At the end of the year, Geta was persuaded to leave his bodyguards behind and meet his brother in their mother's room; there a group of centurions cut him down as he clung to his mother, covering her with his blood.[26] Caracalla claimed to have escaped a plot to poison him and set about blotting out the unnatural brother. According to the historian Cassius Dio: 'If someone simply wrote the name of Geta, or simply spoke it, he was killed on the spot, so that not even in comedy [where Getas was the usual name of the clever slave] did writers use the name any more ... He [Caracalla] felt anger with the stones which carried his [Geta's] images, and he melted down the coinage which displayed him. Even this was not enough for him; at this time in particular he practised the doing of impious acts and compelled the others to murder, as if making a yearly blood-offering to his brother.'[27]

Fraternal vengeance spread outwards through the Empire. In the capital, masons hurried to the triumphal arch of Septimius Severus and did cosmetic work on its inscription; Geta's name vanished, covered over with additional honorifics of his father and brother ('best and strongest of sovereigns') calculated to occupy the same space.[28] Others tackled the reliefs of the monumental arch which the money-changers and merchants of the cattle market had dedicated, only seven years before, to the whole imperial family, and obliterated the murdered brother and indeed the murdered wife (you can still see the blanks in the stonework, now built into the church of S. Giorgio in Velabro).[29] At the periphery, far to the east, in the township of Stratonikeia in Caria, the dead head was scraped off the local coinage.[30] Far to the north, in the frontier province of Rhaetia (Upper Bavaria), the forbidden name was chiselled neatly off a ten-year-old milestone.[31] In Egypt, the viceroy proclaimed the ban: 'By the forethought of the lord of sea and land, our most divine monarch, the designs of his most impious brother have been frustrated. It is therefore for us to abolish all memory of the traitor, so that no public record of him remain.'[32]

The Egyptian bureaucracy did its best. Neither the grand nor the trivial escaped, however remote. Far upriver, beyond the old capital of Thebes, the Egyptian Temple at Latopolis (modern Esna) showed Severus and his family in pharaonic guise: the old Emperor, kilted and crowned and armed with the ritual flail and sceptre, receives life and longevity from Khnum, the god of creation; behind him his wife, then his elder son in full regalia, then the younger son wearing the white crown – once a figure, now only a silhouette where his person and titles have been duly chiselled out.[33] In the far west, where trade came in from the desert and paid toll at the customs post of Karanis, the official seal had shown the two brothers flanking their father; the face of the younger brother was now filled in, so that it no longer left an impression.[34] More widely dispersed were imperial portraits, painted (like the mummy portraits) in coloured wax on wooden panels, a form of secular icon.[35] Such perhaps were the 'little images' of Caracalla and his deified father Severus and his mother Julia Domna dedicated (according to an official survey) in many temples in the city of Oxyrhynchos and in the surrounding villages; each entry puts this dedication first, and then the accumulated offerings of the faithful ('1 purple throw, rotted and useless; 1 bronze folding mirror; 1 bronze platter; 2 statuettes of Zeus and Hera . . .').[36] No mention of Geta here: because these images were made before his public career, or after his disgrace? or because he had been brushed out? One group portrait still survives, painted in lively colours on a wooden disk 12 inches in diameter: Julia Domna with fashionable coiffure, Severus a crowned and bearded figure of godlike benevolence, in front the two sons: the podgy adolescent on the right survives intact, diadem and all; his brother to the left (and this must be Geta) has the face scratched out. Indeed, scratching out was not enough. The face is covered with a green-brown deposit which (according to the original publication) gives off a bad smell when moistened. It seems that a loyal hand daubed the disgraced prince with animal excrement.[37]

At Oxyrhynchos, more centrally, past datings were taken in hand. So with a contract of 28 October 203, in which Tabesammon petitioned to be assigned a guardian (women cannot do legal business without a male adjunct) so that she can borrow money on the security of her vineyard: eight years and more later, the date clause 'Year 12 of the Emperors Caesars Lucius Septimius Severus Pius Pertinax Arabicus Adiabenicus Parthicus Maximus and Marcus Aurelius Antoninus Pius, Augusti, and Publius Septimius Geta Caesar Augustus, Phaophi 30' turned out to contain a forbidden name, which was duly crossed out with ink thick enough to conceal most of it.[38]

In the forest of paperwork, public and private, the axe fell only sporadically; no doubt a systematic search would have been impracticable. So, among the papers carried home by Sarapion alias Apollonianos, an Oxyrhynchite grandee who had been serving as strategos elsewhere, two documents have the name deleted, two do not.[39] Yet the purge, however desultory, extended well back in time, to the imperial visit when the young Geta first entered the Egyptian chronology. In 201, a commission had been appointed to renovate the baths of Hadrian, and the commissioners applied to their juvenile gymnasiarch for the funds. Here Geta's name appeared already in the date – and here too it was struck out when his future collapsed – the name itself, but not the attaching title 'Caesar Augustus', which deserved respect.[40] An extract from the official journal of the town council of Oxyrhynchos (dated AD 201/2?) shows the complexities. The council had expressed its respect for 'our invincible Emperors' Severus and Caracalla and Geta, and Julia Domna 'mother of the camps' (married to Severus), and Fulvia Plautilla (married to Caracalla), and Fulvius Plautianus (her father) the Praetorian Prefect, and Maecius Laetus the Prefect of Egypt . . .' Of these, the over-mighty Plautianus was murdered in 205, Plautilla exiled in fear and poverty to Lipari; she was finally dispatched early in 211, Geta at the end of the same year. All three names have been hatched out, seemingly by the same hand, as if in a single operation – perhaps the later purge gave the opportunity to catch up with the earlier.[41]

There are relatively few examples of *damnatio memoriae* on papyrus. It seems that Geta was pursued with the real zeal of fraternal hatred; other senatorial condemnations may have had less puff. A later target was Caracalla's cousin once removed, Varius Avitus, raised to empire by his local garrison at Emesa in Syria (16 May AD 218). He too took the name Marcus Aurelius Antoninus, recalling his relationship with Caracalla and the virtues of the great philosopher-emperor; but history came to know him by the name of his god, Elagabalus. He had begun as hereditary priest of the Sun at Emesa. In Rome he showed to less advantage – rumour (censoriously recorded by a contemporary historian) said that he prostituted himself in women's clothes and offered a large fee for a sex-change operation. After a reign of four years, at the age of eighteen, he was killed and thrown into the Tiber.[42] His memory was damned, formally and as it seems in popular tradition as well. Here and there in Egypt his name was expunged, witness the document in which the superintendants of dikes report how much earth had been shifted (cubic foot by foot) in work on the embankments of canals near Oxyrhynchos during the week 12–16 March AD 220. Two years later, the Emperor was dead. The document was pulled from the archives, and his most impressive name, 'Antoninus', crossed out. Clearly the name compounded the offence; 'the phoney Antoninus' had been one of his nicknames in Rome.[43]

Astrologers faced a particular difficulty. They needed dates, and the normal system of dating relied on the regnal years of successive emperors. A client aged thirty in year 18 of Hadrian (AD 133/4) would have been born in year 7 of Trajan (AD 103/4). In such calculations the four years of Elagabalus could not be eliminated. One remedy was avoidance: one could count forward from the reign of Caracalla, with the formula 'in year 4 after year 25 of the deified Severus Antoninus' or 'in year 4 after the reign of the deified Antoninus the Great'.[44] Another was insult. One handbook from Oxyrhynchos included a list of Egyptian rulers, Persian, Egyptian, Macedonian and Roman; after Severus and Caracalla comes Antoninus the Little, so distinguished from Antoninus the Great.[45] A set of planetary tables, from which the astrologer could learn in what sign each planet was on each day of each year, heads the page with the name of the reign: Elagabalus appears as 'unholy Antoninus the Little' – 'unholy' alluding to his shameless ways.[46] A set of horoscopes likewise refers to the emperors in short form; but here moral indignation goes beyond allusion – Antoninus/Elagabalus carries the distinguishing epithet (a rare word, from the Alexandrian dialect) 'the catamite'. Astrologers, at least, shared the conventional view of Elagabalus' effeminacy.[47]

'I Appeal unto Caesar'

Such an intrusion of politics, or at least public indignation, seems very rare. For most people, most of the time, the Emperor was there, and the ordinary citizen could do nothing about him. Only perhaps the aristocrats of Alexandria, in their long-continued struggle with Roman authority, might judge and evaluate him.

At some point the Emperor became more real to most of his subjects; and here too the initiative came from Caracalla, the Burnous himself. In AD 212 he declared that all the inhabitants of the Empire, with minor exceptions, should become Roman citizens; in that way, the privileged status which hitherto had been granted as an exceptional favour to non-Romans became the hereditary right of all. This revolution (the 'Antonine Constitution') made little mark on the historians whose work

survives. Dio (or his summariser) includes it as a footnote to the Burnous'
plans to raise revenue from old taxes and new, and notably by increasing
the tax on inheritances – 'for which reason too he designated all those
in his empire Romans, ostensibly as an honour, in fact so that more
income should accrue from this kind of thing also, since aliens did not
pay the majority of these (taxes)'.[48] That may be the spin of a conscientious cynic. The damaged text of the edict (or what is usually
thought to be the edict) gives a quite different context: '... may I
give thanks to the immortal gods, that they have preserved me from
such [*a danger?*]. Therefore I think that in this way I can give
satisfaction to their greatness ... I give to everyone in the world Roman
citizenship ...' Thus the gift to men is a thanks-offering to the gods,
who saved the Emperor from – from what? From sickness? Or from the
murderous plots of Geta?[49]

In Egypt we see an immediate superficial effect. Citizens, now Roman
citizens, adopted a Roman first name, and of course the Emperor's first
name: every Isidoros became Aurelios Isidoros, every Thaisous became
Aurelia Thaisous. In principle, certain new privileges went with the
new status. So far, only the relatively few Roman citizens in Egypt had
had access to the categories and processes of Roman law; all others,
Hellenes and Egyptians alike, had used local law. Now Roman rules
could be invoked by anyone who found them advantageous. Greek
women, for example, could conduct legal business only through a male
'guardian', normally a husband or near relation. Now, as Roman women,
they could assert legal independence, if they had three children – a right
granted long since by the Emperor Augustus as a way of encouraging
citizens to procreate for the fatherland. So, on 15 July AD 263, Aurelia
Thaisous alias Lolliane duly applied to the Prefect:

> Long since have there been laws, Your Excellency, which grant to
> women who are distinguished by the 'right of three children' the
> freedom to be their own mistresses and act without a guardian in the
> business they do, and much more to those women who know their
> letters. So I myself, since I am fortunate in being blessed with children
> and since I am literate and able to write easily to the highest degree,
> address your Greatness with high assurance by way of this my petition
> so that I shall be able to proceed without hindrance in the business I
> do henceforth. I ask that my petition be held in your Excellency's
> office without prejudice to my rights, so that I may enjoy your

assistance and acknowledge my gratitude to you for all time. Farewell![50]

Four years later Thaisous turns up again, buying fields, houses, vacant lots, an orchard and a well, 'acting without a guardian by right of children'.[51]

How far the rights of a Roman citizen – for example, to be exempt from corporal punishment – still held firm in face of despotism, bureaucracy and militarisation is uncertain. Yet there will still have been some magic in the concept. 'I appeal unto Caesar,' St Paul had said; and the right of access to the supreme power may have been reinforced by the Antonine Constitution. This right did not necessarily commend itself to provincial governors, whose jurisdiction it limited. The Emperor Alexander Severus (AD 222–35) needed to reassert it in a letter to the Greeks of Bithynia: 'We forbid procurators and provincial governors to use violence and force against those who seek to appeal and to surround them with an armed guard and in short to fence off their path upwards to our authority. Governors will obey this my proclamation, knowing that I have as much concern for the freedom of my subjects as also for their loyalty and obedience.'[52] The Prefect of Egypt inserted a copy of this in his official Journal; and the Oxyrhynchites took note, since two copies survive among their rubbish.[53]

The dossier of Lollianos the public *grammatikos* (teacher of literature) at Oxyrhynchos illustrates the right, and the practicalities of exercising it.[54] This dossier consists of a single short roll of papyrus, which contains three documents, A and B on the front, C on the back, each copied by a different hand. A is the first incomplete draft of a petition, C is a revised and more complete version of the same. B is the draft (much corrected) of a letter concerning the petition. The roll turned up at Oxyrhynchos; fair final copies may have been sent to their destination, the court of the Emperors Valerian and Gallienus, joint rulers in the years 253–60.

The longer petition reads:

To the masters of the land and sea and every nation of men, Imperatores Caesares Publius Licinius Valerianus and Publius Licinius Gallienus Pii Felices Augusti, from Lollianos also called Homoios.

Your heavenly magnanimity, greatest Emperors, which has extended its benevolence to the whole of your domain, the civilised world, and sent it forth to every corner, has given me too confidence to submit to your divine genius a petition closely connected with both reason and law. It is this:

Your deified ancestors who have ruled at different times, rulers who irradiated their domain, the world, in virtue and culture, fixed, in proportion to the size of the cities, a number of public *grammatikoi* as well, ordering [*that salaries be given to them, so that their care for the children should not be hampered*] . . . [*Yet I find myself*] without even the necessities of life, since, being occupied with the children, one cannot continually persist in demanding payment – I find myself compelled to bring this supplication to your feet, most divine Emperors, a supplication not damaging to the city fund, yet in all justice beneficial to me, namely that your supreme Genius should order that there be given to me an orchard in the city, within the walls, known as the Garden of Diktynos, along with the trees there, and the water for irrigation, an orchard which brings in 600 attikai [2400 drachmas] on lease, so that I may have from this source what satisfies my needs and so be able to have ample time for teaching the children . . .

The background is further explained in the letter:

I send you, brother, this third letter, so that you may perpetually rejoice me by continually writing about your state of health – you will easily avail yourself of those who come in to Alexandria from the Court, if you send [your letters] to Ammonianos, adjutant in the bodyguard, who is to the last degree my friend (he will send them on to me here – the man is [*well-known?*], a relative of His Excellency Theodoros) – and at the same time I have sent you as well a petition very fitting to be granted to your like [?], so that you can obtain the grant for me to provide sustenance for my children . . .; this petition, Ammonios has sent the text by his brother Heraklammon, the clerk [?], with whom too you will consult first whether he had already settled the business, so that the petition is not made twice about one and the same thing. For though I was elected public grammatikos here by the city council, it is not at all the case that I receive the usual salary, on the contrary, if it should happen, it is paid in vinegar instead of wine and in worm-eaten grain, you yourself know how things are with us. So it will be in your power, you who have so much influence, to give me too some assistance, to obtain for me one of the orchards here, which a certain [*predecessor of mine?*] did in fact previously obtain as a grant to himself in place of his salary; the request for which orchard, and the grant, I have sent you, and also the text of our petition, so that ... you may do me this favour ... For you will know the consuls, and generally give a lead in what is advantageous, considering the matter in the interest of one who is a scholar and a friend and in need. And the rescript too is to be unambiguous, so that it cannot be reversed by malignity ...

The petitions are written in sloping approximations to book-script; the letter in a small rapid hand and with the use of a peculiar system of abbreviations – not that commonly used in documents, but that characteristic of long commentaries and similar works of scholarship – the sort of abbreviation, in fact, that belongs to the schoolmaster's own profession. Whether the whole enterprise was wishful thinking, or whether the fair copies were actually sent, we cannot tell, but the covering letter shows clearly that Lollianos had a mind for business as well as for rhetoric. There is ideology: the position of the Emperors as universal judges; the position of a grammatikos in a privileged group established by imperial decree. There is also practical sense. How physically to convey a petition to the distant Emperors? The senior Emperor, Valerian, might be relatively close at this stage, warring on the Persian frontier, close enough, indeed, to require a whole series of Oxyrhynchite villages to deliver oxen ('selected and very suitable for ploughing') to Syria, presumably for the baggage-train of his army.[55] Furthermore, Lollianos had a courier, and one on the inside of the military establishment. That is a good start, but only a start. How then to make sure that the petition comes to the imperial attention? That it receives a formal answer? That the answer (typically short) is unequivocal enough not to be bypassed by an obstinate town council? For this you need a friend at court, and Lollianos thought that he had one (although his earlier letters had been ignored). The upshot, as usual, we do not know. The authorities may have had other things on their mind, since Valerian would soon be defeated and captured, and after death flayed and stuffed with straw. But the whole business illustrates the distant yet close relation of Emperor and citizen: the Lords of the Land and Sea owe justice to the schoolmaster of Oxyrhynchos.

Alexandria and the Roman Tyrant

Thus the imperial authority could be seen as a benevolent arbiter; and, by and large, it was not challenged, practically or psychologically. A garrison (two or three legions, with their squadrons of cavalry) guaranteed Roman rule and maintained order. On the frontiers, the nomads of the Western Desert, and the Nubians and other tribes of the Sudan, made occasional incursions. The only serious invasion came from the east, across the Sinai – another desert people, the Palmyrenes, under Queen Zenobia and her son, took advantage of imperial chaos to occupy Egypt for a few years (AD 270–72). Within the country, focused revolt is rare compared with endemic lawlessness: in the Jewish revolt of 115–17, Greek sentiment would have been on the side of the government; the revolt of the Herdsmen (c.171/2) gives military form to a long history of brigandage (the 'Herdsmen', who operate from the marshes of the Nile Delta, figure also in Greek novels as *banditti* of picturesque savagery).

Serious rebellion threatened only when a pretender to the Empire used Egypt as his base. So Avidius Cassius, who as Prefect had suppressed the 'Herdsmen', set himself up as Emperor against Marcus Aurelius (AD 175). Proclaimed by the Prefect, and recognised at Oxyrhynchos, he reigned three months and six days, until one of his own soldiers took his head.[56] So Domitius Domitianus and his colleague Aurelius Achilleus (297–8) rebelled against Diocletian, and the rebellion had to be put down by the Emperor in person. When Alexandria surrendered, after a siege of eight months, Diocletian vowed to massacre the population until the blood reached his horse's knees. Providentially the horse stumbled as it entered the city, and the surviving citizens set up a statue in its honour.[57]

High politics naturally centred on Alexandria, self-conscious and a law unto itself. Orators took care to celebrate its wealth and glamour, its huge economic power as seaport and factory. Its aristocrats and its mob alike might resent the new occupying power. The mob was potentially huge, in a city enormous (perhaps 500,000 inhabitants) by ancient standards, a magnet for chancers and drifters. The historian Diodorus Siculus witnessed an incident, in the time of Ptolemy XII (c. 60 BC), when a Roman, who had by accident killed a cat, was lynched by the crowd, despite the King's intercession and the general fear of offending Rome.[58] Not long after the Roman occupation, the Prefect

Petronius (*c*.24–22 BC) was attacked and stoned by a mob thousands strong, and saved only by his bodyguard.[59]

The city itself was divided. During the early Empire, at least, there were continual conflicts between the large Jewish community, concentrated in one of the five quarters of the city, and the other inhabitants. In negotiations with the imperial government (which they believed to side with the Jews) the city leaders appealed against Jewish intrusions into their privileged world. This situation was bloodily resolved by the great Jewish revolt of AD 115–17, which spread from Libya (where a Messiah declared himself) to Egypt, Cyprus and Mesopotamia. The rebels fought in Alexandria and as far south as Hermoupolis, against the local population as well as against the troops: 'Our one remaining hope,' wrote an eyewitness, 'was the push of the massed villagers from our nome against the unholy Jews, but now that has had the opposite result, for on the 20th [?] our people joined battle and were beaten and cut to pieces ...'[60] It took two years to restore order, and a century for the Jewish community to recover. No doubt the Greeks took the side of the government, and Oxyrhynchos continued to dwell on its loyalty. Thus the Alexandrian Horion, in petitioning the Emperor Septimius Severus to approve his donations to Oxyrhynchos, where he himself was a large landowner, recommended the city and its people, since 'They possess good will and loyalty and friendship towards Romans, which they showed both by joining in the war against the Jews and by celebrating, even now, each year, the day of the victory.'[61]

Horion exemplifies a type: a rich man whose life and possessions bridged Alexandria and Oxyrhynchos. Among the Oxyrhynchite rubbish we find no explicit politics. Private letters say nothing about emperors or prefects – from prudence? Or indifference? Or despair? Yet private reading might touch on politics. There is apocalyptic literature that looks forward to the expulsion of a godless invader, designed perhaps for the Persian occupation, but still read in Roman Oxyrhynchos – such prophecies of doom always find an audience.[62] There are numerous samples of a sub-literature which has otherwise not survived, political pamphlets which chronicle (with more or less elaboration) the relations of Alexandria and the Roman government – imperial pronouncements, proceedings of embassies sent to the court, transcripts of trials whose form and tone anticipate the Christian martyrdoms (hence the modern name 'Acts of the Pagan Martyrs').[63] It may be that Alexandrians brought them down to Oxyrhynchos. But so many of the pieces show a certain amateurishness in their script and in their format (written on the back of other documents) that they look more like local copies than imports – perhaps private copies for private consumption, and in some cases, to judge from the spelling, consumption by the less literate; perhaps (at least for the more anti-Roman texts) samizdat texts, for which private copying was a matter of prudence not just of economy.

Some of these papyri date, to judge from the script, from the early first century AD. Perhaps there was special interest, at this early stage, in relations with the new masters. So Oxyrhynchites could read the proceedings of the embassy that the city of Alexandria sent to Augustus in Gaul, and the letter in which the Emperor reports his reception of this embassy, in 10/9 BC;[64] and again in AD 12/13, minutes of an audience in which another Alexandrian delegation met the aged Augustus and his advisers, and then minutes of a public meeting in Alexandria in which an imperial prince, probably Germanicus, addressed the crowds.[65] Thereafter they could read more sensational trials, in which heroic Alexandrians confront hostile emperors. The last of these features the Emperor Commodus (AD 180–92); in the third century earlier cases continue to circulate but no new ones are added. The next Emperor, Septimius Severus, flattered the city's pride by opening the Roman senate to Alexandrian nobles; his son Caracalla chastened it, by massacring Alexandrian youth. For one reason or another, it seems, Alexandrian patriotism sought no further confrontation.

The heroes of these pseudo-documents were noble Alexandrians, the villains Roman emperors and their courts; the subjects of quarrel the city's grievances, including the conduct of their governor, the Prefect, and of the Jews, their neighbours and enemies.

Thus before the Emperor Trajan the city's spokesmen denounced the Prefect C. Vibius Maximus (AD 103–7) for usury, extortion, cruelty, negligence and a very public affair with an Alexandrian youth. 'A seventeen-year-old boy dined with you every day. Each of these men here, every time that he was privileged to partake of the meal (and once you turned monarch you used not to grant such favours easily), saw the boy in the dining-room, both with his father and alone, saw also his shameless look and the shameless processions of hairy lovers. So? Every day he was at the morning levee. They swear, my Lord, by your Good Fortune, that as they were waiting to pay their respects and hanging around at the court, they saw the boy coming out of his bedroom alone, showing signs of his intercourse with this man ...'[66] This Maximus was a well-connected man, friend of such Roman authors as Pliny the Younger, Statius and Martial. Yet it seems he lost this battle, or another; his name was hammered out of any inscription that mentioned him.

Under Trajan again, the Alexandrian Greeks and the Alexandrian Jews sent separate delegations to court. The Emperor, influenced by his wife Plotina, showed himself benevolent to the Jews, cold to the Greeks (or so they perceived it). On the Greek side Hermaiskos spoke up, in dialogue with the Emperor:

TRAJAN: 'You prepare yourself to die, despising death, since you answer even me so arrogantly.'

HERMAISKOS said, 'Well, we are grieved that your council is filled with the unholy Jews.'

CAESAR said, 'See here, I tell you for the second time: you answer me arrogantly, trusting to your noble family.'

HERMAISKOS said, 'How do I answer you arrogantly, greatest Emperor? Instruct me!'

CAESAR said, 'Because you have made my council the property of Jews.'

HERMAISKOS said, 'So you find difficulty with the name "Jews"? Then you should in turn help your own people and not act as advocate for the unholy Jews.'

As Hermaiskos said this, the bust of Sarapis, which the envoys were carrying, suddenly burst out in sweat. When Trajan saw this, he was amazed. And a little after crowds rushed together in Rome and multitudinous cries were shouted out and everyone was fleeing to the tops of the hills . . .[67]

So the Alexandrian god performs a miracle, and all Rome dissolves in panic.

At the extreme, it was the Emperor himself, not his prefect or his advisers, who bore the brunt. So it is that, in another sensational pamphlet found at Oxyrhynchos, Appianos, the gymnasiarch of Alexandria, defies the Emperor Commodus:

THE EMPEROR said: 'Now do you not realise to whom you speak?'

APPIANOS: 'Yes, I know: Appianos speaks to a tyrant.'

THE EMPEROR: 'No, to a monarch.'

APPIANOS: 'Do not say that. Your divine father Marcus Aurelius had the proper qualities of an emperor. Listen! – first, he was a philosopher; second, he did not love money; third, he loved the good. In you there are the reverse of these qualities: tyranny, hatred of the good, common ignorance.'

CAESAR ordered him to be led away to execution.

APPIANOS, as they led him away, said: 'Grant me this favour also, lord Caesar ... Order me to be led away in the dress of my noble rank.'

CAESAR: 'You have it.'

APPIANOS took his head-band and put it on his head, and putting the white sandals on his feet, he cried out in the heart of Rome: 'Come running, Romans! Watch while the greatest gymnasiarch of all time, the envoy of Alexandria, is led to execution!'

The Romans murmur, the Emperor calls him back, Appianos remains defiant:

APPIANOS: 'Who has called me back, as I was bowing my head to my second doom and to those who died before me, Theon and Isidoros and Lampon? Was it the senate? Or you, the chief brigand?'

THE EMPEROR: 'Appianos, we too have the habit of chastening the mad and deranged. You speak only as far as I wish you to speak.'[68]

Reading was not rebellion, yet in Roman law at least such material as these 'Acts of the Pagan Martyrs' must have counted as treasonable.[69] Certainly the 'Acts' make a striking contrast with the conventional pieties. In the real world, the distant Emperor reigned supreme. Oxyrhynchites duly prayed for his success, celebrated his birthday, mounted his portrait on their walls, appealed to his justice. In the world of Hellenic self-esteem, the balance was different: the Romans had power, the Greeks had culture. The loyal citizen could still enjoy the fantasy of the noble Alexandrian facing and defying the coarse, corrupted tyrant, and going to his death with Hellenic sang-froid. The public coinage proclaimed the dignities and victories of Caesar Augustus. In the covert papyrus the master of the world dwindles into the boss of a criminal gang.

CHAPTER 6

THE RIVER

• • • •

The Greeks and Romans saw in Egypt a country of ancient wisdom, bizarre superstition and natural wonders. Chief among the wonders was the annual inundation of the Nile. Scientists speculated about the source of the water; naturalists described its consequences for agriculture; tourists and novelists dwelt on its picturesque and paradoxical elements. In their own countries they were used to flash floods, from winter rains, violent and destructive, washing away the ground; in Egypt the river rose, every year, at a predictable time, in the heat of summer, to the benefit of agriculture, depositing new soil. Ancient economies in general depended on two seasons, the sowing and the harvest. Egypt recognised a third season, the season of the inundation, August to November. The inundation articulated the whole pattern of the year. Its height and date affected the livelihood of all citizens, and the income of any government. These factors remained constant right up until the 1960s, when the High Dam at Aswan began to control the water and hold back the silt.[1]

Fertility, the source of Egypt's fabled wealth, was a constant theme. Nile water, it was thought, had nourishing qualities, encouraging the birth of twins or indeed sextuplets; it was exported in sealed jars for the delectation of the rich. The silt which it carried covered the dry, fissured fields, giving moisture and cohesion to the sands. To this silt, wrote Seneca, 'Egypt owes not just the fertility of its soil, but the soil itself'.[2] Water and land joined in natural harmony; the Egyptians spoke of 'the sweat of Osiris', the Greek essayist Plutarch likened it to 'blood mingling with flesh'.[3] The Nile brings soil, wrote Strabo; it also carries away landmarks, and so it was the Egyptians who invented the science of land-surveying ('geometry' in its original sense, and the beginning of mathematical geometry).[4] Nor was every flood of equal benefit. 'The proper rise is of 16 cubits; lower water leaves some areas unirrigated, higher water delays things because it recedes more slowly ... At 12 cubits Egypt senses famine, at 13 it is still hungry, 14 cubits cause cheerfulness, 15 confidence, 16 delight': so wrote the Roman naturalist Pliny.[5] This scale of plenty survived all political vicissitudes. When the Moroccan traveller Ibn Battuta visited Egypt in the fifteenth century, he gave the same report: 'If the rise amounts to 16 cubits, the land-tax is payable in full ... If it reaches 18 cubits it does damage to their farmland and causes an outbreak of the plague. If the Nile rises 15 cubits, the land-tax will be diminished. If it rises only 14 cubits or less, there will be prayers for rain and there is great misery.'[6] A cubit measures the distance from the fingertip to the elbow, 20 inches or so. Thus the optimum flood would reach some 27 feet above low water.

At the same time, the tourist could enjoy (in person or through literature) an extraordinary spectacle. The historian Herodotus was reminded of his native seas: 'When the Nile invades the country, only the cities can be seen projecting above, most resembling the islands in the Aegean, for the rest of Egypt becomes a sea while the cities alone project. So, when this happens, they travel by boat not along the river channels but through the middle of the plain. Thus someone sailing upstream from Naukratis to Memphis sails directly past the Pyramids.'[7] Achilles Tatius, a novelist of the second century AD, was moved to rhapsodise on the symbiotic schedule: 'The great Nile is everything to them, river and land and sea and lake; and the spectacle is a novel one, ship along with mattock, oar with plow, rudder with sickle, habitation of sailors alongside farmers, of fish alongside cattle. You sow where you sailed, and where you sow is a sea being farmed. For the river pays its visits: the Egyptian sits waiting for him and counting his days. And the Nile does not play false: no, he is a river with a deadline, watching his time and measuring his waters, a river unwilling to be caught arriving late ...'[8]

Classical artists took their cue. The Nile assumed the bearded bene-volence of a senior Greek divinity: so in a mosaic from a villa near Leptis Magna, where he rides his hippopotamus, holding his horn of plenty.[9] The crucial cubits become his children, in a statue which was once exhibited in Rome, in the Emperor Vespasian's Temple of Peace, no doubt as a symbol of peaceful plenty; several versions of the theme still survive.[10] The inundation itself offered a picturesque subject, as in the famous Nile Mosaic at Palestrina. There, scattered buildings and hutments stand out above the flooded plain. Around them ply boats and exotic fauna (ibis, crocodile, hippopotamus). By one shack a herdsman looks after his cow, in another arbour a party is in progress, for inundation is a time of rejoicing.[11]

The picturesque is also a reality. Upper Egypt is a flood plain, a valley rarely more than a dozen miles wide, bounded by cliffs. In Lower Egypt, to the north, the river divides to form a delta so extensive that it contains twice as much agricultural land as Upper Egypt. Each year the Nile floods, fed by the summer rains on the Ethiopian plateau. At flood, the volume of water increases on average 15-fold, in years of high flood 45-fold; at Aswan, in the south, the flow rises from 60 million cubic yards at low Nile to more than 900 million cubic yards at high Nile. Each flood carries 110 million tons of sediment into Egypt (30 per cent sand, the rest mud and clay), the water turning red. The flood plain is convex: the river builds up its banks as natural barriers, rising above the plain to either side. The flood rises over these banks, or breaches them, and the waters flow easily outwards towards the edges of the valley. At high water (a period of perhaps ten days) the river may reach 25 feet and more above its low, and the plain is covered to a depth of up to 6 feet. Only dikes, and the towns and villages on higher ground, stand out above the inland sea. The flood drowns roads, except those on embankments; most of the land is now navigable, at least by boats of shallow draft. Men and animals must crowd together on the high ground, and live on their stores.

The Oxyrhynchites, like everyone else, lived to the annual rhythm of the inundation. Many males bore the name Neilos, 'Nile'; some women were called Anabasis, 'the rising of the water'.[12] The citizens lived some 10 miles from the Nile itself, which they called 'the great river', on the side-branch (nowadays Bahr Yusuf, 'Joseph's Canal') which they distinguished as 'our river' or 'the Tomis river'.[13] 'Our river' continues the natural channels which run parallel with the main stream from as far south as Abydos, 200 miles away; it runs northwards for another 60 miles before turning west, through a gap in the bounding hills, to water the fertile oasis of the Fayûm and to connect with its complex of ship- and irrigation-canals. The Tomis river rises as the Nile rises. 'This local river of ours', wrote an official, concerned as always to clear tax-grain from local granaries, 'receives an inflow and abundance of water because of the inundation. So we ask that the boats should be sent at that time and that the villages along the canal should first be cleared by way of this canal . . .'[14]

From mid-June onwards they kept an eye on one of their two Nilometers, stone basins which received the water and measured its level on a graduated pillar.[15] All being well, the water began to rise in late June, in late July it overflowed the banks of the main river, in late August and early September it reached its height, from mid or late September it retreated, rapidly at first and then by slow degrees, returning to its normal bed by November. Then the land could be sown in November/December, and the grown crops harvested in April/May. Such are the traditional three seasons, 'inundation', 'sowing' and 'harvest'; at Oxyrhynchos, for example, it was the inundation that divided summer figs from winter figs.[16]

After the Harvest, Before the Flood

At low water, just after the harvest and just before the flood, there was time and opportunity for various activities. In some of these the government took a strong interest, since they were essential to the economy. In late March 278 the *dioikêtês* (finance minister) Ulpius Aurelius issued a general directive to the strategoi and *dekaprôtoi* (granary overseers) of Middle Egypt:

> Since the time has arrived for the building up of the dikes and the cleaning of the canals, I have thought it necessary to send you the message, by this letter, that all of the farmers must . . . now carry out this work with all zeal in the relevant areas, for the public benefit of all and the private benefit of each individual. Indeed, I am persuaded that everyone knows the advantages arising from these works. Therefore let it be the concern of you, the strategoi and the dekaprotoi, to press everyone to set about this most necessary labour and that there should be chosen the overseers who are customarily appointed for this, from among the magistrates or even the private citizens, those who will compel each individual to carry out in person the relevant works, according to the guidelines laid down in the detailed assignment of the overall target, without any enmity or favour, so that the dikes are brought to the regulation height and width and the breaches

should be blocked so that they can resist the happily about to occur inundation of the most sacred Nile, and the canals be cleaned out up to the so-called standard measures and the accustomed width, so that they may easily receive the coming inflow of water for the irrigation of the fields, this being useful to the whole community, and in no case should anyone be charged money instead of work. For if he dares to try this on or ignores these orders, let him know that, for sabotaging policies designed for the security of the whole of Egypt, he will find himself on trial not simply for money but for his life.[17]

Ulpius Aurelius was ahead of the game, for the inundation was still more than three months away; and the works described would have been in principle part of every year's routine. His circular may reflect the didactic efficiency of the Roman outsider; it may represent an answer to a crisis of authority, for routine maintenance was often the first victim of weakness at the centre. No one doubted that the work was crucial. Octavian, when he conquered Egypt, put his troops to work clearing canals; *chômatikon*, 'embankment charge', is one of the commonest of taxes.

Such maintenance was certainly endlessly laborious; and it had to be done, or at least paid for, by the taxpayer, an actual or commuted corvée. The official handbook defines the obligation: 'Measurement of dikes. Each inhabitant of the countryside digs up five naubia . . . in relation to the assignment of work on the dikes, or less according to what need demands. A naubion is a measure of earth being dug which is three cubits in width, length and depth. Measurement of canals. The canals also are worked on each year, since [*they get silted up*] by the inflow of the river . . .'[18] The standard naubion, 27 cubic cubits, works out at over 5 cubic yards. Five naubia perhaps represent five days' work, since the personal corvée normally lasted five days. If so, they were hard days; five cubic yards of earth would fill a skip 7 feet x 5 x 4 feet, or more than thirty heavy-duty wheelbarrows.

'Dike supervisors' were appointed to see that the work was done systematically and to standard. 'I swear', writes Diogenes, son of Diogenes, 'by the fortune of Imperator Caesar Vespasianus Augustus and by my ancestral gods to take charge of the supervision of the dikes and with all diligence to make the men who have been or indeed will be assigned to this work work each of them the naubia which belong to him, by the appropriate measuring-rod . . . so that the dikes are completed and made watertight as is appropriate . . .'[19] Such supervisors reported the progress in each five-day period. So, for 12–16 March inclusive, AD 220, thirty-three men from the Oxyrhynchite villages of Senekeleu and Seryphis dug $222\frac{3}{4}$ naubia (over 1000 cubic yards), a daily average of 1.35 naubia per man.[20]

Working free for the government cannot have been popular. The unwilling might resist: 'Today being 5 Tybi we approached Soter and a brother of his and whatever their full name is, asking them to carry out the work on their share of the canal. And they attacked us, recklessly, and maltreated us with blows.'[21] They might also find it cheaper to buy their way out. So the village elders of Peenno had complained to the strategos about their dike supervisor 'that he took money from fifty-one men at 4 drachmas each so that they should not work their five-naubia stint on the public dikes and that he covered up for another nine men similarly with regard to their not completing the work'. No doubt the bribers were as culpable as the bribed, and that is why the elders, when the stratēgos demanded names, reported lamely that the thirteen workers they had named had since denied, in writing, making such payments – and of the rest they were (on oath) unable to produce the names![22] The corvée system creaked. But it continued in place, regime after regime, until finally abolished in 1889.

The arrival of the flood had implications for private business too. Theon wrote to Chairemon: 'If you discover that you have a need for threshed straw for Tholthis, move Hekysios' there – just have a lot of chaff mixed in, so that it does not get used up quickly. When the wine from the orchard is sold, you can then buy threshed straw there, since it will perhaps be cheap, with the water approaching. Don't neglect moving the chaff at Tholthis. At this point do not pay hire for beasts for the sake of manure, not until the rise. Do NOT pay hire . . .'[23] The flood, that is, might provide the chance to transport things more cheaply. Its approach might require a fire-sale of bulky goods held on low ground and so exposed to the rising water. Straw served as fodder, all the more necessary when livestock had to be confined to high ground; it also served as fuel, and so a builder repairing a temple noted in his accounts, 'Price of straw, with carriage charge, bought at the season of the flood . . . on the threshing floor, 9 baskets, to fuel the furnace for the rubble and gypsum, 9 drachmas.'[24] Wood, too, always a precious commodity, might be cut before it drowned. Thonis to Choous: 'You too know that our son Apollonios is busy all year and Philostratos has fallen ill, hence we haven't the strength to go after wood for us and I never troubled you about wood. So therefore provide for us at the current price, however you find it, and if you can make your way to Berky before the water withdraws, there are people who have the habit of cutting and selling it, and keep it with you, since often they themselves are cautious in case they are pressed into service. Just act quickly about it in the knowledge that today is their opportunity, with the Nile still approaching.'[25]

During the Flood

The flood made many roads (except those on the tops of dikes) impassable. 'I have passed on the stable-hand to the new security men (curse them!), so that they can give him the horse they took ... and I think that the new wine has already made them too dizzy. So please by all means send the horse to me before the waters take over the earth, since, as God lives, if anything whatever happens to him you will pay the price ...'[26] On the other hand, travel and transport by water, cheaper and generally quicker, became much easier and widespread. The river itself would take boats of deeper draft; canals would be full and overflowing; at high water shallow craft could go cross-country. Theodoros condoled with Kanopos on the death of his wife: 'But what can we do in face of mortality? So please comfort yourself and make the effort and come to me ... I have need of your noble self, and I will have you sent home again by boat. So don't delay, since the water is rising.'[27] 'The other half of the expenses money I lodged at the harbour until the rising of the waters, and I will take it to the monastery in boats.'[28]

Even small cargoes were easier to transport at the flood. So Antas to Phaustos (one of the very few letters to be precisely dated, 26 May 2 BC, three months before high water): 'Take over from Pothos the reeds, the whole lot, and send me word how many bundles you have received and put them somewhere safely so that we can fetch them at the flood ...'[29] So Koprys and Sinthonis to Sarapammon and Syra: 'Theon the father of Petosiris has given you a jar of meat. We haven't found a safe person who would bring it to you. If you write to Theon, inform him that you have received the jar of meat. If the flood happens, I will send it to you by the usual boatmen.'[30] Large loads could conveniently be left until the water rose, but there were always uncertainties about the timetable. Thus, in AD 265, on 24 September, a date which would normally mean high water, the contractor for raising water to the public baths of Oxyrhynchos complained that the slowness of the flood seemed to have produced a shortage of fodder for the beasts which turned the wheel.[31]

On a grander scale, the season was important for a central interest of the state: the transport of tax-grain down to Alexandria. The grain, once threshed, was held in state granaries; from there it travelled to the river, and then by barge downriver to the granaries of the capital. The first stage was often by donkey caravan. The second depended in part on the water-level, for at high water the river was more navigable and the barges could come in closer to the bank. Local officials tried to move things forward: 'The dekaprotos hassles us a lot about the loading of the corn. So send us Dionysios, since he knows the score as regards the delivery. And we did load up, when the river was rising.'[32] The strategos had overall charge of the nome's resources. In one case, the acting strategos was informed that 255 donkeys (and their drivers), sent to transport corn in the Arsinoite nome, had decamped. He was instructed to send the equivalent number 'with tractable keepers', 'so that the transport of corn downstream can be made while the river is still navigable, given that the water is already falling and the need is pressing for the corn to be conveyed down'.[33]

For state peasants and private land-owners, this was a season for vigilance. The flood-water needed to be channelled: embankments held in water, which could be released later in the dry season, or held back water which otherwise would swamp plantations and villages. As the water rose, 'waterguards' watched for possible breaches. Lykarion to Ploutarchos: 'If the pigeons are not laying, let them be sold. Sarapas wrote to me that a new skiff needs to be ordered. So order it straight away. The measurements Sarapas will tell you. Make sure you don't neglect this, as we have need of it for the embankment around Posoous at the time of the water-watch.'[34] This was written on 17 March, well in advance of the inundation. The recurrent dangers are illustrated, sixteen centuries on, by the account of a Victorian engineer, William Willcocks: 'During high floods the Nile dykes are covered with booths at intervals of 50 to 100 yards, according to the amount of danger incurred. In each booth are two watchmen, while in addition to the above every really dangerous spot has a special gang of 50 or 100 men. Every booth has a lantern in front of it, and as the Nile itself is covered with boats laden with stones and stakes all carrying lanterns, all of which are reflected in the water, the scene is full of gaiety and animation.' A serious breach might threaten a whole village:

> The villagers rushed out on to the bank with their children, their cattle and everything they possessed. The confusion was indescribable: a narrow bank covered with children, buffaloes, poultry, and household furniture. The women assembled round the local saint's tomb, beating their breasts, kissing the tomb, and uttering loud shrieks; while every five minutes a gang of men ran into the crowd and carried off something wherewith to close the breach. The fellaheen meanwhile were not in the least confused, but in a steady business-like manner were working in the breach, half of them standing waist-deep athwart the rushing water, holding hands in two rows one behind the other, while the other half closed it from the two sides up-stream of this human wall.[35]

After the Flood

After the flood, the landscape would have changed. 'While I was here,' wrote Dionysia to the Prefect, 'I received a message that all my property had been destroyed by the over-heavy inundation of the most sacred Nile, farms and lands and dikes, and so I ask you, lord Prefect ... to allow me to return upriver so that I may claim my rights. Otherwise I may perish of hunger along with my property.'[36] The swollen river had carried away or eroded existing plots, and created new ones by depositing 'islands' of soil. Depending on the level of high water, it had irrigated some land, but left some dry and useless or dry and usable only with artificial irrigation; other plots might remain waterlogged, or sanded up, or salted by minerals drawn up from below.[37]

Both owners and taxmen had a strong interest in assessing the new situation; owners reported, government surveyors surveyed. Owners put in returns of 'unwatered' and 'artificially irrigated' land, since they could claim tax-relief for the unproductive. Their lessees too could claim a reduction of rent, since their lease often contained the saving clause 'but if (may it not happen) any of the land should be unwatered ...'

Such returns might be on the initiative of the owner; but often the government invited them, with a view to assessing the overall yield. Similarly land-surveys were conducted by the state, sometimes under the overall direction of a special central official.[38]

After the flood, the newly silted soil dried out, and its cracking surface required artificial irrigation. A document found at Oxyrhynchos, but originally from the Lykopolite nome, illustrates the need: 'To [*Dioskourides*] strategos of the Lykopolite nome, from the landowners and farmers of the village of Nebna. [*It is customary that when*] the most sacred Nile recedes, water should be released [*from the reservoir*] onto our fields which lie below it. So, now that the Nile has receded, we ask that instructions be given to release the water to us . . .'[39] The 'reservoir' was a circular earthwork, which filled up at high water, at which point the sluices were closed.

Boats

The Nile and its canals swarmed with boats of all sizes, just as the Nile Mosaic shows it. There were boats belonging to the state; and private boats, often on private business, sometimes hired to the government. River transport had its own hazards, whether in the violence of the high flood or the shallows of low water. Nile boatmen have been an expert group in all ages, as proud of themselves as salt-water mariners. One Oxyrhynchite reader preserved a song about their rivalry:

> You sailors who run over the deep waves,
> Tritons of the salt waters –
> You Nile-men who run over the sweet stream,
> Sailing the laughing waters –
> Tell us, friends, the rival claims
> Of the sea and the fruitful Nile.[40]

Conditions in Roman Egypt would not have differed much from those observed by E. W. Lane in the early nineteenth century:[41]

The boatmen of the Nile are mostly strong, muscular men. They undergo severe labour in rowing, poling and towing; but are very cheerful; for then they frequently amuse themselves by singing. In consequence of the continual changes which take place in the bed of the Nile, the most experienced pilot is liable frequently to run his vessel aground: on such an occurrence, it is often necessary for the crew to descend into the water, to shove off the boat with their backs and shoulders . . . Sudden whirlwinds and squalls being very frequent on the Nile, a boatman is usually employed to hold the main-sheet in his hand, that he may be able to let it fly at a moment's notice; the traveller should be especially careful with respect to this precaution, however light the wind.

In these conditions, those sending freight by water felt it desirable to stipulate for a prudent voyage. Thus:

Anoubas, son of Hermias . . . skipper of the river boat of 500 artabas capacity belonging to Marcus Cornelius Torullus, centurion, hired out to Polytimos, slave of Gaus Norbanus Ptolemaeus, the said boat with its crew, on which too he will load from whichever harbours he chooses in the Hermopolite nome five hundred artabas of arax and for every hundred artabas twelve and a half artabas free of charge, so as to deliver them to Akanthon and Lile in the Oxyrhynchite nome, freight charge mutually agreed twenty-eight silver drachmas per hundred artabas, making one hundred and forty drachmas, of which Anoubas acknowledges that he has received on the spot from Polytimos seventy-two drachmas, and the remaining sixty-eight drachmas of the freight he is to pay him at the unloading of the arax. So, he is to produce the boat ready to sail on the twenty-first of the present month of Sebastos; he is to appear at the harbours of the Hermopolite nome and pick up and take over the arax and set sail without delay and with every precaution, providing for himself on the journey upriver and downriver the complete supplies for the boat in full and sufficient sailors, and he will not be permitted to sail by night or when there is a storm, but he must anchor every day in the safest archorages, the lightering in the Hermopolite being at the expense of Anoubas, that in the Oxyrhynchite at the expense of Polytimos. He is to hand over the arax to Polytimos or his representatives at the harbour of Lile and Akanthon, by whatever measure was used in receiving it, whatever shall come out of the hold belonging to Polytimos, or he is to pay him the price of every . . .[42]

This contract illustrates very clearly the kind of trade involved. The boat belonged to a centurion of the Roman garrison, the cargo belonged to a Roman official high up in the central administration; in the transaction the boat-owner was represented by his captain, the cargo-owner by his slave. The boat was of relatively small capacity, 500 artabas or about 700 cubic feet. As usual, the lading is given by volume, not by weight (500 artabas of wheat would weigh about 15 tons), and to the round hundred, and in fact there was room for an extra 62½ artabas free of charge, effectively a discount on the basic rate. Freight got paid half in advance, half on delivery. The cargo was a bulk crop, arax (perhaps chickling, a kind of wild bean plant used also as green fodder), to be delivered (by donkey) to the most convenient anchorage. The boat came upriver, took its cargo down to Akanthon and Lile (presumably on the Nile), but at neither end of the journey could the boat come up to the shore, so that the chickling had to be moved in skiffs. No sailing in a storm, with the risk of capsizing; no sailing by night, with the risk of running aground (this was mid-September and the river was falling). At the end, the cargo must be fully accounted for, by the same measure (since measures of the same name have different sizes from place to place); and the hold must be emptied (i.e. the skipper could not cheat by asserting that part of the cargo belonged to another client).[43]

The dangers of storms and darkness figure already in regulations issued in the early days of Greek Egypt (probably by Ptolemy II). There too mention is made of 'designated places for mooring': if a crew was forced by a storm to moor on the shore instead, they were to inform the guards at the nearest anchorage, and the commander of the guard was to send them a security force 'so that nothing violent may occur; if representatives of the King are making an urgent voyage and want to sail by night, the guards are to send an escort with them . . .'[44] This hints that boats moored casually in lonely places ran the danger of attack; and even under the Romans authorised anchorages had their 'harbour guards', yet another cadre of amateur policemen doing their compulsory service to the state.

Other contracts dwelt more explicitly on the hazards. Apollonios and associates wrote to Sarapion (Alexandrian citizen), owner and skipper of a 'bedroom carrier' of 800 artabas (24 tons):

I acknowledge that I have hired the said boat from you for the loading of two hundred small Caesarean jars, which you will load at the

harbour [*of the Oxyrhynchite*?] and deliver at the harbour of the aforementioned Herakleopolite nome above Memphis, at an agreed charge
of two hundred and sixty drachmas of silver, which I have handed
over to you forthwith, the dues and costs and expenses on the river
and harbour fees and charge for wood being with me, the hirer. You
will produce the boat fitted out for the voyage, with a sufficient crew,
and you will put off from the city this present day and make the
voyage in customary manner, not sailing by night or in a storm, and
mooring each day at the designated and safest harbours at the proper
times of day, except (may it not happen!) in case of act of god involving
fire from the land or storm or criminals attacking, which if you can
demonstrate you, along with your crew as well, shall be free from
liability.[45]

This specifies more hazards, and hints at others: a fire on board does
make the captain liable, and must have been a good possibility if food
was prepared.

Ships were identified by their owner or captain (sometimes the same
person) and their capacity; and also by their *parasêma*, images
(customarily of a local god) carved on their side at prow or stern.[46] A list
found at Oxyrhynchos, perhaps of corn-transports departing from its
harbour, shows the swarming variety of the traffic. There was the
Ammon, from the Hypselite nome, 93 tons; the *Apollo*, from the Lykopolite, 78 tons; the *Hermes*, from the hamlet of Big Place, 81; the *Dionysos*,
from the Upper Kynopolite, 99; another *Ammon* (a government vessel)
from the Metelite, 54; the *Pythios*, from the Lykopolite, the *Oracle* from
the Leontopolite, the *Ocean* from the Prosopite, and many more. Some
of this traffic came from around Oxyrhynchos itself, and its neighbours
at Kynopolis and Herakleopolis; some from the middle distance
(Arsinoite), some from further away – four from Helearchia in the
Western Delta, others from Metelis and Diospolis Parva in the Eastern
Delta, Leontopolis at the base of the Delta, others from well upriver –
Lykopolis (Asyut), Hypsele, Apollonopolis.[47]

These boats came in all sizes from 500 to 3500 artabas (15 to 105 tons),
mostly in the range 1000–2000; and all of them actually loaded up to 10
per cent more than their stated capacity. The documents very rarely
state dimensions: in one case it seems that a boat 30 feet long and 10 feet
wide could carry 200 artabas (6 tons). In any case, the ships listed are
small fry compared with the huge corn-carriers attested for the Ptolemaic

period, which went up to 18,000 artabas or 540 tons: perhaps Roman pragmatism recognised, as Hellenistic ambition did not, that smaller vessels better suited the difficulties of this river.[48]

Some vessels belonged to named types: a 'fodder-carrier' (and elsewhere we hear of 'dung-carriers', 'wood-carriers' and similar dedicated craft, even a 'corpse-carrier'); a 'multi-oar', a row-boat carrying 20 or 30 tons, and the mysterious *ploion zeugmatikon*, 'linked boat' – a catamaran? Or a vessel in tow? Other documents reveal other types. There was the 'broad-bottom', regularly found in government service; the 'Greek boat', whose name marked it as an import distinct from native patterns; the 'bedroom-carrier', with a cabin amidships, suitable for passengers as well as for cargoes of wood or pottery.[49] The cabined boat does represent an older Egyptian type. It caught the imagination of the Nile mosaicist, and the eye of the geographer Strabo on his Egyptian tour – near Alexandria 'is the marina of the bedroom-carrying boats, on which the Prefects sail up-country'.[50]

Strabo also experienced the *paktôn*, a kind of glorified coracle: 'we crossed to the island (of Philae) on a pakton, which is a small boat put together from strips, so as to resemble woven material. Standing in water or indeed sitting on small planks, we crossed easily; our fears were pointless, since they are quite safe, unless someone overloads the ferry.'[51] This sounds like wickerwork, which of course let in water; but one pakton for sale was 'of willow-wood, length 12 cubits [18–20 feet], with a steering oar and two willow-wood oars'.[52] It was a versatile form, small and drawing little water, suited also to small cargoes (200, 300, 500 artabas). It could carry wine; it regularly ferried corn to larger ships anchored off-shore.[53] It carried passengers, even if Strabo was not alone in feeling nervous: 'If [writes Didymos to Apollonios] we get hold of a boat in which the little one can embark, we will come up, or if you wish send off donkeys to us . . . so that we can come up travelling by night. Just don't leave us the small pakton which I sent up with Isidoros, since the little one did not have the courage to embark on that.'[54] Fragile as they were, their shallow draught made them useful during the inundation, when watchmen could use them to patrol the flooded plain, on the look-out for possible breaches in the embankments.[55]

Even skiffs needed equipment, which might wander unless specified. 'Let them hand over the skiff to the landing-guard,' wrote someone to Apia, 'with 2 oars and pole and fittings.'[56] Even a modest boat (capacity 12 tons) needed a remarkable range of paraphernalia: 'supplied with mats and bedding and planked throughout, with mast and yard and sail and ropes and jars and rings and blocks and two rudders with tillers and cranes and four oars and five punt-poles with iron tips and ladder and a landing-plank and winch and two iron anchors with iron stocks and one single-armed anchor and palm-fibre ropes and a tow rope and mooring-ropes and three grain shoots for corn and one measure and a balance and a Cilician cloth and a cup-shaped skiff with two oars and provided with all the proper gear and an iron spike. . .'[57]

Shipping the Grain

To own a boat and its equipment you would need to put up a sizeable sum. The modest boat above was leased in AD 212 for 50 years (tantamount to a sale) for 1 talent 2000 drachmas, 'perhaps six years' wages even for a well-paid legionary'.[58] The investment brought various returns. There were perhaps tax-privileges, for the state needed boats. This would explain why in Hellenistic and Roman Egypt boats were normally not sold outright but leased for a generation. There was certainly the chance of rental income, for which both private and public business provided many opportunities.

Above all, there was a central need of the state, on the largest scale. All year long, except perhaps at the height of the flood, the 'public corn', the grain which the state exacted in tax, and the 'bought-in corn', the grain which the state requisitioned and paid for at its own estimate, moved in boats and barges downriver to Alexandria, where part would take ship again for Rome and its hungry plebs, whom it fed for four months of the year, and part perhaps would be sold on the private market to supplement the budget. This transport took place sometimes in government craft, sometimes in vessels hired from their private owners. The authorities kept a firm eye on the private boats, since they needed a guaranteed service to keep supplies moving. It was the strategos who received the oath of Clemens, 'skipper of a private boat', to provide such a service. It was the strategos who received the bill from seven skippers (one with his own boat, two representing their owners) who together can handle 4500 artabas (135 tons).[59] Lightering had to be secured, as well as carriage: so Aurelios Herakles, the pakton-builder, acknowledged to the police chief of the nome that he had received back the pakton with two willow-wood oars, 'which I made available for the ferrying of state grain in accordance with the written orders of our most illustrious Prefect Claudius Firmus'.[60]

Given the scale of the operation, the state took a special interest in the hazards of the voyage. The cargo might be accompanied by supercargoes who acted as security: originally soldiers, later civilians recruited under the system of liturgies. But violence was not the only threat. The grain came from the threshing floor, and was always liable to contain some alien matter, even though the government, like private estate-owners, required payment in corn 'new, clean, unadulterated, free of earth, free of barley, sieved'.[61] The judicious thief could still make a handsome profit by abducting some of the grain and mixing in more earth to make up the bulk. That might happen before the cargo was even loaded; it could happen during the long nights of the voyage. The government took early note of this. The cargo itself might be analysed on arrival. In AD 188 the appropriate minister in the central government wrote to the strategos of the Diopolite nome (far, far upriver, round the ancient city of Thebes): 'The shipment brought down from your nome ... to the amount of 2000 artabas of corn turned out, when the samples were lifted, to be impure. I ordered a half-artaba to be sifted for barley and sifted for earth, and it came out deficient by 2 per cent of barley and likewise by $\frac{1}{2}$ per cent of earth. So, at your own peril, exact from the sitologoi who loaded the corn the total difference of $50\frac{3}{4}$ artabas of corn and the extras and the other expenses and add it to the accounts of the operation and inform me.'[62] The shortfall amounts to 30 hundredweight ($1\frac{1}{2}$ tons), a month's ration for fifty men: chicken feed within the overall revenue, but the taxman requires his dues in full.

'Samples' formed an essential part of a checking system which continued at least to the end of the second century AD. From each cargo a sample was taken before its journey began. When the boat reached Alexandria, the sample was analysed for impurities. Sometimes, special officials were appointed to take the sample; sometimes special officers were nominated to carry the sample to the capital (no doubt there was a danger that if the sample travelled with the cargo the same larcenous hand might contaminate both).[63] The sample went in an earthenware jar. One such survives, dated at Oxyrhynchos in 2 BC, with all the details inked round its sides: 'Ammonios, son of Ammonios, captain of a state boat whose ensign is Ajax [?], by his supercargo Lucius Vuclatius, soldier of legion XXII cohort II century of Maximus Stoltius, and Hermias son of Petalos, captain of another boat whose ensign is Egypt, through his supercargo Lucius Castricius, soldier of legion XXII cohort IV century of Titus Pompeius. This is a sample of what we embarked from the produce of the 28th year of Caesar . . . and we have jointly sealed it with both our seals, the seal of Ammonios which has an image of Ammon and the seal of Hermias which has an image of Harpokrates . . .'[64] The analysis of the sample would reveal the proportion of foreign matter in the corn as loaded. It might also reveal that further adulteration had occurred en route, despite the watchful supercargoes.

Fishing

The Nile remained a lifeline. It provided natural and regular irrigation; it provided the quickest and cheapest transport; it provided also a renewable source of food, all the more vital in a country which had only limited pasture for livestock. Of course, fresh fish has a short life in a hot climate, but pickled or salted fish in jars makes a welcome part of the diet. Psais and Syra, expecting a visit from their son, promised fish as well as pork: 'So far we have not slaughtered the piglets. We are waiting for you to arrive. You know that last year we did not make fish pickle, but this year we did it, and if it works out I will have it ready by the time you arrive . . .'[65]

There were fish everywhere, not only in the river but in the canals, reservoirs, ponds and marshes which broke up the cultivated land. The autumn and winter were a good time to fish, with the river returned to its bounds and inland waters restocked by the inundation. Fish were valuable, and fishing rights also, whether the rights of a private owner with a lake on his land or the rights of the city or the state to exploit public waterways.[66] Fishing could be done on foot, or from a boat; with spear or hook and line, with hand-nets or cast nets or seine nets, by the use of traps or weirs or barricades.

Fishing was a profession, and fishermen might specialise. Thus the three 'seine-fishermen' from a nearby village, elected representatives of their group, who reported on oath to the strategos of the Oxyrhynchite; or the eleven 'sacred net-fishermen' of the Temple of Athena Thoeris, Greatest Goddess, taken in ones and twos from seven different quarters of the city, whose full names some bureaucrat registered.[67] With a group, fishing could be done on a systematic scale. So, in October of an unspecified year, an accountant recorded three weeks of uninterrupted fishing with a net (the account is headed 'Good Luck'). Most days began with a single 'night-time' cast (did the dark make it too difficult or dangerous to repeat?), and then a series of casts – two, three, four, five and at the end of the month as many as ten or eleven in a day. A few casts produced fish for pickling, the rest presumably was sold fresh.[68]

Of course, some fish were sacred and therefore untouchable. The idea amused the belletrists of Old Greece, since it confirmed their image of Egyptian superstition: the Oxyrhynchites, they say, did not eat fish caught with hooks, in case the hook should have touched a sacred fish.[69] Here, in fact, there was an element of truth. A document of AD 46, not actually from Oxyrhynchos, confirms that the oxyrhynchus fish was taboo: the secretary and thirteen elders of the fishermen of Narmouthis and Berenikis Thesmophorou swore by the Emperor Claudius that 'we never have connived, and never will connive, with persons fishing or dragging a net or casting a net to catch the images of the divine *oxyrhynchoi* and *lepidôtoi*, in conformity with the public written agreement made by us and the other fishermen. If we swear truly, may it be well with us; if falsely, the reverse'.[70]

The authorities exploited their fishing rights through superintendents (liturgists again) and later through tax-farmers, for fish in canals and around their sluices.[71] Individuals could lease out the rights to private ponds. Thus on 28 December AD 161 Sarapion son of Hierax, mother Arsinoe, from Oxyrhynchos, leased to three men 'for the present year only, the catching of all the fish which are in the ponds belonging to him at the said village of Seryphis ... at a rent of one hundred and seventy two silver drachmas and eight drachmas gratuity, which sum totalling one hundred and eighty drachmas Sarapion acknowledges that he has received on the spot in full at the same time as the writing of the lease ...'[72] In some cases there was a kind of auction, and the leases went to the highest bidder.[73]

The lessor could benefit from the product as well as the money-rent. Ammonios wrote to an Oxyrhynchite notable: 'I engage to lease for six years from the incoming second year the fishing of the fish forthcoming in the places under water in your estate at Terythis in the Eastern Toparchy, you providing stakes, me providing for myself the nets and the other necessaries, at a yearly rent of two hundred and forty silver drachmas, and on the side thirty jars of fish pickle, two jars of shad, two jars of mackerel, one jar of tilapia, one jar of bream . . .'[74] Some leases presuppose individual labour, in others lessor or lessee engages to provide fishermen, boats, nets.[75] The rent might be in cash only, or in cash plus fish, or by simple division of the catch. Leases apply to defined areas of water, and usually to a single year, or indeed to 'the inundation of the present year', since it was the flood which restocked reservoirs and canals.[76] Two leases give specific permission 'to whirlpool': to fish, it would seem, in the swirling water at the bottom of sluice-gates, where no doubt the extra oxygen attracted the fish and the barrier restrained their escape.[77]

Such valuable resources naturally attracted poachers, witness the aggrieved narrative of Hermon son of Demetrios, who had a pond in the middle of his land. The fishermen Paysis and Papsious and his brother and Kales and Melas and Attinos and Pasois and their associates, 'being not few in number, bringing with them also Titios a soldier, advancing on our pond with many nets and scrapers, they fished with gaffs and pulled up fish worth altogether one talent of silver, and when I had words with them they came close to me as if they were going to scrag me . . .'[78]

Worshipping the Nile

The Nile provided, the annual inundation above all, since on it depended the difference between hunger and plenty. The inundation was a sign from heaven, of divine favour or divine anger. A low flood represented a natural disaster of the first order, and all the world knew it. 'If the Tiber rises into the city [Rome], if the Nile does not rise into the fields, if the heavens stand still, if the earth moves, if there is famine or plague, at once the cry is "The Christians to the lions"' – so wrote Tertullian in the early third century.[79] Eschatologists included a good flood in their future paradise: when the benefactor comes (says the Oracle of the Potter), 'the survivors will pray that the already dead too should be resurrected, so that they may share the good things; and at the end of the bad times he will water what is dry . . . and the water-short Nile will come in fulness, and winter, which has taken on a new discordant guise, will run in its proper cycle, and then the summer will take its proper course and the breaths of the wind will be orderly. These things shall be.'[80]

Prophets predicted the height of the flood as they predicted the death of emperors: 'The King will die in his own house ... and the beggar shall be exalted and the rich shall be humbled, there will be hunger and sickness in many places ... After this the King will be great and take revenge on his opponents. Talisman for the year: draw on a linen rag ... OUÊREBÊÊ ... Measure of the inundation: 14 divine cubits, 4 hands [x] fingers'.[81] The flood (no more than acceptable) was 'predicted' to the inch. It does not require much cynicism to suppose that such 'prophecies' were composed after the event, so that verifiable predictions for a fake future added credence to predictions of events in the real future. In any case Oxyrhynchites could nourish optimism, or indulge the pleasures of pessimism, with such texts by their sides.

'The most holy Nile', they called it. The river had all the characteristics of a deity – powerful, potentially beneficent, unreliable and to be placated. In the festivals of Oxyrhynchos, the Nile was celebrated alongside other gods, with processions and feasting.[82] Leading citizens organised the cult: such was 'Zoilos, son of Zoilos and grandson of Dionysios mother Sarapias also called Arsinoe, former Clerk of the Market in the said city, high priest in office of the most holy Nile'.[83] These festivals cost substantial sums (some contributed willy-nilly by the magistrates themselves). One provided for grooms, a crier, a trumpeter, and for those who carried the statues of the gods, and the statue of the Nile, in noisy procession.[84] Another included two pairs of all-in wrestlers and a group of ball-players, along with priests, Nile, throne and grooms – the Nile's statue enthroned on a cart and drawn by horses?[85]

The higher administration also took care to promote this popular and age-old cult. One high official noted, for his own use, and with file-references, the letters he was writing on important issues – irrigation, the transport of pure and unadulterated grain, the sacrifices to the most holy Nile.[86] The strategos himself conducted the ceremony with all the trimmings: 'For the sacrifice to the most holy Nile, Payni 30. 1 calf, 2 jars sweet-smelling wine, 16 wafers [?], 16 garlands, 16 pine-cones, 16 cakes, 16 green palm-branches, likewise 16 reeds, oil, honey, milk, every type of incense except frankincense.'[87] In the villages too the inundation was an essential part of prosperity: hence the 'customary sacrifices' at Sinkepha 'for our lords the Emperors and their Victory and the rise of the Nile and the growth of the crops and the temperateness of the

imate'.[88] The coming of Christianity did not destroy the traditional
:lebration. In AD 424 a party of minor officials received two jars of
ine with which to celebrate the festival of the Nile.[89]

It was natural, then, to make the Nile the subject of hymns and
anegyrics. A serious poet, in classical hexameters, celebrated the hardi-
:ss of the persea tree: 'it perceives the advance of the river; but if it
ils, it draws in more water, as if by thinking intelligence, through
rge roots . . .'[90] At school level, too, a wooden note-book in the Louvre
irries (along with alphabets, mathematical exercises and a list of tax-
iyers) an address to the Nile, in Greek hexameters and invoking Greek
ythology, but unmistakably from an eyewitness. 'Hear me, father of
vers, and hasten onto your land! The sun calls you to bring us your
immer-born surge; the earth, stripped bare of the full fruits of harvest,
retches out its back and awaits the golden flow of your water. Men
anding by your pouring stream invoke the dear water of the divine
ile, and children, singing all together the yearly hymn, call you,
eseeching, to show yourself in fullest form . . .'[91]

The 'hymn' too, like the festival, continued into the Christian epoch.
papyrus found at Antinoe carries twenty-four lines, beginning with
ie letters of the alphabet in consecutive order, a magical simulation
the whole universe, 'Nile, delight and providence of all nourishment
the good, most fortunate Nile – smiling you have watered the land –
ghtly we offer you this hymn.'[92] A parchment amulet (a pocket-sized
ook of nine leaves) in the British Library contains a Creed, 'I believe in
ie God', and Psalm 133, 'Behold, how good and pleasant it is for
rethren to dwell together in unity!', but before these the familiar
ivocation – 'O Nile, King of Rivers, rich in rain, great in name . . . Rise,
ile, come up those cheerful sixteen cubits.' The magic number is still
ie same; and in the title we still read 'the most holy Nile'.[93]

CHAPTER 7

MARKETS

• • • •

For a town of perhaps 20,000 inhabitants, Oxyrhynchos maintained
good population of specialist tradesmen.[1] Its scatter of surviving docu
ments, over the three centuries of the Empire, take for granted a wid
range of goods and services. There were workers in glass, honey, lead
oil, vines and yeast. There were sellers of beer, books, condiments, egg
figs, fish, fish-sauce, fruit, gourds, linen, medicaments, oil, perfume
porridge, salt, vegetables, wine, wool – even a seller of everything (a
emporium where you could buy cheese, olives, pickled fish, meal, mat
mattresses, wrought iron, bed-feet, purple wool, pine-cones and plaite
fish-baskets).[2] There were bakers, barbers, bathmen, bleachers, boa
makers, brick-makers, builders, butchers, carpet-makers, confectioner
doctors, donkey-drivers, dyers, embroiderers, fishermen, fuller
garland-weavers, grooms, hieroglyphic-carvers, irrigators, key-maker
leather-workers, locker-room attendants, millers, money-changers, pla
terers, potters, poulterers, pub-keepers, sack-makers, sailors, she
herds, skippers, smiths (bronze, silver and gold), stokers, stone-mason
tailors, tow-handlers, undertakers, weavers, and wine-merchants. It wa
mostly a man's world, but not entirely: one could deal with wome
bakers, dyers, fullers, millers, undertakers and, of course, wet-nurses

Craftsmen operated sometimes as a cottage industry, sometim
(perhaps increasingly) on a more industrial scale, their products on sa
from home, at market stalls, through shops and workshops (often th
same place). They recruited labour from their own families, or throug
hired workers, or by taking on apprentices who produced while the
learned. They might function individually, or as a family busines
sometimes they related to the government through a collective or guild

To judge from other towns, such guilds, whose members paid a sub-scription and attended monthly meetings, provided for mutual assist-ance and mourning, but also for common action in fixing prices and paying taxes.[3] It is not clear whether certain crafts occupied certain streets or quarters, but certainly different craftsmen could be found living side by side. An extract from a survey shows two fishermen, a builder, an embroiderer, a dyer, a linen-weaver and a carpenter as near neighbours.[4] As in medieval times, the crafts and trades occupied a prosperous space in town society. When the World Association of Sacred Victors came to Oxyrhynchos for the Capitoline Games, no doubt an expensive occasion, those who 'gave' included Neilos the carpet-maker, Pammenes the perfumer, Ammonios the dyer, Philosarapis the gold-smith, Sarapammon the bronze-worker, Heras the oil-seller, Papontos the carpenter, the sons of Syros the baker and the son of Demeas the wine-merchant – the sons more enthusiastic for sporting glamour than their fathers?[5]

It remains a question how far these craftsmen produced for a wider market, as well as for local consumption. Egypt itself represented a substantial internal market; and Egypt in turn exported, via Alexandria, to the rest of the Empire (a local poet celebrated its linen, papyrus and glass).[6] At Oxyrhynchos, weaving was a flourishing business, perhaps indeed the main industry. One document seems to show 1,956 items being exported from the city (or its nome) in a single week – 'adult tunics 584, children's tunics 1036, cloaks 172, blankets 99 . . .'[7]

The Marketplace

At the same time the city itself consumed: goods and services from its own workers, food mostly from the surrounding country. The market-place was a central feature of Oxyrhynchite life. The strategos walked round it on his way to the office.[8] There might be other markets: by the fifth century, certainly, a whole quarter of the city took its name from the leather-workers' or shoe-makers' market.[9] But 'the market' par excel-lence would be the market by the great Temple of Serapis, to which several documents refer, a public space with a speaker's platform.[10] There was a concentration of shops in the area: an oil shop in the market, an emporium on the avenue leading to the temple, the vetch-seller and the beer-seller on the Eastern Colonnade.[11] Livestock was perhaps sold elsewhere: at any rate buyers and sellers of donkeys came from Hermopolis, 60 miles upriver, to 'the market of the Oxyrhynchite nome'.[12]

Those who sold at the market were subject to dues, some perhaps as a sales tax, some for the right to sell or the lease of a stall. For the latter, at least, the authorities appointed a pair of superintendents, who had for guidance an official schedule of dues payable. The superintendents were responsible for reporting yearly on the proceeds. One pair, Sarapion the younger and Pasion, drafted their report for the year 142/3 in rapid and much-abbreviated script on recycled papyrus, stating the total for each month and then the grand total of 2,968 drachmas 3 obols.[13] They copied in the schedule, which shows that the gymnasiarch was ultimately responsible for collection and that the revenue came under the heading 'temple taxes', perhaps that is payable to the Temple of Serapis itself. The schedule includes two broad categories of payer. There were craftsmen and shopkeepers: bakers of fine bread (per establishment) and coarse bread, dealers in wool and grain, sellers of rushes and wood and olives, makers of clothes and shoes and yarn, garland-weavers and tinsmiths, individuals selling around the city, butchers and shoemakers and vegetable-sellers organised in guilds or unions – and brothels, which paid a charge each month 'per workplace'. Then there were those 'who import things and sell them', their produce taxed at so much per unit: olives, dates, cucumbers, marrows and vegetables (per bundle), spices and beans, natron (per 100 artabas), rock-salt (?) (per boatload?), pottery, green fodder, wood, dung and cowpats, dates again (per basket) ... The superintendents clearly cast their net widely. Retailers in the second category effectively paid import dues. For those in the first the basis is not clear, but a similar account shows more detail: traders are listed profession by profession ('cucumber-sellers', 'marrow-sellers'), and each pays a fee per day of trading, perhaps indeed the minimal one obol a day.[14]

Of course, trading conditions might vary from place to place. A nervous and cryptic letter, found at Oxyrhynchos, hints at this: 'Please, my very dear Potamon, write to me about the market where you are, since that in the Oxyrhynchite is foreign to surpluses, since orders arrive there every day. Greetings to all your people and to my lord Apollonios the only friend.'[15] In the early Byzantine period, an interventionist time, the authorities even gathered comparative prices (whether actual or prescribed). Thus salt and chaff (used as fuel) cost the same at Oxyrhynchos and at Aphroditopolis, which lies 30 miles south along the Bahr Yusuf; but wheat cost 42 per cent more at Aphroditopolis, and meat 25 per cent more, barley 23 per cent less and lentils 24 per cent less.[16]

Those who went to market could refresh themselves at the local bars, kept by publicans known technically as 'dealers' (*kapêloi*) – a term by now specialised as 'dealers in drink'. Such was Diodoros, to whom Loukios wrote on urgent business: 'Please go off to Aretion the baker and receive from him four talents he got from us when he himself was in Alexandria.'[17] Such was Aurelios Horion, who in AD 261 proposed to lease working space 'in the city's Capitol, below the Eastern Colonnade, in which to open a bar ...' The Mayor duly published the offer, in the hope of attracting better bids.[18] Landlords (occasionally landladies) stocked Egyptian wine, a regular item of consumption since the immigrant Greeks had introduced the vine to Egypt. There was a 'wine of Oxyrhynchos', and its poor relation, 'sour wine of Oxyrhynchos', a *vin* more than *ordinaire*: cheap, thirst-quenching but not for finer spirits (the schoolmaster Lollianos complained that the town council tried to pay his salary in kind, 'sour wine instead of wine, and worm-eaten wheat').[19] More up-market establishments offered more reputable imports: wine from the Thebaid, a long way upriver, wine from the Oasis – presumably the Small Oasis (now Bahariya), a hundred miles from Oxyrhynchos across the Libyan Desert.[20]

There were also vendors of fast food. Some sold *orbia*, the bean-like fruit of the vetch (just as now, in Rome, you can buy a cone of lupin-beans from the stalls on the Gianicolo), or a thick purée made from them. Some sold the gruel or porridge called *athêra*, meal or flour boiled with milk or water. (Both categories paid a tax for the privilege of vending.)[21] *Athêra* had a Hellenic pedigree;[22] the comedy-writer Pherecrates, in the fifth century BC, had visualised an afterlife of perpetual feasting, in which gurgling rivers of porridge poured into the mouths of the dead without any effort on their part – the fast food to end fast foods.[23] It continued to be thought specially suited for the toothless, young and old; it could also be used as a poultice. The Romans saw it as typically Egyptian, and so the physician Galen, in discussing the prevalence of elephantiasis at Alexandria, included it in his diagnosis of unhealthy diet – 'they eat athera and boiled lentils and snails and much preserved food, and some of them even donkey meat and other such things'.[24] A household might buy it in along with its regular supplies of salt and pepper, meat and vegetables,[25] but it seems to count as food for the lazy, when Sempronios, reproaching Kephalon the priest for many dishonesties, summed up with 'You should not be chomping porridge on my signature.'[26] The vendors would have done good business. We know the name of a 'handler' in the porridge business, Isidoros son of Hierax: ironically enough, he died of disease in Alexandria, and his wife hastened to cancel his liability to poll-tax.[27]

Regulating the Market

Markets were of, course, regulated. The imperial government might intervene, notably in AD 301, when the Emperor Diocletian tried to freeze prices Empire-wide. This universal decree was inscribed on stone and displayed city by city; it enjoined the population to observe its provisions for the public good and on pain of death.[28] One fragment of an inscribed copy has been found in Egypt, and one papyrus refers to the edict in passing.[29] Otherwise there is a notable silence. However, the basic strategy of setting prices may lie behind a whole series of documents, dating from the period c.310–60, in which retailers submitted monthly schedules of their 'prices' – not, it seems, the prices at which they sold their products but the prices at which they bought their materials, for bakers recorded the price of wheat, brewers of barley, oil-sellers of vegetable-seed, silversmiths of bullion silver.[30]

The local authority had a more immediate concern. The city needed to be fed, for its well-being and to avoid the public disorder that a hungry population might cause. The town council included a Clerk of the Market and a Director of Food Supply. If the free market failed to provide adequately, it might be necessary to lean on suppliers. So, in AD 228, Aurelios Sarapion, 'retailer', swore to the Mayor that he would provide the city with fish 'without default' 'for as long as the fishermen of the hamlet of Monimou are working'.[31] So in 275, a seller of 'fine oil' swore to the strategos the imperial oath that 'I will provide daily in the workplace I have on the marketplace fine oil for retail sale and the provisioning of the city, so that no fraud occurs, or may I be liable to the consequences of the oath.'[32] Some fifty years later, in 327, an egg-seller swore with equal solemnity that he would 'conduct the retail sale of my eggs in the marketplace, publicly, for retail sale and the provisioning of the city, every day, without intermission, and it shall not be possible for me in the future to sell secretly or indeed in our own house ...'[33] In times of shortage, of course, and in times of inflation, suppliers had all the more temptation to hoard and force up the price. No doubt any hint of fixed prices increased the temptation to sell on the black market.

Above all, there was the question of 'daily bread', the staff of life yet always exposed to the vagaries of the harvest. Rome had set the example of a dole, a monthly distribution of free wheat to citizens who qualified for a ticket, up to 200,000 people in the early third century AD. Alexandria too possessed such a system, at least in the third century. Oxyrhynchos followed suit at some stage, it is not clear whether to handle particular shortages or as a continuing gesture of municipal grandeur; what we have is an archive of documents from the period 268–72. Those entitled to draw their one artaba per month came largely from two groups – those who had performed state service (liturgies), which normally fell on men of means (limited to 1000 at any one time), and those who qualified by ancestry to enter the privileged (and partly tax-exempt) group of 'metropolite citizens' (limited to 3000 at any one time). This 'dole', that is, represented not a charity for the have-nots but a bonus for the haves.[34]

In any case it did not address the more deep-seated problems of supply, which from time to time required direct intervention. In AD 116 a group of bakers drafted an agreement with officials to maintain the supply of bread, in part from wheat provided to them by the Clerk of the Market: 'and we shall produce for you loaves which are baked, seasoned and acceptable ... each loaf two pounds weight, 30 loaves being reckoned to each artaba, and we shall receive as commission and for pounding flour [?] and all expenses 10 obols for each artaba; and similarly with the 856 artabas which we have received from [...] Clerk of the Market in office in the city of Oxyrhynchos, in three instalments, by the public measure, we shall make flour from them and we shall make loaves from them whenever we are ordered and we shall put them out for sale publicly with the normal sellers ...'[35]

In AD 199 the need was for flour. The city's Director of Food-supply agreed with his five colleagues (all of them among the city's grandees) that for the next month each of them should fix up a bread-bakery: they were to provide fodder and barley for the donkeys, so that they ground corn each day in each workplace up to 20-something artabas – the five mills together processing 3 tons a day.[36] We do not know what kind of crisis this was. There was the possible hazard of a state visit from the governor, or a body of troops temporarily encamped near by.[37] Worse still, there was the possibility of famine: that might account for the emergency measures of AD 246, when the central government required that all private stocks of wheat in the city and the nome should be registered within twenty-four hours; in case of evasion, the treasury would confiscate both the wheat and the house in which it was found.[38]

Daily Bread

Greeks had originally divided their diet into two: bread, and what you eat with the bread (if anything). For the Oxyrhynchites, bread remained central, and bread-making a central part of the domestic routine.[39] Egyptian bread had been made from barley or the cereal called *olyra* (emmer wheat?). The immigrant Greeks introduced, or at least favoured, the cultivation of durum wheat; wheaten bread had become the norm by the Roman period, though there are scattered references to *kyllêstis*, the traditional Egyptian loaf. The wheat needed to be milled; the flour produced came in different qualities – whole wheat, refined (sieved to remove bran and other impurities), even the fine white flour made from Italian wheat and designated by a Latin name (*silignion* or *selignion*) which reveals its status as an import. From this could be made ordinary bread, with a fair measure of bran and perhaps also of stone-dust (hard on the teeth); 'pure bread', a white loaf of higher quality; and the luxury loaf of Italian flour. This was far from the great gastronomic world, in which the learned foodie Athenaeus could list fifty varieties of bread.[40] Still, it invited social discrimination. White bread might be bought specially for children.[41] When the diplomat Theophanes travelled, he and his friends ate 'pure bread', while their slaves ate 'ordinary loaf'.[42] The top-quality silignion might suit festivals; when the military visited, it was provided for the officer, simple 'bread' for his men.[43]

The process began with wheat. Traditionally, one artaba of wheat provided for one man for one month: one (standard) *artaba*, that is just over a bushel or nearly 5 stones by weight. One text suggests that one artaba would produce thirty loaves (one loaf a day for a month), each weighing about one and a half pounds.[44]

Much bread was made at home. This was traditional women's work
~~i~~d indeed work for women slaves in better-off households, and it
~~re~~quired early rising. When, in AD 185, Glaukios rented out a female
~~sl~~ave to Achillas, for whom she would work as a weaver, he reserved
~~th~~e right to this service: 'if her master suffers by night a need for her to
~~b~~ake bread, he will send for her, nothing being deducted for this reason
~~fr~~om the sum paid by Achillas to hire her'.[45] For this you would need to
~~bu~~y in flour, or send out your wheat to be ground, or grind it yourself
~~in~~ a mortar or with a quern; at need a quern could be rented.[46] Once
~~m~~ade, the bread must be baked: on the fire, on a griddle, in a portable
~~o~~ve – not, it seems, in fixed ovens.

At the other extreme was the commercial baker, known earlier as
~~ar~~topoios, 'corn-maker', later as *artokopos*, 'bread-basher'. The older term
~~m~~ight apply equally to millers and bakers, and no doubt many combined
~~b~~oth businesses. In the Roman period there were signs of specialisation:
~~m~~illers and head-millers, oven-men, makers of fine bread, cake-makers
~~(o~~ne at least charged with assault and battery), a 'confectioner to the
~~st~~rategos'.[47] But in fact many bakeries continued as one-stop businesses.
~~T~~he 'baker' milled the wheat, baked bread and cakes, sold them on to
~~th~~e consumer. Such were the bakers of AD 116, mentioned above; such
~~th~~e bakers of AD 359, who declared their one raw material as 'wheat'.[48]
~~W~~hen Kalasiris the baker presented his account, he listed as goods
~~su~~pplied: '5th: 5 large loaves, 20 pairs of crisp-cakes, one measure of
~~fin~~e flour, cakes. 6th: one measure of fine flour. 7th: 40 section-cakes, 40
~~lar~~ge *selignia*, 28 pairs of small *selignia*, 2 measures of fine flour.' This
~~ho~~usehold clearly had guests on the 7th, which required large quantities
~~of~~ top-quality bread.[49]

This sort of business required premises and equipment, wheat and
~~sa~~lt and water (a well was useful), and for some kinds of bread, also
~~ye~~ast. The equipment need not be extensive: in one bakery, three
~~o~~vens and two mills and a pounding-stone with mortar and a grinding-
~~st~~one with mortar.[50] These mills were hand-mills (*muloi*); other docu-
~~m~~ents give more detail, 'a Theban mill with base and handle', that is
~~an~~ upper stone of Theban granite, with a projecting lever with which
~~to~~ rotate it on a flat stone base. More industrial production required
~~an~~ industrial mill (*mulaion*), a conical lower stone, an upper stone
~~fit~~ting onto it (with a hole into which the wheat was poured) and
~~eq~~uipped with capstan-like arms so that it could be turned by a
~~do~~nkey. Such a mill could process 20 or more artabas a day, that is

12 hundredweight of wheat.[51] The stress on such mills must hav
been considerable; references to them often find it necessary to specif
'in working order'.[52]

Baking itself seems often to have been done by the portable stove
called *klibanoi*. The normal word for 'oven', as applied to the firing
pottery, does not appear in connection with bread-making.[53] As usua
the documents do not describe the object, since it was familiar to al
We see only that it could be bought from a potter, and had its place a
much in private houses as in commercial premises.[54] A specialised ope
ator (*klibaneus*) might do the work, like the Horion who turns u
(probably) in two different documents of the early fourth century – a
illiterate shopping-list ('Horion says: Buy me four obols of oregano') an
an illiterate letter (festival time: try to get the authorities to supply th
bakers!).[55] Essentially, the klibanos is a terracotta shell. You place yo
dough on a clean, hot surface in the fire, cover it with the klibanos, an
sweep the hot ashes around it; holes in the sides may help to condu
the heat. Modern examples are still sold to ambitious home-baker
under the name 'baking-cloche'; the cloche 'traps the steam and giv
the crust a beautiful sheen and a thick, chewy texture. The slow he
penetration also creates additional oven spring. The result is a loaf
uncommon beauty.'[56] At a more homely level, the process has bee
observed in modern Yugoslavia, with shells from 8 to 20 inches i
diameter; the bread is turned once, and the baking takes about thirt
minutes altogether.[57] If this is a fair guide, an Oxyrhynchite bakery wit
three ovens could have produced six loaves an hour. That seems we
below the likely demand, and the fact that *klibanos* was apparently use
sometimes to refer to a building may suggest that the name was extende
to more ambitious facilities.

The produce was quite various. Bread (standard, 'pure' and superfin
normally came in loaves (small and large), and loaves in pairs. A pair
loaves could represent a day's ration for one man, equivalent that is t
the '2-pound' loaf mentioned above. The use of 'pair' suggests tw
(smaller) loaves joined together, like the eight-shaped double loaf yo
can still buy in Rome today: a day's allowance of dough could be roughl
divided, but not separated, before baking, to produce more crus
Pharaonic practice may provide a clue. One hieroglyph shows an oblon
loaf with rounded ends, and in the middle a circular depression
opening: perhaps the product might be sold entire, or broken at th
opening. On the other hand, the Egyptian pyramidal loaf was regularl

divided vertically into two, as tomb-paintings show: was the division so regular that the whole loaf counted as a couple?[58]

Cakes also: the standard flat-cake (*plakous*), cakes with honey and nuts chopped up (*koptai*), crumbly cakes with honey and sesame (*itria*). Naturally, the sweet things were in demand for celebrations: so flat-cakes and fritters (*lagana*) for the Festival of the Nile.[59] Naturally they were a special treat for children. 'I received from Korbolon the big cheeses. But I didn't want big ones, I wanted small ones ... Goodbye! Payni 1. Send me one obol of honey-cake for my sister's child.'[60] 'Pigeon for the children, 1 ob. White bread similarly, ½ ob. To Sekountos, for *itrion* for the children, ½ ob., and for dry flour, ½ ob. Milk, ½ ob. Myrrh for the burial of Pasis' daughter, 1 dr ...'[61]

Honey and Fish-sauce

'Not by bread alone': there were certainly those who could afford a more varied diet. When the Prefect himself visited Hermopolis, assorted groups of citizens were charged to assemble provisions: after bread, 'pure' and ordinary, came meat (veal and pork), wine (good and *ordinaire*), geese, oil and lentils, poultry and game, olives, pickled fish, cheese 'and other things from the general store', vegetables and fish.[62] This was a grandee, but even a citizen could enjoy more enterprising menus: 'For dinner on 5th: a Canopic cake, liver. For dinner on 6th: 10 oysters, 1 lettuce, 2 small loaves, 1 fatted bird from the water, 2 wings ...'[63]

Oil was important; oil-sellers produce it from vegetable-seed.[64] So too was honey, the ancient equivalent of sugar, and that depended on intensive bee-keeping. A tale of sabotage shows the scale of the business, with hives disposed in groups around the countryside:

To Herostratos the strategos, from Heraklios and Onnophris both sons of Sarapion, of the beekeepers of the city of the Oxyrhynchoi. We, and the sons of Heraklios, own four hundred and eighty-seven beehives, of which we kept eighty-seven hives in the village of Toka in the Middle Toparchy at a place called Petne in the house of Diogenes, in accordance with the declaration we made in the past 2nd year of Tiberius Caesar Augustus. On 17th of the present month Sebastos of the 3rd year of Tiberius Caesar Augustus, when we arrived at the aforesaid place to inspect the hives, we found part of the hives destroyed, and the remaining hives in a weakened state so that they were in danger of being abandoned. We at once asked Diogenes the house-owner about this, and he told me that, by the doing of Sarapion, the man of Theon the gymnasiarch, with those whom he brought in secretly with him by night, all the hives had been blocked up with mud on the inside for several days and the hives have no way in and out . . .[65]

Other provisions were on sale. The fish-sellers stocked 'all kinds of fish'.[66] There were fruit-sellers and vegetable-sellers and some specialists – pumpkin-sellers and gourd-sellers.[67] Butchers (the same word means 'cooks') handled beef, veal, mutton and pork, some specialising in pork or veal.[68] All parts of the animal could be eaten: 'Butcher's bill [Cook's account?]. Thôth 4th, 24th year. Meat, 4 minai [about 4 lb]. Trotters, 2. Tongue, 1. Snout, 1. 6th. Half a head with the tongue. 11th. Meat, 2 minai. Tongue, 1. Kidneys, 2. 12th. Meat, 1 mina. Breast, 1. 14th. Meat, 2 minai. Breast, 1. 16th. Meat, 3 minai. 17th. Meat, 2 minai. Tongue, 1. 18th. Tongue, 1. 21st. Paunch, 1'.[69]

Inevitably, in a hot climate, there was much pickling and preserving. One student (probably in Alexandria) received from home 'a full jar of sour wine and 126 pieces of preserved meat'.[70] The results may have needed extra flavour. Garlic could be had (introduced early on by the Greek immigrants).[71] The condiment-seller stocked spices and flavourings: sesame, oregano, mustard, safflower, dried coriander, two kinds of cummin.[72] The sauce-seller sold *garum*, a piquant fish-sauce of classical credentials (mentioned indeed by Sophocles) and by now popular all over the Empire. Fish-guts and small fry, well salted, were fermented in a jar, out in the sun, for two or three months; the mixture, shaken or stirred from time to time, was finally strained to produce the sauce. It could be made at home, but factories manufactured it in bulk and distributed it in jars wherever there was a market. There was white garum and black garum, top quality and second quality, famous garums from Pompeii and Klazomenai and Leptis Magna, from Cartagena and Barcelona. 'Almost no other liquid, except perfume, has come to be more valued', says Pliny the Elder, and an austere philosopher deplored 'that costly blood of evil fish' which 'burns the guts with its salty infection'.[73] The garum-sellers of Oxyrhynchos said nothing about the quality or origin of their stock – just generic garum, perhaps locally produced.[74]

The sauce-seller bought in his sauce ready-made, so the business was simple retail. Other businesses processed a simple ingredient: bakers bought in wheat, beer-sellers bought in barley. The largest stock attested belongs at the luxury end of the market. No party was complete without garlands, bought from the garland-makers, and scented oils. The perfumers, it seems, made their own blends, from a stock which included (apart from oil) pepper, incense, malabathrum, tall and dwarf storax, costmary, mastic, amomum, bdellium, cassia, cassamum, zedoary, elecampane, myrrh and ginger, as well as the cosmetic white lead which served as face powder.[75]

Pots and Bricks

Businesses were small, but by their own standards they were capable of production on an industrial scale. The glass-workers, commissioned to glaze the windows of the Baths, could handle 6000 pounds of glass.[76] Pottery and brickmaking also represented a volume trade. Daily life depended heavily on pottery. Indeed, in Egyptian mythology, the god Khnum, who created the universe, was himself a potter. The potter provided cooking pots and storage jars, even the narrow-mouthed nesting boxes which lined the walls of the dovecotes. You could buy domestic pottery in the market. The guild of 'potters of pottery pots' mention only pitch (two varieties) among their raw materials – did they buy in jars and pitch them before sale? Or did they pay nothing for their primary material, since clay could be had for the asking in any irrigated place?[77]

There was also a huge demand for larger pots, above all for the wine trade. Manufacture on so large a scale clearly benefited from a country site, which offered clay in abundance, space to dry the pots, and proximity to the wine they would contain. In AD 243 Aurelios Paesis, 'potter of wine-jars', agreed with two rich ladies

> to lease for a period of two years from the present month Thôth of the current 7th year the wine-jar pottery which belongs to you in the big farmstead of your estate around the village of Senepta, together with its store-rooms and kiln and stone potter's-wheel and other appurtenances, on condition that each year I make for you and fire and

refire and pitch what are called Oxyrhynchite jars of four chous capacity to the number of fifteen thousand, one hundred and fifty double-jars, one hundred and fifty two-chous jars, you providing the friable earth and sandy earth and black earth and at the kiln sufficient kindling and water in the cistern and for coating with pitch twenty-six talents of pitch in weight by the measure of Aline per ten thousand jars, while I provide for myself sufficient potters and assistants and stokers. I am to receive as wages for the single jars alone thirty-two drachmas per hundred, and as special extra payment per ten thousand two jars of wine, two jars of sour wine ... If I make other jars beyond the aforementioned number, and you have need of them, it shall be possible for you to take them provided that I receive from you the same wage and the pitch and the rest proportionately with the above quantity. If my offer to lease is confirmed, I shall deliver the above jars on the drying-floors of the said pottery, of winter manufacture, well baked and coated with pitch from base to lip, not leaking, without any that have been repaired or are defective, each four-chous jar holding up to its lip twenty Maximian *kotulai*. And at the end of the period I will hand over the pottery clean of dust and sherds.[78]

This neatly illustrates the complexities of the process. This pottery belonged to a country estate; jars would be in high demand there, and the raw earths needed could be obtained without too much transport. Manufacture took place in the winter, so that the product was ready for the new vintage. The basic mix contained three kinds of clay. Each pot must be fired twice; its inside must then be thoroughly coated with pitch to make it impervious (the pitch affected the flavour of the wine, making it perhaps more like modern retsina). Pitch had many uses and sources; another lease specifies that half the quantity should be Troadensian pitch, the other half from Siris, a city far away in southern Italy.[79] If they were not on site, pitch and clay and chaff (for firing the kiln) cost money to transport, as emerges from the letter of a dissatisfied customer:

Anthestianos to Psois the potter, greetings. It was only recently that I again sent Sarapammon to you so that now at last you can make amends for the sins you have committed time and again and hand over the sums you owe for the remaining cost of chaff and the hire-charge of the donkeys for the transport of the said chaff and similarly

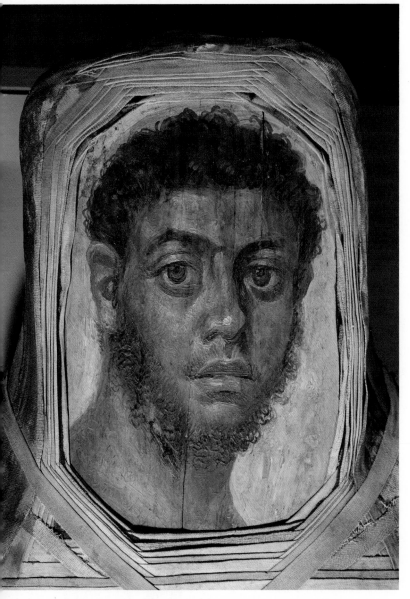

13. Mummy portrait. These mummy portraits were painted on wooden panels in wax-based pigments, and inserted over the face of the corpse within the mummy-wrappings. A man in his prime, swarthy and curly-haired (often known as 'The Nubian').

14. Mummy portrait. The melancholy sitter shows all the signs of wealth: hair carefully set, earrings of emerald and pearl, a heavy necklace of precious stones set in gold. Gold leaf was applied for her wreath and the neckline of her dress.

15. Mummy portrait. A youth with unruly curls and a first moustache. His victor's crown has been added in gold leaf, which also covers the background, as often later in Christian icons (in Egyptian belief gold symbolises eternity).

. This life-size painting (6 feet tall), water-based pigment on linen, shows the dead ─man, Greek in features, dress and stance, being received by the black jackal-faced ─nubis (shown in profile, as in Egyptian painting) and presented to the mummified Osiris. A shroud? Or a funerary hanging?

17. The monumental centre of a Graeco-Roman city, of the grandeur aspired to by Oxyrhynchos: arch and colonnade at Palmyra.

18. BELOW: A bijou residence at Oxyrhynchos: architect's plan of a house, ink drawing with colour wash (see page 52).

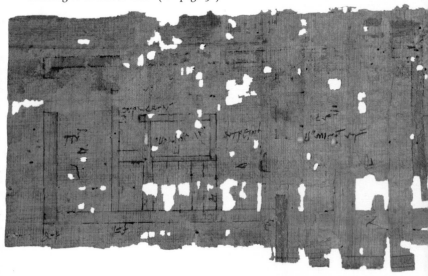

19. OPPOSITE: 'Mummy C' from the Valley of the Gol
Mummies in the Bahariya (Small) Oasis. The body is banda
face-mask in gilded plaster, pectoral of papyrus cardbo
painted with Egyptian deities. The tightly curled black
and the victor's crown, are Greek features; the uraeus ser
on the forehead is purely Egypt

20. *Damnatio Memoriae*. Emperor Septimius Severus and family, Greek style: painon wood. The face of the younger son, Geta (lower left), was scratched out and da
over after he was murdered by his brother Caracalla (see pages 68–70).

21. *Damnatio Memoriae*. Emperor Septimius Severus and family, Egyptian style:
relief in the Temple of Esna. The Emperor (left of centre) is facing the ram-headed
god Khnum. The figure of the younger son, Geta (extreme left), was chiselled out
after his murder.

Damnatio Memoriae. Tattered fragments from the minutes of the Town Council of Oxyrhynchos (AD 201/2?). Ten years later, the name and titles of , and other murdered relations, were vigorously inked out.

23. The famous mosaic of Palestrina gives a fantasy panorama of Egypt during the annual flooding of the Nile. In this detail are farm-building with towers (top); papyrus hut and herdsman sheltering on high ground; party-goers celebrating the flood in a pergola covered with grapes.

for the transport of earth, at present seven hundred drachmas ... You took no notice of Sarapammon but said to him, 'Let me off just now, since I have arrived from abroad with my pitch' – just so that you recognise my evidence. So I had to ask my friend Dionysios to demand from you what you owe or give it to him in jars. I've written also to Sarapammon to visit you again so that you don't battle on in this shameless way, refusing to comply with my demand and making excuses: just make sure to comply, otherwise I may treat you differently and send for you through an officer of the law ...[80]

Many of the same conditions applied to the making of bricks. Brick was the normal building material, made from mud. 'Raw brick' would be dried in the sun, 'baked brick' fired for greater toughness. Builders might make their own. Horion wrote to Pagenes, 'If Pinoution the builder is still with you, encourage him urgently to stack and fire the baked brick belonging to Eudaimon son of Plotinos. Now, don't treat this as a side issue. The job must be done urgently. The baked brick is at Valens' farmstead. Goodbye.'[81] This is cottage production. Professional brick-makers produced tens of thousands. Indeed, on the great landed estates of the Byzantine period, the needs of cottages and farm-buildings and cisterns required an almost industrial production (one account records 160,000 in a single entry).[82] Baked brick will naturally have cost more; builders working on the Great Praetorium of Oxyrhynchos (a three-storey building) used both baked and raw brick, no doubt for the more and less load-bearing elements. At the top of the range came 'well-baked brick', often used to line wells and cisterns and presumably baked for longer to make it impermeable.[83]

Apprentices

Some crafts trained new generations, as we did until quite recently, by apprenticeships. Among the documents from Oxyrhynchos there are twenty-odd contracts, in which a parent or guardian 'gives out' his child, or an owner his slave, to learn a trade: ten in weaving, one in 'linen-weaving' and one in 'linen-weaving by those sitting down', two in wool-carding, one to a bronzesmith and one to a house-builder; and two as shorthand-writers.[84] Certainly there were similar arrangements in other trades, as witness the excited letter of a barber newly employed: 'Agathangelos to Panares the barber, very many greetings. I greet Heliodora as well. I make obeisance for you both before the gods of this place, and I make obeisance for you every day. The gods willing, I am already cutting the hair of the master, and I am cutting the hair of everyone in the household. Any day that I cut hair, it is my custom to make the obeisance. Give my greetings to all my fellow learners!'[85] Agathangelos may well have been a slave. Now trained, he had been bought to barber a whole household. He was proud of this new status, and therefore remembered his old master (and his master's wife) in his prayers.

Apprenticeships were set up by contracts which specified in great detail the obligations of the parent or owner and the master (male, with only one exception) and the conditions under which the apprentice (a juvenile, often in fact a minor, with no legal voice) would learn and work. Thus:

> Aurelios Polydeukes, son of Alexandros, mother Apia, from the City of the Oxyrhynchoi, and Thonis son of Peteuris, mother Thaisous, from the same City, head weaver, make an agreement with one another that Polydeukes has consigned to Thonis his daughter Aurelia Aphrodite, mother Dionysia, a minor, to learn the trade of weaving, for a period of four years from the new moon of the following month Tybi of the present 12th year, for which period the father will make the girl available to remain with Thonis, not sleeping away from his house or absenting herself by day, the girl being fed and clothed for the entire period, in lieu of wages, by Thonis, as they have established between them. Polydeukes agrees that he has received from Thonis as advance payment for his necessary purposes four hundred drachmas of silver, which after the period of four years he will return to Thonis without interest; it is not open to him to take his daughter away within this period, nor after this period until he returns the four hundred drachmas of silver in full ...[86]

Weaving was one of the great traditional crafts of Egypt, and perhaps the only one in which a substantial part of the workforce was female. Among thirty or so recorded apprentices, three-quarters were boys (almost all free-born), but a quarter girls (almost all slaves). The free-born, once trained, could work for themselves, the slaves would work for their master or be hired out by him. Aphrodite, like many other apprentices, was a minor, i.e. under fourteen. What made her exceptional is that she was free-born. The period of four years was standard. So was the regulation that she should reside permanently in the master's house, which no doubt contained the master's workshop, which to judge from his title, *headweaver*, employed a number of workers. She was not to be paid directly, so that the master retained any profit arising from her labour. However, he would pay to feed and clothe her, and make her father an interest-free loan of 400 drachmas, which might otherwise have brought in (at the usual rate of 12 per cent per year) 192 drachmas.

Such contracts show a range of standard topics: the term of the apprenticeship, the place of residence, the provision of food and clothes, any wages payable to the apprentice, replacement of days lost by idleness or indiscipline or illness, holiday entitlement, penalties for breach of contract, signatures of the parties. The term ranged from two to five years. The apprentice might live at home (in which case the parent usually fed and clothed him) or with the master (who then normally took on this responsibility) – the choice may depend on distance, though all these arrangements took place within the one town, or on the nature of the business, for an apprentice present twenty-four hours a day could be called upon for shift-work. Wages might be paid to the apprentice, as his work profited the master, therefore not necessarily from the beginning and generally on a rising scale. The masters received no cash payment direct, except those who taught the less immediately profitable arts of flute-playing and stenography. It was for the apprentice to 'do everything he is instructed to do'; for the parent to guarantee performance; for the master to teach the trade 'complete' or 'as he himself knows it'. Holidays (specified only in five contracts, all from Oxyrhynchos and all to do with weaving) came out at 18 days (a slave girl) or 20 days (a free boy) a year, even three days a month (the son of a Roman veteran) – was weaving especially privileged?[87] We do not know how much holiday Aphrodite enjoyed, since the rest of her contract is lost.

The signatures show, as might be expected, that master craftsmen need not be fully literate: so Dioskoros son of Athenodoros, linenweaver, apparently got someone else to sign for him and then, half-way through, took over himself in spindly capitals and demotic spelling.[88]

Within the general framework, unusual terms might reveal special situations. Aphrodite, in the contract quoted, was free-born; all other girl-apprentices were slaves. Her father received money in advance, not as elsewhere an advance on her wages but simply as a loan. What lay behind these clauses? Polydeukes needed the loan so badly that he put his daughter to a trade, where she would effectively be live security to the lender, day and night for four unbroken years? Another contract of the same period, to a linen-weaver and for five years, shows that the balance could be different. Here too the father received 400 drachmas in advance (no mention of interest), to be repaid at the end of the apprenticeship. However, the apprenticed son, though his name is not stated, enjoyed more favourable conditions. He lived at home, fed and clothed by his father, and went to the master each day 'from sunrise to sunset'; after six months without wages 'in return for tuition' he got paid, on a scale increasing year by year; he would enjoy quite generous stated holidays – at least three separate weeks, plus two days for the Festival of Serapis.[89]

This all sounds like an easier life than Aphrodite's: perhaps a tribute to the situation of the boy's father, who had no 'necessary purposes', or to the social standing of his grandfather, who had been Market Clerk of Oxyrhynchos. Beyond economic pressure and social standing, affection too might bend the terms. When Taseus apprenticed her son Heraklas, still under fourteen years old, to Seuthes the weaver, it was specified that the master would feed and clothe the apprentice; but 'if the boy does not wish to be fed by the master, the master will pay the mother five drachmas a month for his maintenance' – the boy, that is, might choose (unusually) to stick with home-cooking.[90]

Banks: Cash and Corn

The Serapeum hosted the market. It also attracted banks, as temples do (remember the money-changers in the Temple at Jerusalem). In the Ptolemaic kingdom, all banking had originally been a monopoly of the state, though private banks began to develop later. In the Roman province, the state or 'public' bank continued. The 'public bank' of Oxyrhynchos, located at the Serapeum, was run by a board of 'public bankers' with a named director, 'Didymos and partners', or later 'Didymos and associates'. By the second century the board could count up to five members, all liturgists; in the third ultimate responsibility moved to the new municipality, and in the reform of 245–8 the number of bankers was reduced to two – a sign of how onerous an imposition this was, for the bankers had to guarantee the probity and solvency of the bank with their own fortunes. The public bank held public moneys, and disbursed it on public business. When the state owed money to liturgists, the strategos authorised the public bankers to pay (we have a file of such documents from the strategos Phokion).[91] When the state made a compulsory purchase of grain, the individual claimed reimbursement from the strategos, the strategos authorised payment, the individual issued a receipt to the strategos (in duplicate) and to the public bankers.[92] In both cases, the authorisation came jointly from the strategos and the Royal Scribe, another precaution against malpractice.

Other banks, however, are described as 'private'. Some documents refer also to the Serapeum; a whole series refer to 'the bank at the Serapeum by the City of the Oxyrhynchoi', with the name of the banker in charge. It may be that there were only two such banks, managed successively by different groups of bankers, and from the second century only one; and that seems to have been taken over by the city in AD 153/4, since from that date its administration was farmed out to 'superintendents'. After 201/2 we hear no more of it, only of an equally old but apparently more specialised institution, the 'exchange bank'.[93]

'Exchange' was indeed a normal function of the banks of Oxyrhynchos.[94] What that means emerges from an order issued by the strategos in AD 260: 'the officials have had a meeting and accused the bankers of the exchange banks of closing them down from a desire not to accept the divine coinage of the Emperors. Therefore it has become necessary for an order to be issued to all those who own the banks to open them and to accept every coin, except the really spurious and counterfeit, and to change them into smaller denominations, and not only to them but also to anyone who in any way conducts business transactions, who should be aware that if they do not comply with this order they will experience the penalties which his Highness the Prefect fixed for them already in the past.'[95] This was no doubt a crisis of a kind familiar in more recent history: a crisis of confidence caused by the debasement of the standard coinage. But the exchanges will have handled imperial coinage from outside (documents occasionally mention denarii), foreign currencies and indeed bullion, as well as a basic business of giving change for larger denominations.

Banks played an essential role at the higher levels of commerce. At lower levels, no doubt, much trading was done by barter; some was done by the use of locally issued tokens. Archaeologists have commented on the relatively small number of coins found on even well-populated sites. But for larger transactions, and for payments due to the state, there were two parallel resources: the official currency (issued by the Alexandrian mint), and wheat, the widespread medium of payment in kind.

Banks handled the former. They needed to cope with coin, which in quantity becomes cumbersome. The standard tetradrachm, called 'imperial silver' though even at its best it contained no more than 20 per cent precious metal, weighed nearly half an ounce; thus a payment of 500 drachmas weighed about $3\frac{1}{2}$ pounds. Practicality recommended paper transactions instead.[96] Sums could be transferred from account to account: 'I acknowledge receiving back from you through the bank of Agathos Daimon and partners at the Serapeum at the City of the Oxyrhynchoi three hundred silver drachmas of capital and interest at 12 per cent per year from Hathyr of the past year to the present day ... [Endorsed at the end] Through the bank of Agathos Daimon the transfer has been made.'[97] A local account-holder could issue an order to the bank to pay a certain sum to another of its accounts; this amounted to a cheque. At longer distance, the bank could accept instructions to pay against an account in another bank; this amounted to a letter of credit.[98]

Corn functioned alongside money as daily currency, and public granaries similarly functioned alongside public and private banks.[99] The state maintained granaries in villages throughout the nome, each directed by a board of 'corn-collectors'. Taxes paid in grain were paid into these granaries, from which by donkey and then by boat the collected yield made its way down to Alexandria. But it was possible to keep a private account there too, and to arrange payments into and out of such accounts. The holder could write a cheque on his account: 'Horion to the *sitologoi* of the Upper Toparchy, Monimou district, greetings. Transfer to Herakleides son of [—] the eighteen artabas, that makes 18 art., which you hold on deposit for me from the wheat-crop of the 22nd year of Antoninus Caesar our lord. [Date, signature]'[100] Here, and in the equivalent transfers of cash, the sum payable is written twice, in words and then in figures – a security precaution still observed on modern cheques. This document went to the sitologoi. The sitologoi then notified the recipient that the transfer had been credited to his account. Both orders and notifications could become negotiable instruments, a form of paper currency. Thus in AD 158/9 Sarapion son of Mnesitheos was notified of three separate transfers to his account, totalling 16 artabas. A second hand adds: 'I Sarapion, the aforesaid: transfer to Herakleides the aforesaid 16 art. in respect of an advance loan in the Sko district.' A third hand adds: 'I Herakleides the aforesaid: transfer to Zoilos son of Sarapion the aforesaid sixteen artabas'. So the papyrus passed from hand to hand, and the legal ownership of the corn with it.[101]

CHAPTER 8

FAMILY AND FRIENDS

• • • •

Achillion to Hierakapollon his brother, greetings. Since I was in process of sending for my sister, I write as in duty bound via those whom I have sent over for this purpose, first saluting you and my sister and our son Dionysios, then exhorting you to write to me about your health and what you need from here. If you do this, you will have done me a favour: for we shall have the impression, through our letters, of seeing one another face to face. I pray for your health.

> [On the back an address, 'To Hierakapollon, his brother', and a docket, 'From Achillion, governor of Marmarike.']¹

Letter-writing had a special place in ancient society. It was among the prime duties owed to friends and relations, as well as a prime instrument of business and government. Travel was difficult and even dangerous – fifty miles represented a substantial enterprise, whether by road or by river, a matter of two days' journey. Letters served as personal contact, and letter-writers as well as ancient theorists of letter-writing make it clear that a letter constituted a virtual visit, a conversation in writing, a face-to-face (as Achillion says) at a distance.² Even grammar reinforced intimacy: ancient letter-writers characteristically described their present doings in the past tense, since that is how their reader would see them – not 'Today I am going to market' but 'Today I was going to market', the writer thus putting himself in his correspondent's shoes. The business-like might date their letters, but the majority of correspondents felt no need, and that too adds to the sense of informal immediate communication.

Writing a Letter

Large numbers of letters survive among the papyri, a sample great enough to indicate how frequent the practice was, and that despite the practical difficulties. At first sight, the letter-writer needed only pen and ink and papyrus and literacy. Achillion belonged to a prosperous minority, a career civil servant at the height of his career, even though Marmarike, all rock and sand, bounded by the Libyan Desert and the treacherous North African coast, would not have been an easy billet, and his letter, a careful concatenation of civil nothings, is personal only in an official sense. He dictated it to a secretary, who wrote a handsome chancery script. Achillion then signed it, in a much less elegant fist, with the final greeting 'I pray for your health'. On the back, the secretary added the address, and the recipient or his secretary scribbled the docket before filing the letter away.

Even in ordinary correspondence, it was widespread practice to write only the signature oneself, an autograph which also guarantees authenticity; just so St Paul adds a final greeting 'in my own hand, which is a token in every letter: thus I write'.[3] Others might write the whole message in their own hand, sometimes a good educated hand, sometimes the tottery capitals of the semi-literate.[4] Those who cannot write (or feel too lazy) might turn to a literate friend; so Taesis sent her husband a long letter of domestic detail, written on both sides, which only at the end reveals the hand on the pen – 'I Alexandros wore myself out writing you the letters'.[5] Perhaps also we should envisage public letter-writers (though the papyri do not mention them), to whom the illiterate passer-by could dictate, like those who nowadays sit by the roadside in Ankara or (known as *evangelistas*) in the Central Station in Rio.[6]

Some kept a supply of letter-papyrus (sold in rolls and then cut into sheets), or used remnants from longer documents – so Ptolemaios got all his business ('buy me a pair of girl's full-size shoes made of hair') into a strip $1\frac{1}{2}$ inches wide, at ten letters a line.[7] Fashions in format came and went – the Greek of the Ptolemaic period wrote shorter letters on wide, shallow strips, the Roman age prefered narrow, deep pages, Byzantines reverted to the wide format even if it meant writing across the fibres, a bumpy ride for the pen. For economy, you could recycle obsolete material and write on its blank back. When Apollonios had agricultural instructions for Sarapammon ('So get the water-wheels ready, so that we may be prepared after the rise of the Nile'), he used the back of an old slave-sale.[8] When Dionysios needed help for his brother Demetrios, since he himself was dangerously ill, he cut up an old account and wrote his three letters on the back of the bits.[9] Papyrus-saving is a general habit. At Arsinoe, Alypios tried washing off an old memo, then gave up and turned it over – 'Since for the moment I couldn't find a clean sheet, I wrote on this.'[10] Not that literature remained sacred either: at Theadelphia, the estate-manager Heroninos and his correspondents dismembered texts of Homer and Demosthenes and New Comedy and recycled the backs for business letters.[11]

Those who could not afford papyrus at all, or were remote from supply, used bits of broken pottery instead. Indeed, it is a potsherd found at a grim military post, on the desert road from the Nile to the Red Sea, that preserves an appropriate appeal: 'Please, brother, when you come bring me 8 obols' worth of letter-papyrus.'[12] Of course 'No papyrus' looks like a conventional excuse, and a determined correspondent might need to call the bluff – 'Although I have often written to you,' wrote Theoninos to Didymos, 'and sent you papyrus for letters, so that you would have the chance to write to me, you have simply not thought fit to remember me in any kind of way. Well, of course, you exult in your wealth and your great abundance of possessions and so you look down on your friend. Don't be like that to your brother Theoninos: write us letters more frequently . . .'[13]

A finished letter got folded over and over, or rather rolled up, the right-hand edge inside, and then squashed flat. The exposed left-hand edge, being liable to damage, should be tucked in. The resultant spill made a small, flat packet, easy to stow away. The address, if any, was written on the outside panel or panels, sometimes in two parts with an inked pattern between. The pattern marked the place where a tie (some papyrus thread) went round to keep the packet closed. It seems that the drawing was done after the tie had been applied, and over it; when the tie got removed, it left a narrow, blank channel in the inking, clearly visible on the letter once opened. No doubt this was a precaution against tampering (it corresponds to the modern practice of signing across the joins of a sealed envelope): any unauthorised opening could be detected, since it would be difficult to replace the tie in exactly the right position.[14] Such packets were easily portable, alone or in bundles (Cicero speaks of receiving bundles of letters): 'to each the letters tied up with this one,' wrote a daughter to her mother.[15] The method allowed enclosures: 'I have rolled up a copy of the contract with this letter.'[16] What remains is delivery, a haphazard business. Letters might arrive damaged or late or not at all. Harpalos, for example, twice writing to Heras to send him important documents, specified on both occasions 'by a safe person'.[17]

Delivery

The imperial post, with its relay-stations, carried official correspondence, but private persons could not use it, unless indeed they had a friend in the system. The local administration too had its own arrangement; at village level, and again at the level of metropolis, individuals might be required to serve as 'letter-carriers' and convey official reports and letters.[18] Such dispatch-riders could always take on private business, whether from good will or for a sweetener. 'We received from Trophimos and the priest,' wrote Koprys and Sinthonis, 'six jars [of wine] – and we are being charged 6 drachmas 6 obols freight from Dikomia and 3 drachmas 3 obols in duty – and a flask and four pairs of sandals, and we received from the letter-carrier your letter and a rag in which there are gold leaves . . .'[19] The official touch perhaps offered reliability: 'Don't neglect to send me Apollonios' tunic,' wrote Isias on the back of a sheet cut from a handsome library-catalogue. 'I know that you too care for him like a son. Whether through the letter-carrier or someone else safe I'm sending you in haste a pound of wool for my Dalmatian cloak . . .'[20]

Most people, however, will have depended on casual messengers, very often on travelling friends. Achillion used his own servants; for the more ordinary it was a matter of chance, even in the most grim of crises. 'Since I found someone coming up your way,' wrote Titianos, 'I was impelled to write to you about what happened to me, that I was taken ill for a long time so that I couldn't even stir, and when my illness relaxed my eye festered and I had trachomas and I suffered terribly in other parts of my body too so that it almost came to an operation, but thank God . . .'[21] Sometimes the messenger knew the recipient, so that the address could be purely formal; if no address was written, it might mean that the letter travelled inside a parcel.[22] Sometimes more was needed: 'To the house of Theon son of

Apollo[nios?] the banker'; 'In the Teumenous quarter, in the alley opposite the well'.[23] Towns, of course, have no street-signs, and finding an individual in a strange town may need elaborate enquiries. So someone in Oxyrhynchos, setting off to deliver letters from Rufus in Hermopolis, required step-by-step direction – 'From the Moon Gate walk round as if towards the granaries, and if you enter the first lane on the left turn behind the baths ... Go westwards. Go down the steps and go up ... and turn right and after the precinct of [*Hermes?*] on the right there is a seven-storey house and on top of the gate-house [*a statue of Fortune?*] and directly opposite a basket-weaving shop. Enquire there or from the concierge and you will be informed. And give a shout yourself ...'[24]

'I was delighted to get your letter and know that you are well': the recipient often responded after reading the letter, or having it read to him. Recipients might be illiterate: 'Of the two jars of soap I sent, give one to Harpokratiaina, since I now remember that when I was leaving she gave me an order for this. Have this part of my letter read to her, so that she doesn't think I've been negligent.'[25] Occasionally they might not understand Greek: 'Whoever you are', wrote Ptolemaios, 'that read this letter, take a little trouble and translate for the women what is written in this letter and pass it on!'[26] Business-letters might require more action, and there were additional hazards. Letters might miscarry or arrive water-logged or otherwise illegible.[27]

Above all, however, it was crucial that they were authentic. Some letters carried seals, like legal documents (so when Serenos replied to the letter from his wife which 'could have shaken a stone', he applied a seal),[28] but even seals could be counterfeited. The provident might therefore include a 'Sign' – a reference to something known only to the two parties and thus a guarantee of authenticity. Not surprisingly financial transactions particularly need this sort of security. Sinpsansneus to his son Leonidas: 'Please transfer at your place in the Oxyrhynchite to Aurelios Herakleides son of Kephalon the poulterer who lives in the same street as our brother Leonides, nine hundred drachmas of silver in imperial coinage, against which I have received the equal amount in full of nine hundred drachmas here in the village of Sesphtha, but do not hold him back. By way of Sign, the fact that I loaded up for you three hundred linen pieces when you embarked with Alexandros the linen-worker. This note of credit is binding and in answer to the formal question I have agreed to it.'[29]

Friendship, Business, Social Duty

n life and business and society, letter-writing, and replying to a letter, could be a matter of courtesy as well as convenience, even a matter of morals. 'For many days now,' wrote Theon to Ammonios, 'I haven't had etters from you and I ask you to inform me why. That I myself write to you unfailingly, of this certainly you are persuaded.'[30] Friendship – and friends were a practical necessity, not just an emotional footnote, in the many uncertainties of the world – carried obligations as well as privileges. That is why ancient philosophers devoted much space to Friendship, something that we should not regard as a subject of ethical enquiry. Before all else I pray for your health,' wrote Horis to Horion. 'This is he second letter I'm writing to you and you haven't written back a single one. I love you always, but you rate me nowhere ...'[31] 'For my part I never leave off enquiring every single day how things are with you, as regards your well-being – but you in writing to my sister didn't mention me even once'.[32]

Even a routine letter might be a tonic. So Harpocras wrote to his father, in a letter which he took the trouble to date (a rare occurrence): Knowing that you will be delighted, I felt bound to write to you that here's nothing wrong with me, well, I was rather dim for just a very few days and felt better long since and there is nothing wrong with me. was greatly delighted reading through your letter, in which I saw that you were in the best of health, my lord father, and because since I was n swaggering spirits at receiving your letter I at once thought it could be an oracle from god and I am all the more remarkably healthy. Receive from Petechon, who is also bringing you this letter, a pair of sandals worth 4 drachmas ... Year 8 of Vespasian, Mecheir 2 [28 January AD 76].'[33]

Indeed, friends and family tended to merge in polite address. Older friends were called 'mother' and 'father', contemporaries 'brother' and sister'. Wives and husbands too could call one another 'sister' and brother', sometimes perhaps in literal truth (the Ptolemaic kings had taken over the practice of sister-marriage from the pharaohs – it put them on a par, as court poets did not fail to point out, with Greek gods ike Zeus and Hera – and some of their subjects followed suit), more often to express their integration in the family.

Friendship could be made by letter: 'I have often written to you,

seeking your friendship, but you have written me only one letter, an
you did not write back to me, instead you wrote to my father, threatenin
me not a little . . .'[34] Friends did favours: 'You must help him for the sak
of the friendship we have for each other.'[35] Friends did errands: 'Kee
the rest of the money, which isn't much, for the linen-weavers, it wi
do you no harm. It's in these things that the active benevolence of one
friends shows itself.'[36] Friends gave advice, not always welcome: 'I tol
you, face to face as well, what to do about the servant girls, but yo
think that I have other feelings about you and was not advising you a
a friend, although I myself have suffered from them . . .'[37]

The letter-writer, whether his purpose was business or pleasur
would frame his message with conventional formulae. Letters bega
most often with 'X to Y, greetings', and ended with 'Goodbye', or the
variations. 'Greetings' is literally 'rejoice'; 'Goodbye' is literally 'B
strong!' (or 'I pray that you are strong') – that is, 'Keep well!' Thes
formulae went back a long way, to the fourth century BC and beyon
Originally, you began with 'X tells Y to rejoice'; the letter, that is, sai
in writing what the letter-writer would say face to face, 'Rejoice!' Lat
(already by the third century BC) 'tells' dropped out, leaving a sho
formula whose truncated grammar came to be debated by later scholar
So conventional was it that writers could make a point by changin
letters of condolence avoided 'Rejoice' in favour of 'Be of good courage
'Keep well!' in favour of 'Farewell'; letters to and from philosophe
preferred the moral commitment of 'Lead the good life!'

The basic framework lasted at least seven hundred years, with mod
fications from changing social norms. Standards of politeness develope
as time went by. 'X to Y' gave place to 'To Y, X', that is, the recipient
name before the writer's, in official letters (a mark of deference) an
later in Christian letters (a mark of humility). In Byzantine times th
prescript might be dropped, but deference was expressed through a
elaborate system of abstracts, the ancestors of our own 'Your Majest
and 'His Worship' – 'Your glorious brotherly learnedness should hav
helped my insignificance,' wrote one lawyer to another.[38]

Within this frame, there was a second set of recurrent element
At the beginning, 'Before all else I pray for your health'; sometime
especially when the writer was in a strange city with different b
potentially powerful gods, 'I bow down on your behalf before the go
of this place.' At the end, 'Look after yourself' and 'Best wish
from . . .' and 'Give my best wishes to . . .' – best wishes to a list

ames, or 'all my friends', or more altruistically 'all your friends'. Within his inner frame came the meat of the message.

There is no strict evidence that letter-writing was taught in schools; t may be that the conventional forms got passed on by precept or osmosis. Certainly the rebellious schoolboy Theon (known to his family by the pet-name Theonas, to which he reverted in the address) had no difficulty with the framework, however rocky his grammar. 'Theon to Theon his father, greetings. A nice thing to do, not taking me with you to the city. If you refuse to take me with you to Alexandria, I shall not write you a letter or speak to you or wish you good health. So: if you go to Alexandria I shall not take your hand or greet you ever again. If you refuse to take me, this is what happens. And my mother said to Archelaos, "He's upsetting me, take him away!" A nice thing to do, sending me these grand presents, a hill of beans. They put us off the track that day, the 12th, when you sailed. Well then, send for me, I beg you. If you don't send for me, I shan't eat, I shan't drink. There! I pray for your health. [Address] Deliver to Theon from Theonas his son.'[39]

Beyond the day-to-day, there were occasions which required a more formal letter: death, and ambition. The letter of consolation, and the letter of recommendation, were social gestures, and the educated had guides to composing them, partly no doubt from tradition and practice, partly from formal manuals. Several columns survive from such a manual of the third or fourth century AD, perhaps originally from Oxyrhynchos. The specimen letters, Latin version and Greek version in parallel, illustrate a systematic range of social exigencies; the bilingual form may suggest Empire-wide circulation.[40] Letters of Thanks: to someone who has responded to a Letter of Recommendation. Letters of Advice: to someone who has received only a minimal legacy from a dead friend (three models). Letters of Congratulation: to someone who has received a legacy (six models); to a slave who has received his freedom. Such handbooks continued to fulfil a social need. Two complete collections in Greek, one of them originally composed in Egypt, survived into the Middle Ages.[41]

Individuals might well not need a complete manual, but schemes for the commonest types of formal letter could come in useful. Thus someone, somewhere, copied out a model Letter of Consolation, in which you have only to insert the names to achieve a usable product; the copy is misspelled and syntactically abrupt, showing perhaps the hand of a writer with more ambition than education: '—— to ——, be of good

heart. When the terrible news was signified to me about th
deceased ——, how I was distressed with all my household I cann
describe in words. You, brothers, as rational people who know what
in store for all of us and how you are neither the first nor the last
suffer this, bear what has happened courageously. I would have wishe
to meet you face to face, but I had no opportunity to set foot in th
village. In remembering my fellow-feeling for the deceased and his goo
deeds, which he performed unstintingly for all, so I beg you not
hesitate to write to me about what you need . . .'[42]

In the event, of course, the actual letters vary greatly in style an
sentiment. The basic fact, helplessness in the face of death, may itse
serve as consolation. Irene to Taonnophris and Philon: 'Be of goo
courage! I felt as much grief, and wept as much, for the deceased as
wept for Didymas, and I did everything that was proper and so did a
my people, Epaphrodeitos and Thermouthion and Philion and Apo
lonios and Plantas. Yet one can do nothing in face of such things.
comfort yourselves. Farewell!'[43] On the same day, Irene wrote the
another letter, to say that she had sent them 340 drachmas, which the
would please give to Parammon, her workman, and a portmantea
(containing dates and 25 pomegranates under seal), which they shoul
send back with two drachmas worth of white bread (?). Again on th
same day she writes to Parammon to confirm the arrangement.[44] H
mind, clearly, is full of daily business, but it seems that she thought
proper to handle business and consolation in different letters.

Not everyone had such scruples. Menesthianos' mind shifted fro
condolence to revenge to his own loss of a valuable slave:

> To Apollonianos and Spartiates, be of good heart! The gods are my
> witness that when I heard the news about my lord our son I was
> distressed and mourned just as for my own child, he was so lovable.
> I was on the way to setting out in your direction, but Pinoution
> restrained me, saying that you, my lord Apollonianos, had sent him a
> message that I should not come up since you were going to the
> Arsinoite nome. Well, bear it bravely; this is something that even the
> gods have in store. In everything, my lord Apollonianos, I owe you
> gratitude, because you stand up for me as for yourself. I too, although
> I can now get even with Chairemon for the way he treated me, held
> back until I informed you. He acted inhumanly. He himself, with
> others, made trouble, but so far is saying nothing at all, treating us

beyond human endurance[?]. So let me know what you think. I'm not easy myself. However I have sent over to you by hand of the acquaintance whom I've sent a copy of the contract, so that you know. I too have lost [?] a house-born slave worth two talents.

What begins as consolation ends with a copy of a document relevant to the quarrel with Chairemon. The recipient is an influential man, a former strategos and gymnasiarch.[45]

The letters of recommendation represent friendship in its most concrete aspect.[46] 'God willing, I hope to live frugally and get transferred to a cohort. However, nothing will happen here without money; letters of recommendation will have no effect unless one helps oneself,' commented a Roman soldier, serving with the Alexandrian fleet.[47] But this disillusion simply shows how central such letters were to success within the network. Often the letter goes with the person recommended. It might serve simply to introduce him. 'Theon to his most honoured Tyrannos, very many greetings. Herakleides, who delivers this letter to you, is my brother. Therefore I ask you with all my strength to regard him as introduced to you. I asked [your?] brother Hermias too in writing to give you an account of him. You will do me the greatest kindness if he obtains your favourable notice. Before all else I pray that you enjoy good health and the best success free from the evil eye. Goodbye!'[48] It might ask a favour for him, however self-interestedly. 'To my lord brother Heras, Ammonios the centurion, greetings. Ph[ ], who delivers my letter to you, is at present a tenant farmer of mine. He says he has been nominated to public service in the village of Dositheou, i.e. to the levy of tunics and cloaks, but has not yet been entrusted with the levy. So exert yourself, brother, to rescue him from this service; and also to give him your favourable attention, doing me a great kindness in this, and furthermore in the future also not to allow the villagers to injure him in other things or to nominate him to other services: let him testify to me what has been made available to him by your good will. I pray for your health for many years, my lord brother.'[49] Ammonios was a centurion, Heras governor of his district: officer and official could do business.

Here too, no doubt, there were model letters to be imitated. Certainly such letters written in the Christian age, as brothers and sisters wandered from one community to another, followed a fairly set pattern. 'To our beloved brothers and fellow ministers in each place. Welcome in peace our daughter Germania, who is in need of help, when she arrives with you! Through her I and those with me greet you and those with you. Emmanuel! 99. I pray for your good health in the Lord, beloved brothers.'[50] ('99' means 'Amen', a Christian cryptogram dating back to times of persecution.)[51] Such letters might develop into a chain. One recommender added, 'and if you can, don't delay to write to the others about them, so that they welcome them at each place'.[52]

Love and Anger

Such formal letters represent a social duty, and social needs dictated not only the framework but some or all of the content. More ordinary correspondence naturally allowed a much wider range of tone and matter, reflections of personalities and lifestyles. Sometimes, indeed, a letter seems to speak with the individual voice of its sender.

Here, for example, is Akulas writing to his friend Sarapion, 'the philosopher'. He has a Roman name, an elaborately literary style, and sentiments of the most morally improving sort. Only the puppy brings him down to real life:

> I was overjoyed to receive your letter. Our friend Kallinikos was testifying to the utmost about the way of life you follow even under such conditions – especially in your not abandoning your austerities. Yes, we may deservedly congratulate ourselves, not because we do these things, but because we are not diverted from them by ourselves. Courage! Carry through what remains like a brave man! Let not wealth disturb you, nor beauty, nor anything else of that sort: for there is no gain in them, if Virtue does not join her presence, no, they are vanishing and worthless. Under divine protection, I expect you in Antinoopolis. Send Soteris the puppy, since she now spends her time by herself in the country. Keep well, you and yours! Keep well![53]

Here, by contrast, Serenos writes to Isidora, 'his sister and lady', the distant and apparently estranged wife. No moralising, but the misspellings do not conceal the direct emotion:

> Before all else, I pray for your health. Every day and evening I make your obeisance with the goddess Thoeris who loves you. I want you

to know that from the time you went away from me I have been mourning, weeping by night and grieving by day. Since we bathed together on Phaôphi 12 [9 October], I never bathed or anointed myself until Hathyr 12 [8 November]. You sent me letters that could shake a stone, so much your words have moved me. I wrote back to you on the spot and gave the letter, sealed, to the messenger on the 12th with your letters. Apart from your words and letters, 'Kolobos has made me a whore,' he said 'Your wife sent me a message, "He himself sold the necklace and he himself put me on the boat."' You say these words so that I shall no longer be trusted with loading my boat. Look how often I have sent to you! Let me know whether you are coming or not coming.[54]

Diogenes, like his namesake the philosopher, seems to have been a grouch. His letter is addressed to 'his very dear friend' Apollogenes, but the business in hand does not admit of politeness. 'A thousand times I've written to you to cut down the vines at Phai [?], as Demetrios the gymnasiarch and Adrastos and Sotas decided. But today again I get a letter from you asking what I want done. To which I reply: cut them down, cut them down, cut them down, cut them down, cut them down! There: I say it again and again . . .'[55]

Business certainly did not exclude bad temper. Apollonios splutters to Artemas:

I am amazed that all that money went on olive oil. You rolled a double six! Here Ammoniac oil costs 220 drachmas and oil from the Oasis 200 drachmas. Therefore, if you can buy to supply another need that can benefit us, please do. You wrote to me that I am cutting you down in your absence, and this too worse than at the start. Well, if it's only recently that you know my opinion, you shouldn't be rated a human being. Other times too I've written to you that I did not detain Hermias' camel nor anyone else's. If this is what you want me to write, I'll write it to you, since perhaps you aren't reading what I write to you. All that Ammonas and the automata-maker, Anthropas, and all the rest suffered here on account of the Koptos camels, you can hear from your brother. Your accursed brothers-in-law are kicking over the traces and I've put in several appearances on their behalf, thanks to you . . . I'll tell you my plan, face to face, otherwise you'll think I'm writing a lot! I pray for your good health.[56]

Most letters focus on business. They are part of day-to-day survival. They do not linger, and certain subjects are notably missing. The letters often report arrival in strange places, but they do not paint touristic scenes; occasionally they order books, but they do not discuss literature.[57] When the papyri touch the great events of history, they do so only from the viewpoint of small personal convenience. One writer referred in passing to a 'cannibalistic' war,[58] another noted the entry of Titus Caesar into Alexandria – but only as a postscript to a letter about pig-fodder.[59] We hear nothing about political attitudes, nothing about the deeds, characters or deaths of great men. That may be a matter of prudence; it may be a matter of indifference – why remark on what you cannot change? We might expect love and jokes to play a part in the life of the people, but romance and scandal rarely surface. Just occasionally the frivolous breaks in. One slip of papyrus contains what purports to be a letter, duly folded and addressed; when opened, it turns out to contain a joke *billet doux* which also parodies the language of official edicts: 'Apion and Epimas say to their very dear Epaphroditos: "If you let us bugger you and it's OK with you, we shall stop thrashing you – if you let us bugger you." Keep well! Keep well!' An anatomical drawing illustrates their intentions.[60]

'Business', of course, reflected life, and lives at very different levels. Onesimos lived in a world of paperwork, with a touch of luxury in the purple dye. The tone is brisk and confident: 'Herewith the documents, completed. Before this I sent you by the hand of Osorapis the priest the ounce of purple and before him books [papers?] by the hand of Polydeukes. Let me know about them. Give my best wishes to your son (may he avoid the evil eye) and all those in your household. I pray for your health.' No address: probably this note was enclosed in the packet of documents.[61] By contrast, Ptolemaios concerned himself with old clothes, small objects and avoiding starvation. 'I received the saddle-cloths from Sarapas and a grey outfit half-worn and mended and a striped garment similarly half-worn and for my boy a brand-new purple hood and another tunic, emerald-green, all of these in a new linen wrapper, and a glass basket and a jar of pickled fish and a mattress and . . . a child's white tunic and a chest and a rod . . . I have pawned the white cloaks to get the money for corn, so that we can eat.'[62]

None of this, the bustle of trivia and the conventions of correspondence, excluded human feeling. Didyme, writing to her husband, turned even the stereotyped beginning into a love-letter: 'Didyme to

Apollonios, her brother and sun, greetings. Be aware that I do not see the sun, because you are not seen by me: for I have no sun but you . . .'[63] Affections generally remain unspoken, or cloaked in a final 'love and kisses'. Yet when time allows, the serious emotions of family and friends find their own eloquence.

Herkoulanos, who carried the first name Phlaouios, an honour (since it is the first name of the Emperor Constantine) which suggests substantial status in the government or the military, wrote, to 'his sweetest and most honoured' Aplonarion:

I rejoiced greatly when I received your letter, the knife-maker having given it to me; but the letter you write that you send me by Platon, the son of the dancer, I have not received. Well, I was very upset that you didn't arrive for the birthday of my son, both you and your husband, since you could have enjoyed yourself with him for many days. Well, certainly you had better things to do, that is why you scorned us. For my part, I want you always to have a good life just as much as myself, but I am also upset that you are away from me. If away from me you are having not too bad a life, I rejoice that you are having a good life, but at the same time I am worn down with not seeing you. Do what suits you! Any time that you want to see us, we will welcome you most gladly. So please come to us in the month of Mesorê [July/August], so that we actually see you. Greet your mother and your father and Kallias. My son greets you, and his mother, and Dionysios my assistant, who helps me in the record-office. Greet all those who love you. I pray for your health. [Address] Deliver to Aplonarion from Herkoulanos her patron.[64]

'Her patron' indicates that Aplonarion had been his slave before she was freed – a slave, clearly, perhaps his son's nanny, who is very much missed.

Apollonios and Sarapias were not just well-to-do (they dictated their letter) but generous in their message 'to Dionysia wife of Alexandros':

You filled us with joy by telling us the good news of the wedding of the most excellent Sarapion and we would have come at once to serve him on a day greatly longed for by us and to share in his delight, but because of the assizes and because we are recovering from illness we couldn't come. There are not yet many roses here, in fact they are scarce, and from all the estates and from all the garland-weavers we only just managed to collect the thousand that we sent you by Sarapas, even by picking the ones that ought to have been picked tomorrow. As to narcissi, we had as much as you wanted, hence instead of the two thousand you wrote for we sent four thousand. We wish you wouldn't condemn us as stingy by writing that you have sent the money, which is an insult when we too regard the kids as our own children and value and love them more than our own and rejoice just as much as you and their father. Write to us about anything else you want. Give our greetings to the most excellent Alexandros and to his children (may the evil eye not touch them!) Sarapion and Theon and Aristokleia and to Aristokleia's children. Sarapas will confirm to you about the roses – that I did everything to send you as many as you wanted, but we didn't find them.[65]

Letters like these bring ordinary Oxyrhynchites vividly to life. Many private letters survive from ancient Greece and especially ancient Rome, but by and large they survive because written by great men and collected after the writer's death by his admirers (so with the uncombed correspondence of the orator Cicero), or by the self-admiring writer during his own lifetime (as with the smug, stylish epistles of Pliny the Younger, lawyer and administrator). Greek Egypt offers something uniquely different, a huge random mailbag of letters to and from small people whose names have not otherwise entered history. We possess no portraits of Akulas or Serenos or Didyme or Apollonios and Sarapias. Even their gravestones have vanished. Yet through their letters we still hear them speak.

CHAPTER 9

POETS AND PEDANTS

• • • •

The notion of 'a classical education', which for us may have a Victorian ring, is in fact almost as old as the Classics themselves. Already in the heyday of the fifth century BC, Athenian schoolboys (even some schoolgirls) studied Homer; the well-taught could explain the rare words and strange expressions of a canonical text which was already archaic. The third century BC, in the new world of the Hellenistic diaspora, created scholarship. At Alexandria and elsewhere, the Greek literary inheritance was collected, studied systematically, equipped with explanatory commentary. There emerged a canon of the best authors, and its correlative, a list of set books for schools. This process no doubt arose precisely from the diaspora, from the need to define a Hellenic culture for Greeks now living among the barbarians and eventually for all Greeks as they fell subordinate to the engrossing power of Rome.

To the citizen of Oxyrhynchos, therefore, Hellenic education carried wide implications. It was useful: 'Letters are the best start in life', a maxim used as a copying exercise by those learning to write. It gave status, within the Greek-speaking community of the city and against the Egyptian-speaking peasants of the villages. It linked its products to elites outside Egypt, the educated classes of the Greek East and indeed of the Latin West (whose educational system had been founded, at least, on Greek models). The most ferocious of grammatical drills appears, in full fig, in a textbook written by Theon of Smyrna in the first century AD. A simplified form of the same turns up in Egypt, two centuries later, on three separate school tablets. The true Greek might detect, on a visit to Oxyrhynchos, an Egyptian accent (confusing D and T), he might look about uneasily for such unHellenic practices as animal-worship and sister-marriage. But when it came to grammar, they all shared the same hymn-sheet.

Not, of course, that the central, or indeed the provincial, administration prescribed a pattern of schooling or a curriculum to be followed. Nonetheless, the imperial government maintained an interest in the learned professions. The Emperor Hadrian, himself an intellectual, as his beard proclaimed, confirmed that philosophers, *rhetors*, *grammatikoi* and doctors should be exempt from all local offices (expensive and time-consuming). His more practical successor, Antoninus Pius, limited the number who might enjoy exemption in any one city, according to its size, and as it seems deleted the philosophers, who were to rely on support from the rich ('and if they should argue too precisely about their substance, it will become clear there and then that they are not engaged in philosophy'). This policy was well enough known for Lollianos, the 'public grammatikos' of Oxyrhynchos, to appeal to it, when he invoked the emperors against the city council.[1]

It applies, clearly, only to teachers at secondary and higher level. The Emperor Diocletian's *Edict on Maximum Prices* (an attempt to halt inflation by fixing the cost of goods and services Empire-wide) provides an economic view of the pecking order in AD 301: per month, per child, the *paidagôgos* received 50 denarii, the 'teacher on the ground' also 50, the teacher of arithmetic 75, the teacher of shorthand also 75, the Greek or Roman *grammatikos* or geometer 200 denarii, the *rhetor* or sophist, for each pupil, 250 denarii.[2] At the bottom of the ladder, then, we have the *paidagôgos*, the male nanny (often a slave) who escorted the young master to school and oversaw his deportment and behaviour, an important figure who might remain confidant and bear-leader for life. On a par with him, the elementary teacher, who instilled the elements of literacy – the very name 'teacher on the ground' (in Egypt they use, until late on, the less picturesque 'teacher of letters') suggests humility: he sat (or had once sat) on the earth, whereas his seniors taught more comfortably from what we still call the professorial 'chair'. He faced an all-too-familiar pattern of indiscipline. *Philogelos*, the surviving anthology of old Greek jokes, preserves a typical scene: 'The schoolteacher suddenly looked towards the corner and shouted, "Dionysios in the corner is misbehaving". And when someone said, "He isn't here yet," the master replied "When he is, he will."'[3] What qualifications teachers needed, we do not know: only that, in those Egyptian exercises in which the teacher wrote out a model for the pupil to imitate, there was more than one teacher who wrote beautifully but could not spell.[4]

As to pay, we see that the teachers of practical skills, accounting and shorthand, earned more than the teacher of letters; and the privileged, grammatikoi (who still teach 'children') and rhetors (who teach 'students', a step up in the age scale), were paid at least four times more than the basic rate. According to the astrologers, it was all in your stars. Those born under Mercury were suited to the professions – Mercury at the most important points of the zodiac produced sophistai, grammatikoi, educators; at the more inferior points, solicitors and speech-writers and 'teachers on the ground'.[5]

The Edict articulates the social and economic skeleton of a whole Empire. From Egypt we have no systematic overview of schooling. We do have, as usual, the worm's-eye view – scattered exercises, abandoned notebooks, fragmentary textbooks, some showing the hand of the pupil or the teacher or both. Broken pottery ('ostraca') represented the cheapest medium for school-exercises. In fact one group of exercises from far-away Thebes clearly come from one and the same broken pot, so that the editor envisaged the class as meeting at the city dump, where ostraca were plentiful – 'or possibly, if it is more in accordance with educational dignity to imagine the school as held among more savoury surroundings, we may have here the contents of the waste-ostrakon-basket which were deposited on the dust-tip after a day's work'.[6] Wooden tablets were a traditional part of the pupil's equipment, especially tablets infilled with wax, whose surface could be smoothed and reused. Groups of tablets, bound together with ties through holes in one edge, served as exercise-books for pupils and sometimes as note-books for teachers.

Going to School

How many Oxyrhynchites went to school, and with whom, and at what ages, we do not know. School-teachers there were, but we have only two names: Dionysios, a 'teacher of letters', who had a school in the West Colonnade, and Lollianos, a 'teacher of literature', whose salary the town council failed to pay.[7] These professions corresponded to two stages of education. Dionysios' pupils would be 'learning letters', and 'letters' (literally 'things written') is a wide concept. At the most basic, letters mean the alphabet, the atoms of written communication: so an illiterate person, facing a document to be signed, got someone else to write for him 'since he himself does not know letters'. Yet this stage covers a wide range of ages: there are boys of 14 (the age of majority) learning letters,[8] indeed boys aged 15 and 19 who already took part in a competition to show their skills as herald and as poet.[9] That suggests a wider interpretation of 'letters': not just the three Rs, but some study of set texts as well. More serious work on literature would fall to the grammatikos, 'the man of letters', whose province was classically defined as 'knowledge of speaking correctly and explication of poets'.[10] Beyond that a possible third stage, higher education: here the best paid, the 'rhetor or sophist', took students and taught them rhetoric, the techniques of stylish writing, artful presentation and public speaking, all indispensable for professional and political success.

Another term occurs: *kathêgêtês*, which I doubtfully translate as 'tutor'. It may be a different name for the same thing, but it may be that the 'tutor' specialised in individual instruction. His pupils might be boys or girls, young or relatively mature. 'Now too I write to you to keep your mind on the work in the fields so that it is not neglected and if anything is getting neglected inform the tutor,' wrote Demas to Agathos Daimon, who was clearly old enough to be left in charge.[11] 'From tutors one gets nothing useful, except the pointless paying of large fees,' wrote a disillusioned student of rhetoric.[12]

It is not clear how much the gymnasium, a central institution and a critical link with the Hellenic tradition, contributed to education as such. This was more than a gym, and indeed more than a country club. Membership was hereditary; the members, the city's aristocracy, pay a reduced rate of poll-tax. Parents put forward their sons at age fourteen (the age of majority and the beginning of tax-paying), adding proof that the family's ancestors figured on the register drawn up in the reign of Vespasian. Very rarely something was said about the boy's education. 'What is your craft?' asks the interviewer. 'Letters,' replies the candidate[13] – letters, one would guess, in the more substantial sense of 'literature', on a par with other careers. Not that they represent a full-time occupation. There will be time for the sports with which the Gymnasium is preoccupied – one applicant is described as 'runner, learning letters', another as 'learning letters and wrestling'.[14]

Dionysios' school was near the city centre. However, not everyone lived near a school or a tutor, and in some cases education might mean living away from home. For 'higher education', as with our universities, that could be required by the distribution of resources. However, even secondary education might take the pupil away; even finding a suitable teacher might be difficult. A mother wrote:

to my son Ptolemaios ... don't hesitate to write to me also about whatever you need from here. I was distressed to discover from the daughter of our tutor Diogenes that he has sailed downriver, since I was not anxious about him as I know that he will attend to you to the best of his ability. I took care to send and enquire about your health and discover what you are reading, and he said "Book VI", and he said many favourable things about your paidagogos. So, child, you and your paidagogos must take care to put you in touch with a suitable tutor. Your sisters send you many greetings, and the children of Theonis (may the evil eye not touch them), and all our people by name. Greet your most honoured paidagogos Eros.

This is the archetypal schoolboy world: his tutor, the trusted paidagogos who takes care of him, his set reading, Book VI, no doubt of the *Iliad*, the famous episode in which Hector parts from his wife and infant son.[15]

Naturally there were parental anxieties. In one letter, Aurelios Dios (in a strange city) formally greeted his father Aurelios Horion (in Oxyrhynchos): 'I make your supplication every day with the gods of this place. So don't worry, Father, about our studies. We work hard and we relax, it will be fine with us. I salute my mother ...'[16] In another, Kornelios wrote to his 'sweetest son' Hierax about various practicalities. There is a touch of Shakespeare's Polonius about the tone:

All of us at home salute you gladly and all those with you. As to the person you often write to me about, don't get involved until with any luck I reach you with Vestinos and also with the donkeys. If the gods will it, I will come to you quite soon, after [the beginning of?] the month of Mecheir [January/February], since I have urgent business in hand. See to it that you do not clash with anyone in the house; just study and stick to your books and you will profit from them. Receive through Onnophras the white cloaks which can be worn with the purple capes, the others you will wear with the mulberry ones. By Anoubas I will send you also money and rations for the month and the other pair of scarlet ones. You delighted us with the fish. I will send by Anoubas also the cost of them, however until Anoubas reaches you pay out for your and your people's provisions from your own cash until I send it . . .'[17]

The clothes sound fashionable; at the same time, the letter was written in January, when a double layer might be called for (in Cairo nowadays winter temperatures range from 9°C at night to highs of 25°C, or 48°–77°F). The fish, to be a special treat, should be sea-fish. Perhaps, then, the son is in Alexandria, and brought his father's letter with him when he returned to Oxyrhynchos.

Thonis too went away to school, and reported to his father, in a letter with several crossings-out and misspellings.

To my lord father Arion, Thonis sends greetings. [His father's name first, his own name second, as politeness requires.] Before all else I make a supplication for you every day, praying also that I may recover you in good health and all our people, before the ancestral gods where I am a guest. Look, this is the fifth letter I'm writing you, and you have not written to me except just once even about your health nor come to me. You promised me, 'I am coming,' but you did not come so that you could also find out whether the teacher is taking care of me or not. And in fact he himself enquires almost every day about you, 'Isn't he coming yet?' So I say one thing: 'Yes.' So hurry up to come to me quickly, so that he can teach me as he is eager to do. If you had come up with me, I would have been taught long ago. So when you come, remember what I have written to you often. So come to us quickly, before he goes away up country. I send many greetings to all our people by name with those who love us. I send greetings also to my teachers. Good health, my lord father, and good fortune to you for many years, I pray, along with my brothers (may the evil eye not touch them!). PS Remember our pigeons.[18]

Again, the teacher was on the move. He had been waiting for the father before teaching the son. Probably we should read another factor between the lines – no teaching until fees have been paid.

Fees there must certainly have been, but also less formal (or more feudal) contributions. You could send your daughter's tutor a box of grapes,[19] or 'the baby pigeons and other small birds that I don't usually eat . . . Anything at all that I didn't eat . . . send to my daughter's tutor, so that he takes pains with her.'[20] Lollianos represented a special case: he was a grammatikos, and he was on the city pay-roll – another gesture to the city's status, and another privilege for its privileged citizens. Whether he made a further charge to his students we do not know. We do know that the city (or so at least he claimed) failed to pay him his due. His private papers (see above, pp. 73–5) illustrated both the squalid circumstances and the glorious pretensions of the profession.[21]

'Learning Letters'

Primary education followed a systematic pattern which we easily recognise, since it continued to be the norm in European schools well into the twentieth century. Children learned to write and to read in logical order: letters, then syllables, then words, then sentences. First the alphabet, from beginning to end and then from end to beginning. Next, syllables, the basic units of words: one child used an ostracon to write BA BE BI BO BU and the like – the stuff of reading, and also a canon of writing, for convention set the syllabic boundary after the vowel not the consonant (so I-SI-DO-ROS, not IS-ID-OR-OS), and only illiterate writers ignored this rule. We do not know whether the class recited syllables as well as writing them. In classical Athens, Callias had written a 'grammatical tragedy', whose female chorus sang 'Beta alpha, BA – Beta epsilon, BE – Beta iota, BI'. Clearly this 'tragedy' was meant to be comical, and it would make a suitable joke if the chorus sang, in operatic cadences, what everyone had uttered in the schoolroom.[22]

A wax tablet of unknown provenance illustrates the process.[23] On one side, on ruled lines, the teacher has written out a double maxim in a full oval script. Below, closer and closer together, four sets of parallel lines between which the pupil has copied it twice. The pupil clearly has difficulties. Letters lean this way and that, and letters made in multiple strokes often do not cohere – so for example O, which is written as always in two movements, a concave and a convex curve joining at top and foot, but in the pupil's performance not joining but overlapping. Φ gives particular difficulty; the pupil's version leaves the central loop disjointed and the upright short and crooked. You can find similar wobbly and painful attempts also among semi-literate adults, those who describe themselves as 'slow writers'. The use of single or double ruling illustrates a hierarchy, if we can judge from later practice. Sigismondo Fanti, in his *Theory and Practice of Writing* (1514), says that an absolute beginner 'must be made to use two lines to contain the bodies of their letters ... You will see such a man learn to write in thirty days. Then make him write on one line for fifteen days, and without any lines for a further fifteen. By this method he will become a competent writer.'[24] At the same time, the conscious elegance of the model does not conceal the teacher's own ignorance: he misspells the last word, confusing epsilon with alpha iota (pronounced the same, as they are in modern Greek).

Once arrived at continuous text, the beginner could practice with QUICK BROWN FOXes, sentences, normally a hexameter verse (the metre of Homer) or a trimeter (the metre of tragedy and comedy), created to contain every letter of the alphabet at least once. And not only beginners; it is clear that these confections remained in the mind, and even grown-up literates or trainee calligraphers could recall them. Thus one possessor of a practised official cursive turned over his document and on the back, in two different formal scripts, wrote out the hexameter, 'He fired an altar to the gods, and a powerful fiery flame poured out.'[25]

At the level of the sentence, maxims played a large part, the pocket moralising intended to improve as well as to practise the learner. Some of these, naturally, concerned education itself. One potsherd, written by an ambitious but inept hand, offers: 'The farmer tames his land, the philosopher tames his nature. Those who are to become good men must exercise their body at the gym, their spirit with literature.'[26] Another, this time in letters so elegant that it may be the teacher's model, conveys the teacher's particular concern: 'Since you are young, work hard.'[27] This is the liberal version; elsewhere the exemplary text reads, 'Work hard, boy, or be skinned' – written once by the teacher and copied four times by a pupil 'doing his lines'.[28]

Many maxims connected with literature; they were quotations, and often in verse. The longer-winded could copy a whole series; so a 'cramped and ugly' hand wrote out, with several mistakes, an alphabetic series (but broke down at N):

> Alone is this true virtue, Kleitophon:
> Both parents to regard with faithful love.
> Consider that your father gave you light;
> Decent to love your mother from your birth ...[29]

Not that such things were always taken seriously. One document contains, on the front, a standard report to the strategos from a collector of money taxes, for November/December AD 229. On the back a 'thin and straggling' hand has added another date, perhaps Wednesday 8 March 243. Above that a maxim, 'It is our habit to think the rich fortunate'; below, a rectangle with criss-crossing strokes, and a face with large, long ears. This second writer may have been a schoolboy, or an adult 'slow-writer', but it seems that his irony was more developed than his script: the rich (the tax-payers on the front) are thought fortunate – yet consider wealthy King Midas, whom the god Apollo endowed with ass's ears. As to the rectangle – does it show an abacus? Or a gaming-board?[30]

Longer passages of the Classics survived, in writing and sometimes in spelling inept enough to suggest a school exercise – in copying? In writing to dictation? In writing out a passage learned by heart ('internal dictation')? Such, say, may be the 'crude and heavy hand' which wrote out the prologue of Euripides' *Phoenissae* with some uncertainty about where one verse ended and the next began.[31]

Pupils, of course, learned to read their letters as they learned to write them, and in parallel they could move on to words and sentences. Here there is what seems to us a particular and unnecessary difficulty. The Greek book consists of a single string of letters; there are no spaces between words. Latin texts originally did divide words, by writing a dot after each one. But the Romans gave this up sometime around the beginning of the Empire, perhaps in imitation of Greek practice, which still carried a weight of cultural glamour, perhaps in sign that those who could read at all could now read fluently without the aid of dots. In the event, it is not until the tenth or eleventh century AD that written texts normally divide their words.[32] We can make too much of this (after all there are still languages – Thai, for example – which present an undivided text), but it must have increased the difficulty of reading difficult texts. With the average maxim, the word-ends are easy to find, and with that the overall structure of the sentence. With the archaic dialect of Homer, grammatical entities are less easy to isolate, and the texts (at least from the second century BC) make some attempt to help – not by dividing words, but by writing stops, which divide sentences, and accents, which reflect the shapes of words or distinguish between homographs. Overall, we are tempted to think that even practised readers may have been reduced to spelling out their text; and this assumption has served to support a general theory that ancient readers (all or most) read aloud even when reading by themselves. This sounds all the more plausible for a culture in which literature was often designed for public performance, in declamations or at poetry-readings. However, the evidence is largely anecdotal and may therefore be untypical. We do not need to assume that ancient libraries were abuzz with readers muttering to themselves.[33]

Grammar had a necessary place, both accidence (declension and conjugation) and syntax. There were grammars to be studied and learned: so the rubbish yields an odd sheet (written on both sides, so perhaps from a codex) with full conjugation of the verb γράφειν, 'to write' – enough misspellings and mistakes to suggest a learner's transcript.[34] Such texts and exercises show a remorseless thoroughness: they include all forms found or possibly to be found in the literary Greek of the classical period, seven or eight centuries earlier. The schoolboys of Oxyrhynchos learned the dual number (a form used in referring to two persons), which had been totally dead in the spoken language for five hundred years. They learned the optative mood, whose function had been long forgotten and served now, if for anything, to add a note of cultural pretension to educated utterance. They did not learn, as beginners do nowadays, the verb λύειν 'to loose', because it shows no particular difficulties; they were after all being educated in their own language. But they were exercised in anomalous verbs – those with consonant stems, those with contracted endings – and exercised with a view to understanding Homer or Plato, authors as remote from their ordinary speech as Chaucer or Shakespeare are from ours. The results showed in composition too. The well-educated man could write Homeric verses, or a Demosthenic speech, in near-perfect imitation of the original language.

All this knowledge could be tested by an exercise which must have been widespread, since it turns up on one wooden tablet (complete with projecting knob, so that it could be hung on a nail on the wall) and two wooden exercise-books, all of uncertain provenance,[35] and also in the *Progymnasmata* of Theon of Smyrna, a widely circulating textbook which survives to this day.[36] The pupil was given a complex sentence, and a set of short formulae which, prefaced to the sentence, would change its grammar. Thus (the tablet, now in the British Museum, has it written out in full, with a verb conjugation on the other side): SENTENCE 'Pythagoras the philosopher, having disembarked and teaching letters, advised his pupils to abstain from beans.' TRANSFORMATION: (1) 'They say *that* Pythagoras . . .'; (2) 'It is related *of* Pythagoras . . .'; (3) 'It seemed good *to* Pythagoras . . .'; (4) 'O Pythagoras . . .' So the original subject of the sentence (nominative case) was turned into the accusative, the genitive, the dative and the vocative, and the rest of the grammar had to be modified accordingly. This exercise, which one grammarian thought very suitable for young people proceeding from the poets to rhetoric,[37] must really have sorted the sheep from the goats. Even the vocative of the dual had to be mastered: 'O you two Pythagorases you pair of philosophers . . .'

Reading the Classics

Schoolboys and adults alike dieted heavily on the Classics, that is, the Greek literature of the classical and early Hellenistic period. The authors most represented in the papyri are authors of the third century BC or earlier. It is as if, from our point of view, their taste had stopped with Dryden.

These authors required not only an effort of imagination but an effort of comprehension. It was not just the complexities of genius but also the vicissitudes of language. The spoken Greek of the second century AD had much in common, grammatically, with the Attic Greek of the fifth and fourth centuries BC. Yet that was not enough to make Demosthenes easy reading. Schoolboys at least found the long, involuted sentences hard going, certainly in the standard texts which articulated the stream of undivided words only with rudimentary punctuation. So one reader or teacher of Demosthenes needed eleven different lectional signs to make sense of the First Speech against Philip.[38]

Homer, the centrepiece of education and culture, to Hellenes the Bible and Shakespeare in one, presented the special problems of alien dialect, archaic grammar and forgotten vocabulary. Even the Athenians of the classical period required scholarly guidance. The schoolboys of Oxyrhynchos, reading themselves across a millennium into their heroic past, needed all the help they could get. And help was to hand. There were Homeric dictionaries, glossing the poet's words in alphabetical order. There were Homeric vocabularies, glossing the text in sequence word by word. There were Homeric commentaries, explaining the text in detail for the scholarly reader. There were also Homeric summaries, narrating the plot for the less scholarly reader who had forgotten it.[39] The pupil was expected to construe the text line by line, but also to know its content. Thus on one piece a thick, clumsy hand has written, on recycled papyrus, a series of educational items.[40] First, a quiz on the *Iliad*: 'Who was the Trojan general? Hector. Who were his advisers? Polydamas and Antenor. Who were his heralds? Idaios and Eumedes, the father of Dolon, and perhaps also Dolon. Who were the seers? Helenos and Kassandra, the children of Priam.' Then a narrative of the events leading up to the Trojan War. Then the first line of *Iliad* I, followed by a summary of the book.

The pupil could now read on, with this sort of programme-note informing his mind. He needed to make sense of ΜΗΝΙΝΑΕ-ΙΔΕΘΕΑΠΗΛΗΙΑΔΕΩΑΧΙΛΗΟΣ (μῆνιν ἄειδε, θεά, Πηληι-άδεω ᾿Αχιλῆος, as a modern text would print). He reached for the vocabulary, generally set out in two columns, Homeric words to the left and their modern interpretation to the right. The first word is archaic, 'wrath'; the vocabulary explained 'anger'. The third means 'goddess': the vocabulary explained 'i.e. the Muse'. The fourth is a patronymic; the vocabulary duly expanded it to 'son of Peleus'. The fifth is the genitive case of 'Achilles', but in Ionic dialect; the vocabulary gave the form in current usage. There are many copies of such vocabularies, and when we find two relating to the same passage they often differ in the items they think worth explaining – they are, that is, individual compilations by the teacher or by the pupil.[41] Every student needed one. 'My lord Isidoros,' wrote a fluent hand on a potsherd (always cheaper than papyrus), 'When you come, bring me the vocabulary to *Iliad* Book I, as I asked you.'[42]

'University'

The last phase, rhetoric, was even more likely to take the student away from home. One long letter gives a partly familiar picture of what we would call undergraduate life – a world of depression, scandals, cramped digs, unsatisfactory tuition and financial difficulty (alleviated only by a slave who could be sent out to work, and extensive food-parcels from home). Son wrote to father, apparently in his own hand (for the final greeting is by the same), a spiky subliterary script. The father was a respectable figure (High Priest of the Nile), probably in Oxyrhynchos, where the letter was found; the son, to judge from his sniffy reference to 'the country', was in the big city, that is Alexandria.

You freed me from the [*deepest*] depression by indicating that you [*don't mind*] what happened about the theatre. [*I was hoping*], by going early downriver, to find glittering [*prizes*] – [*and what*] have I achieved for my enthusiasm? As it is, [*in my search*] for a scholar, [*I found*] both Chairemon, the tutor, and Didymos, son of Aristokles, with whom [*there was some hope that I too*] could make a success, no longer in the city – [*only*] offscourings, with whom [*the majority*] have taken the direct road to ruin. I wrote to you earlier as well, [*just as I also*] wrote to Philoxenos and co., to [*consider the*] matter, and by them [*I was introduced*] to the famous man, whom . . . you at once disapproved of, just as I too condemned him [*as having a totally defective*] attitude. When [*I*] communicated your view to Philoxenos, he did indeed [*think*] the same, saying that he sympathised with the city only because of this shortage of intellectuals, but he said that Didymos, who as it seems is a friend of his and has the time to spare, would take care of the rest when he came downriver, in fact he persuaded the [sons?] of Apollonios son of Herodes to fetch up with him, for they too up to now are looking for a cleverer tutor, the scholar whose pupils they were having died.

As for me, if I found worthwhile tutors, I would have prayed not to see Didymos even at a distance; it is precisely this that depresses me, that this man, who was a tutor out in the country, has decided to compete with the others. So, bearing in mind the fact that, apart from paying numerous fees to no purpose, there is nothing to be gained from a tutor, instead I rely on myself, write to me quickly what you think. I have Didymos, as Philoxenos too says, always giving me time and providing whatever he can. Further, by listening to those who give public declamations, one of whom is Poseidonios, perhaps, the gods willing, I shall do well.

But it's the depression these things cause that makes us neglect our body, on the ground that those who are not yet achieving anything shouldn't even look after themselves, and especially when there are not even people to bring in money. Then, good old Heraklas – damn him – used to bring in a few pennies for days at a time, but now, as soon as he got tied up by Isidoros, as he deserved, he escaped and has, I think, come up-country to join you. Be quite clear that he would never hesitate to plot against you, for he had no shame in spreading the news about the theatre in the city, in front of everyone, with glee, and telling lies which not even a professional informer would utter, and this when he wasn't suffering his just deserts but had been freed and was doing everything as a free man. Well, all the same, you can, if you don't send him back, at least hand him over to a carpenter – I hear that a young man makes two drachmas a day. Or else attach him to some other work, from which he will make more money, so that his bit of wages can be collected and sent to us from time to time. You know that Diogas too is learning letters. While you are sending the little one, we will look out for more space in a private house, for so as to be close to Dionysios we have been in a very small place.

We received the basket, which contained safely everything you wrote, and the vessels with the half-jar, in which we found, instead of 18 choes, 22. And I sent with a letter a half-jar to each of those you wrote. I got the six measures of whole lentils, and a Coan jar full of vinegar wine, and 126 pieces of preserved meat, and those in the jar, and the 30 roast pieces. Good health! Choiak 4 [30 November].[43]

Books, Libraries, Readers

It was a bookish education. But there is no clear reference in the documents to a public library at Oxyrhynchos, or to a library attached to the gymnasium, although such things would have been standard in the great Hellenic cities whose institutions the Oxyrhynchites of the third century AD seemed so anxious to imitate. No doubt there were private libraries, but we know them only by inference from their discarded contents.

Such probably was Grenfell and Hunt's find of 13 January 1905.[44] The twelve book-rolls, torn up before being discarded, include standard classics – Thucydides, Isocrates, Plato (two copies of his *Phaedrus*, one of his *Symposium*). However, they include also a number of major rarities – among them, the *Paeans* of Pindar, Antiphon *On Truth*, Euripides' *Hypsipyle*, and an extensive History of Greece which continues Thucydides (its authorship still a mystery). Six of the twelve look like economy books, the literary text copied on the back of a roll formerly used for an administrative document. These documents, when their origin is clear, come not from Oxyrhynchos but from the Arsinoite nome, some 60 miles away. It can be guessed that some career administrator, sent from Oxyrhynchos to govern the Arsinoite, brought back recyclable official papers and had personal copies of favourite texts made on their backs.[45] A personal library, in that case – until (after the owner's death?) someone put all the rolls in one basket and took them to the dump.

A larger hoard turned up three days later, a hoard of lyric poets (Sappho and Alcaeus and Ibycus, Pindar and Bacchylides), plus poetry of the Hellenistic age, the elegantly learned Callimachus and the satirical moralist Cercidas. The dig stopped short, to avoid disturbing the tomb of a local saint, Sheikh Ali El Gamman, and it was only in December 1931 that the Italian excavators resumed work in the same area; among their finds were additional fragments of papyri recovered by Grenfell and Hunt twenty-five years earlier. Fifty more books turned up – another library or libraries? This time they found the books mingled with documents, and documents from a rather grand family. In three successive generations, the head of this family was named Sarapion-Apollonianos (the double-barrelled name itself shows social status). Each of the three held high civic office and served as gymnasiarch. Sarapion II held administrative office outside, in the early third century, as strategos successively in the Arsinoite and Hermopolite nomes. Of course this mix of books and papers may represent separate discards dumped together. Yet it is tempting to think that grandees like these had literary leanings; in their studies official papers rubbed shoulders with classical poets. They may even have worked on their books: some of the rolls, the notoriously obscure poems of Pindar, for example, have extensive annotation in the margin. The books themselves date from the second and third centuries AD, the Sarapions also; other documents in the same find date from the fifth century, so perhaps this treasure-house of rolls survived for two centuries before being discarded – at a time when the roll itself had become obsolete.[46]

A small group of texts nestles round another aristocratic lady.[47] Aurelia Ptolemais was probably the daughter of Aurelios Hermogenes alias Eudaimon, Mayor and much else of Oxyrhynchos. His will, dated AD 276, divided his estate among his five children. To Ptolemais he left a share of a vineyard and corn-land and her pre-agreed dowry and 'my slave named Loyalty'.[48] Ten years later she leased land to no less grand a figure than the strategos.[49] That lease was found with two rolls of Homer (one informally written on the back of a document, the other handsomely written and well enough thumbed to need strengthening strips pasted on the back), and a history of Orthagoras, tyrant of Sikyon, an episode in the archaic history of mainland Greece.[50] The will, on the other hand, turns out to be a private copy, written on the back of a book-roll. This time the book is a modern work, *Charms*, a learned miscellany at epic length by the Christian polymath Africanus, dedicated to the late Emperor Alexander Severus (murdered in AD 235). Someone in the family, it seems, had catholic tastes. And someone held *Charms* in low enough esteem to recycle the roll within a generation of the author's death.

Who read books in the City of the Sharp-nosed Fish? We can't estimate the number of the really literate (there would be more who are functionally literate – able to sign their name, or even spell out a short message, when the business of life called for it); and certainly there will have been different levels within this select group. There will have been schoolboys reading Homer; these might continue reading in later life – or they might have added one more Homer text to the mass that we find in the dumps. There will have been serious readers of standard texts: if the books thrown away were proportionate to the books being read, middle-brow taste was very conservative – after Homer (four times more papyri than anyone else), and his rival in antiquity, Hesiod, the favourite authors were the great names of classical Greece – Plato, Herodotus and Thucydides, Demosthenes and Isocrates, Aeschylus, Sophocles and Euripides. To those add the major poets of the third century BC, Callimachus and Apollonius, and the morally entertaining comedies of Menander. Here and there we find fragments of more modern classics, like the famous prose-writers of the Roman period; the essayist Plutarch was certainly being read at Oxyrhynchos within a generation of his death. But these are rarities. The old favourites remained the best sellers.[51]

This leaves the frivolous reader, and the intellectual reader.

There will have been those who read for pleasure, the picaresque adventures of Iolaos the pretended eunuch, for example, or the classic pornography of Philainis, *On Indecent Kisses*,[52] even comic books like the parody *Labours of Hercules* with its ink-and-wash illustrations[53] – this is a time before illuminated manuscripts, when only vulgar texts and technical manuals carried pictures. Such people could go to the theatre for a burlesque that parodied Euripides, while the more serious went to see the real Euripides' *Kresphontes*.[54]

At the other extreme stood the card-carrying intellectuals, philologists and philosophers. Philosophers even advertised their passion. 'Sarapion the philosopher' received from his friend Akulas, in the serious-minded epistle quoted above, the proper encouragement to self-discipline and avoidance of worldly things.[55] 'Herakleides the philosopher' received from his friend Theon a letter and a parcel of serious reading: 'Just as I contribute every effort to supply books which are useful and most relevant to life, so I think it becomes you too not to be negligent in reading them, since there results from them a more than common utility for those who are zealous to be helped. The ones sent, via Achillas, are those listed below. Good health! I myself was in good health! Greetings to the proper people. – Written in Alexandria: Boethos, *On Austerity* III–IV; Diogenes, *On Marriage*; Diogenes, *On Freedom from Pain*; Chrysippos, *On Relations with Parents*; Antipater, *On Relations with Servants* I–II; Poseidonios, *On Exhortation* III.'[56] These are latter-day Stoics; the books are classics of Stoic philosophy, composed some three centuries earlier.

Another intellectual group shows up in the letter, already quoted, about copying books: Pollio, Diodoros, Harpokration. These were in a different class: Roman citizens, and citizens of Alexandria, who left their name on the historical record as experts on the Attic oratory of the classical period (indeed, Harpokration's lexicon still survives). Diodoros, Pollio's son and a Fellow of the Museum (the All Souls of Alexandria), still had strong connections with Oxyrhynchos. There, about AD 173, he bought a boat;[57] there too lived Ophellianos, to whom he wrote a letter introducing the nephew 'of a very close friend of mine, who was a philosopher of things Epicurean'.[58]

Authors and Illiterates

Education was no doubt for the few. Of course, we have no statistics of illiteracy, only the anecdotal evidence of individual documents and their signatures. There were types and degrees.[59] Most Master Weavers could not write enough to sign their contracts at all; but Aurelios Dioskoros, after someone else had written two lines for him, suddenly plucked up courage and added the last two lines in his own spindly capitals, drawn rather than written.[60] The 'reader' of a Christian church near Oxyrhynchos declared himself 'illiterate' – in Greek, that is, but presumably not in the Coptic of his village congregation.[61] A city's elite has a better chance of literacy than its traders, but there is no rule. Thus Aurelios Demetrios, former High Priest of Arsinoe, deposited money with Aurelios Sotas, former gymnasiarch, and held two written acknowledgments. But when Demetrios came to reclaim the deposit, Sotas 'tried to do a dirty trick with a view to defrauding me, because I am illiterate'.[62]

Illiteracy therefore carried risks, in a system so dependent on the written record. However, it did not carry social disapproval, let alone social exclusion. Private letters could be read out to the recipient;[63] here and there we hear of a 'reader', whose function was perhaps to read out documents before the illiterate agreed to them.[64] Those who could not write would get someone else to write for them. Those who could hardly write would at least sign their names, describing themselves frankly as 'slow writers'. In life and in business, friends and family stood ready to help.[65]

At the other extreme, we meet those who wrote and read with ease. There were practical advantages in this, and for women even legal advantages, as we see in the case of Aurelia Thaisous alias Lolliana, who applied under Roman law for the right to conduct her own affairs without a male guardian, in virtue of having three children and of being literate – 'knowing letters and able to write with the utmost ease'.[66] 'Lolliana' is a rare-enough name: was she related to her contemporary, the grammatikos Lollianos, a man equally insistent on the privileges due to education?

Literacy represented the first stage, but only the first, of a literary education; and literary culture carried further privileges. To know your classical poets could represent pleasure, self-improvement, or the parole of an educated and influential elite. That study was reflected in domestic versifying, which too might have a public face. Here and there we seem to have the author's own manuscript. One such preserves a rhetorical exercise, 'What Hesiod would say when he received his inspiration from the Muses'; and on the other side (it is an economy to write on both sides) the praises of Hermes and Antinoos – Hermes, the messenger of the gods and patron of the Gymnasium, Antinoos the drowned favourite of Hadrian who provided Greek Egypt with its own peculiar tragedy.[67]

Another offers alternative titles, *Praise of Hermes* and *On the Magistrate*. Hermes must inspire the poet to celebrate the young Theon, who provides plenty of oil and bread for the boys in the Gymnasium, and other good things which show his culture as well as his wealth. We have a handsomely written fair copy, with corrections in a hasty scrawl which may be the poet's own fist, inspired to change 'For those are the soothings of empty wealth' to the more emphatic 'For the gifts of empty wealth are empty boasting'.[68] Both these compositions, it seems, were occasional pieces for the occasions of the Gymnasium.

Inspiration and occasion were not the only spur to the Muses. There was also competition. Oxyrhynchites took part in a competition in the grand old city of Naukratis, well to the north in the Nile Delta, which gave prizes for performance as herald, trumpeter and poet.[69] The Capitoline Games elsewhere included competitions in versifying as well as in athletics, and it may well have been the Oxyrhynchite Games of AD 285 which called forth two more sets of hexameters – one looking back to the glamour of a more stable epoch and that enduring myth, the drowned Antinoos, the second facing new political realities – the accession of the Emperor Diocletian, the arrival of his new Prefect, Diogenes 'saviour of cities', and the virtues of the Procurator of the Seven Nomes, who was perhaps present for the occasion.[70]

All this local poetry exhibits the educated virtuosity of the poets, who reproduce without error the epic dialect and hexameter metre that Homer had used a thousand years before – a dialect long since obsolete and a metre all the more difficult to use now that the pitch accent of classical Greek was giving way to the stress accent of modern Greek. The ability to pastiche classical models would continue well into the Byzantine Empire. But how little it should be taken for granted is shown, for example, by the extraordinary collection of Christian poems contained in a codex in Geneva, in which Dorotheos' vision of the Kingdom of Heaven is described in hexameters of brutal barbarity.[71] This traditional education, and this preoccupation with classical poetry, bore dubious fruit later. About AD 400 the historian and biographer Eunapius could write that 'the Egyptians are really mad on poetry, but serious Education has deserted them'.[72]

The wider popularity of such poets, in the fourth and fifth centuries, won some the immortality of surviving the Middle Ages. We still possess Triphiodoros' *Capture of Troy* and Kollouthos' *Rape of Helen*, digestible mini-epics on Homeric material. We can still read Claudian of

Alexandria, who changed his language from Greek to Latin and exercised his talent for flattery and invective at the court of the Western Empire, and Nonnos of Panopolis, who narrated the conquest of India by Dionysus, god of wine – a flashy, fleshy poem as long as the *Iliad* and *Odyssey* together, loaded with epithets and preoccupied with snakes, which combines poetic technique, polished rhetoric and arcane mythography in a verse orgy well worthy of the god. Others too, whose works are now lost, enjoyed fame enough in their time to wander the Empire, marketing their skills; the rich and powerful could always use an epic on their exploits, a panegyric on their characters, or a marriage-hymn for their weddings.[73]

Copyists and the Survival of Literature

Behind every book read, there is a copyist. Such was the world before the invention of printing. The poems of Homer survived from the sixth century BC until they were first printed in Florence in AD 1488: this voyage of survival depended entirely on their being copied and recopied by hand through generations of scribes.

Of course, the very word 'scribe' can mislead. It suggests a professional member of a sacred calling. Such was the Egyptian scribe, proudly depicted in sculpture, transmitting texts and informing administration under the eye of Thoth himself; or the monastic scribe, with his special place in a religious institution, governed by firm rules of professional conduct, and portrayed at one remove in the Evangelists from whom his calling descends. By contrast, the book-transcriber of Roman Egypt had a low profile: anonymous, uncommemorated in art, featureless except in the rare aside to the reader. In the classical period, Athenian vases often show boys or men writing on tablets; so far as I know, they never show men writing on papyrus. That is the contrast between the author, who composes, and his secretary, who makes the fair copy. The same snobbery continued in the Greek diaspora.

We owe our literary papyri to these copyists. We do not know their names, we do not even know how their profession was designated on the ground. We do not know whether they were free or slave, working for themselves or for a master, taught by a colleague or a father, alone or in a scriptorium, to order or to supply a bookseller. One document refers to payment: a copyist who copied three classical dramas (that is, about 4000 lines of verse) received 12 drachmas, a sum which would buy (in the best market conditions) seven litres of wine or enough corn to make bread for a month.[74] Copyists do not sign their work, as medieval scribes sometimes do. Very rarely they speak, not as individuals but as professionals. A copy of *Iliad* III–IV ends with the conventional title and ornamental squiggle (*korônis*); then (in verse) 'I am the coronis, the guardian of the letters. The pen wrote me, the right hand and the knee.'[75] These are the essentials: the copyist sharpens his reed-pen, spreads the fresh papyrus over his knees, and proceeds to write – somewhere near by is his pot of ink (soot mixed with gum), somewhere the exemplar from which he copies – on a stand, perhaps, unless indeed someone else dictates it to him. The posture must be strenuous (only afterwards do desks come into fashion);[76] some later images show the left leg crossed over the right, which may explain why in many rolls the columns of writing slope outward towards their base, following the thigh-line. A minor poet depicts the physical suffering of it all: 'my eyes are tired, my sinews, my spine, the base of my skull and my shoulders'. The veteran may end with shaky hands and clouded sight.[77]

Oxyrhynchos supported its own copyists. As usual we do not know their names, but we do recognise their hands. When in the rubbish we find different rolls of different authors copied in the same individual script, we can reconstruct the graphic profile of the single copyist who produced them and (given the range of his activity) identify him as a professional. Some of the thirty-odd copyists so identified may have worked elsewhere, and exported their work to Oxyrhynchos, but many will surely have been local. So, in peopling the city, we can include craftsmen like 'the Euphorion scribe', whose nervous angular writing shows up in copies of Herodotus and Plato as well as of early Greek song-writers and the Hellenistic riddler Euphorion; and 'the scribe of the flat-bottomed omega', a solid fist which transmitted standard works of Isocrates and Aeschines but also one of the most remarkable of Greek poems (another treasure now rescued from oblivion), Erinna's lament for a childhood friend.[78]

Professional copyists were not the only makers of books. There were no doubt schoolteachers turning an extra penny, someone's secretary adding to his duties, the poor scholar copying in his own blood the books he cannot afford to buy. A private letter illustrates the distinction between private and commercial copies: 'Hypsikrates' *Characters in*

Comedy Books VI and VII, make copies and send me. Harpocration says they are among Pollio's books, and it's likely that others have them too ...' Here another hand adds a note: 'Demetrios the bookseller has them, as Harpocration says.'[79] A rare work, that is, might be found at a bookshop – otherwise it was tracked to a private library, from which the user or a friend could make his own copy. In either case, it was the symbiosis of reader and copyist that kept the book in circulation. Without the interest of the one and the labour of the other no author could expect immortality.

The City of the Sharp-nosed Fish exemplifies the culture of a whole Empire. We owe to this culture the rare books and long-lost works which survive only in that literate rubbish, but also the whole traditional corpus of Greek and Latin literature which successfully ran the gauntlet of the Dark Ages to re-emerge from its monastic retreat in the fifteenth century. The lowly copyist was the saviour of the high culture, and we can sympathise with the defensiveness which made one of them add, at the end of his own copy of Menander's *Sicyonians*, a message of his own:

> Do not laugh at my writing ...
> Anyone who laughs, [*I'll break*] his leg.
> How gladly I have rested my three fingers.[80]

CHAPTER 10

BUREAUCRATS

• • • •

The kingdom of the pharaohs had always depended on writing. Some two thousand years before the Greeks arrived, a satirist, or perhaps a realist, had reviewed the various trades. His son, he thought, had good reasons to go to school and learn to write. That would qualify him to become a scribe, a civil servant attached to the palace. 'Look, nothing excels writing; it is like a loyal man ... The scribe, whatever his place at the Residence, he cannot be poor in it ... So I would have you love writing more than your mother, and have you recognise its beauty. For it is greater than any profession; there is none like it on earth.'

By comparison, the life of the craftsman or the labourer is miserable. The reed-cutter is slaughtered by mosquitoes; the brick-layer is filthy and exhausted; the washerman 'does the laundry on the shore, neighbour to the crocodiles'; the gardener 'spends his morning drenching leeks, his evening in the mire ... So it happens that he rests dead to his name, aged more than any other profession ... I see the coppersmith at his toil, at the mouth of his furnace, his fingers like crocodile skin, his stench worse than fish eggs ... The barber shaves into the end of the evening, continually at the call, continually on his elbow, pushing himself continually from street to street, looking for people to shave. He does violence to his arms to fill his belly, like bees that eat at their toil ... The mat-weaver lives inside the weaving house, he is worse off than a woman, with his knees up to his stomach, unable to breathe in any air. If he wastes any daytime not weaving, he is beaten with 50 lashes. He has to give a sum to the doorkeeper, to be allowed to go out to the light of day.' The peasant fares worst of all: he 'complains eternally, his voice rises higher than the birds, with his fingers turned into sores . . . He is too exhausted to report for marsh work, and has to exist in rags . . . He reaches his home in utter poverty, downtrodden too much to walk.'[1]

The conclusion is clear: 'if you know how to write, that is a better life for you than these professions I describe . . . Look, no scribe will ever be lacking in food or the things of the House of the King, may he live, prosper and be well!' So high officials represented themselves with a roll of papyrus on their knees, or kneeling before Thoth the baboon, god of writing. There was magic to writing, but also a practical mastery. Ancient Egypt and Babylonia, like China and India, early developed systems of writing and so of record-keeping. In these societies, which depended for survival on the organisation of irrigation (so-called 'hydraulic civilisations'),[2] scribes, scripts and files provided the essential underpinning of a centralised economy.

The Greeks inherited a different tradition. In the remoter past, the great palaces of the Mycenean age maintained scribes who kept the paper-work (in fact, on clay tablets) of a bureaucratic economy. The written record, so far as archaeology has recovered it, consists entirely of documents, with no hint of a written literature, which no doubt did not need recording – poetry sticks in the memory, accounts do not. This phase, similar on a small scale to the scribal regimes of Egypt and Babylon, collapsed and disappeared about 1200 BC, and writing disappeared with it. Four centuries passed before the new beginning: the same language, Greek, now written in a new script derived from Phoenicia, the alphabet from which our alphabet descends. Even then the passage from an oral culture to a literate culture was slow and desultory. Classical Athens, in the fifth century, was a centre of trade and of culture; yet written documents were not taken for granted, and the comedy-writer Aristophanes made jokes about 'books' as a new-fangled toy of the pretentious. The vase-painters of the fifth and fourth centuries show people reading from papyrus-rolls. They show people (mostly schoolchildren) writing on wooden tablets, the handy reusable notebooks on which children practised and authors drafted. They do not show people writing on papyrus-rolls. The reason, I guess, is that such people would be secretaries and copyists and legal draftsmen, below the required level of glamour. That is, the ability to write did not in itself qualify a man for distinction. That ability, to our mind, would be less difficult to acquire for the Greek alphabet than for the complex Egyptian script of 800 hieroglyphs, even in its streamlined cursive forms. It might also be less useful, since the Greek world, politically and geographically fragmented, had no call for a systematic, centralised bureaucracy.

Once set up as rulers of the Near East, the Greeks found themselves manning and supervising just such systems, and adapting to their need for the written record. In Egypt even Greek script shows the effect. The traditional alphabet consisted of capital letters, written separately. From that evolved more cursive letter-forms, under the law of least effort: E (four movements of the pen) becomes ϵ (two movements) and then Ω (a single movement). The same law conditions the writing of letters in groups: ETOYC ('year') contains five letters; but make each letter cursive, and ligature them together, and the whole word can be done in a single movement, $\sim\!m\!\gamma\!\supset$. The effect is long lasting: the cursive script, in the late formalisation called 'minuscule', provides the basis for that still used to write Greek ancient and modern. It can be argued that it was precisely the needs of the Egyptian bureaucracy, and others like it, that encouraged the development of faster writing, the better to service the elaborate hierarchy of officials on whose activities the government depended.

Hierarchy

At the top of this hierarchy stood the Roman grandees, career civil servants who might move from post to post, and province to province, on their way up the ladder. The Prefect governed the country and commanded the legions there, as viceroy. He held office at the Emperor-Pharaoh's pleasure, but there was no doubt that some royalty attached to him – he lived in the palace of the Ptolemies and, like the pharaohs, he was forbidden to sail the Nile during the season of flood. Even in imperial terms, this was an exceptional post: for the first hundred years, the highest available, and thereafter second only to the praetorian prefecture (for the Praetorian Prefect, as commander of the imperial guard at Rome, was responsible for the Emperor's safety). The Prefect, like British viceroys of India, might arrive with no experience of his province; and since the tour of duty was short, perhaps four or five years on average, the experience gained did not serve for long. He had the usual friends, who served as a kitchen cabinet. He could call on local lawyers for advice on local law. He must have depended heavily on his personal staff (the satirist Lucian served as Prefect's secretary) and on a permanent secretariat, like the solidly titled 'Overseer of prefectoral letters and other things'.[3]

The Prefect was absolute ruler, supreme judge and commander-in-chief. Below him in Alexandria were subordinate Roman officials with departmental responsibilities: for law as applied to Greeks and Romans, for the administration of the courts, for temples and domain lands and imperial estates, for the shipment of grain to Alexandria and thence to Rome. Below him were the *epistratêgoi*, with responsibility for the main divisions of the country, the Delta, Middle Egypt and the far reaches of the Thebaid. That, with the legions, made up the Roman presence. Below them administration fell to Greeks, some professional, some amateurs. The professionals formed a civil service of their own, the amateurs functioned under the Roman system which imposed administrative duties ('liturgies' in the original sense of the word) on well-to-do citizens as unpaid service to the state – with their own property at risk if they failed to perform.

That administration followed geographical logic. The main divisions (*epistratêgiai*) were divided into counties (*nomoi* or nomes), which had once, 3000 years before, been independent princedoms and still maintained their special deities and individual customs (even under Roman management, the form for the regular census has different wording in different nomes), each nome subdivided into *toparchies*, each toparchy into villages. In parallel, each nome had its governor, with the traditional title of 'general' (*stratêgos*), and his assistant, the 'royal scribe'. Each toparchy had its *toparch*. Each village had its elders or its *comarch* and its secretary. Orders came down the pyramid, from the capital to the village; information, and taxes, went up the pyramid from the village to the capital – written orders, and written information, based on an elaborate system of written records, collated by scribes and preserved in archives.

The citizens of Oxyrhynchos had on occasion to deal with the Roman grandees. Above all, they could take their grievances, by way of petition, to the Prefect. But the always present symbol of authority was the strategos, who occupied a central position in the hierarchy and its responsibilities; together with his deputy, the royal scribe, he ran the nome.[4] Both offices had roots in the landscape; the strategos' title goes back to the Ptolemaic kingdom, the royal scribe much further (his title

Statue of the Nile as a classical river-god; swarming over him the putti which
~~~resent~~ the sixteen cubits of an ideal inundation.

A traditional Egyptian 'corpse-carrier' for use on the Nile: wooden model (to be
~~~ed in a tomb) of *c.*2000–1900 BC.

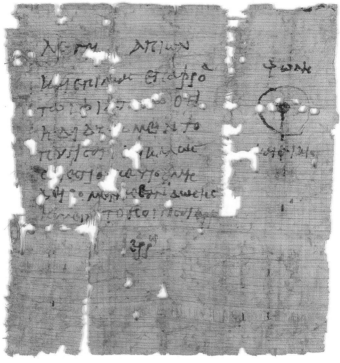

26. Papyrus letter, from Theon to his father Theon. 'If you don't send for me I won't eat I won't drink so there.'

27. Papyrus 'letter', from Apion and Epimas to their very dear Epaphroditos. 'If you let us bugger you and it's OK with you, we shall stop thrashing you' – with illustrative drawing.

Learning to write on a wooden tablet covered in wax. The first two lines are schoolteacher's model. Then the pupil copies them twice, between double lines ting smaller and smaller).

'King Midas has ass's ears.' A primitive hand doodles a maxim about the piness of the rich, then draws what may be a gaming board and a head with ears (see page 145).

30. A kind of comic book in verse, which illustrates the Labours of Hercules with pen and wash drawings. Upper right: the naked hero strangles the Nemean lion.

Bureaucrat as icon: the 'scribe' of Egyptian tradition, papyrus on his knees, under eyes of his patron god, Thoth the baboon, inventor of writing. (Stone statuette, 70 BC.)

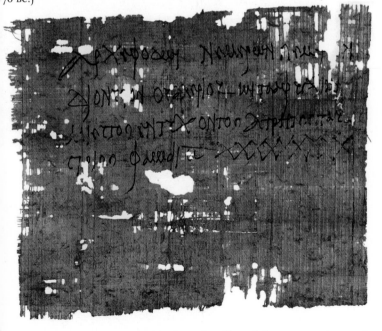

Bureaucratic routine: papyrus chit, from the office of the strategos, instructing a ...ceman to 'send' two defendants in a legal case. The row of XXXs at the end was ...revent any unauthorised additions.

33. Tyche ('Luck'), an important Greek
deity, on an Alexandrian coin of AD 138/9.
Her left hand holds the cornucopia of good
things; her right the rudder with which
she steers the world.

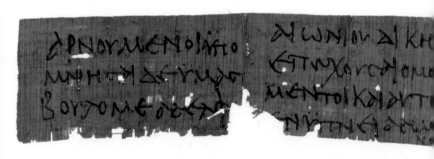

34. Double leaf from a miniature codex of the Epistle of Jude (the
shortest book of the New Testament), probably intended to be carried
(or slung round the neck) as an amulet by an early Christian
(third/fourth century AD).

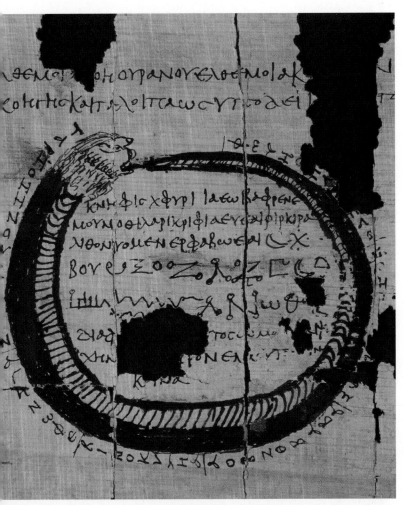

Design for a self-help amulet 'against demons, against apparitions, against every sickness and suffering'. Draw the *ouroboros* (snake swallowing its own tail), and inscribe inside the correct magical names and symbols and then 'Protect in health the body and the soul of ————' (insert your name).

36. Egyptian Christianity produced an art of its own. This splendid tapestry (sixth century AD) shows the Virgin and Child on a jeweled throne between the archangels Michael and Gabriel. Above, Christ enthroned in heaven; in the border, apostles and evangelists (named in Greek) amid fruit and flowers.

translates an Egyptian one). A strategos occupied a career-post. He might serve in any nome, except the one in which he resided (this presumably to avoid insider deals and local enmities). Tenure varied (at one stage limited to three years), but normally he had no time to identify too deeply with one area before he moved on to another. When official papers from another nome turn up in the rubbish of Oxyrhynchos, we may guess that a serving strategos brought them home from office elsewhere: so Heras also called Dionysios had done duty in the Saite nome, Ammonios in the Arabian (on the canal leading from the Nile to the Gulf of Suez), Aurelios Kalpournios Isidoros also called Harpokration in two different nomes of the heartland, Arsinoite and Memphite.[5] No doubt such officials retained some official papers for security, in case of retrospective enquiry, or as scrap paper (some such rolls have their blank backs reused to copy literary texts – an economical way of adding to one's library).[6]

The strategos, like other major officials, kept an official diary, which recorded his activities day by day and summarised his decisions.[7] He was a public figure. He walked round the marketplace before going to his office. There he might preside over the opening and reading of a Roman will.[8] He took the lead in public ceremonies, in the theatre or at the temple of the imperial cult, with sacrifices and acclamations to the emperors. The god Ammon invited him, as guest of honour, to the rose-festival in the village of Seryphis.[9] He was in charge of public funds: it was he who ordered state bankers to disburse moneys owed (the Royal Scribe countersigned).[10] He was responsible for tax-collection and its complications: it was he who corresponded with other strategoi when a person who lived in one nome owed tax on property in another.[11]

The strategos was also law and order. When a house burned down, or a water-wheel was found damaged by fire, he was notified in case of future proceedings. An accidental death was reported to him, so that his assistant could check the body.[12] He investigated on the spot the disappearance of some shepherds and the wounding or death of one of them.[13] His diary would include details of more complex cases, and litigants could obtain extracts with this information. In one famous case Tiberius Claudius Pasion, strategos of the Oxyrhynchite, was called on to act as Solomon: Pesouris had picked up a foundling boy from the rubbish dump, and entrusted him to a wet-nurse named Saraeus, who had a son of her own. One baby died, and the survivor was claimed by Pesouris as his foundling and by Saraeus as her natural child. Pasion judged that the baby looked like Saraeus, and awarded him to her.[14]

Petitioners (and he might receive petitions direct, or by reference back from the Prefect or epistrategos) might call on him to get their opponent to court; and no doubt it was his office that sent out the formal summons which survive in large numbers. Thus: 'To the head watchman of Mermertha. Send Eros the wine-merchant at the petition of Dioskoros. XXXXX [seal attached].'[15]

Such chits, which brought in defendants from the outlying villages, had their own economy. They did not normally state the authority which issued them, or the place to which those summoned should be sent, or whether an escort was required; this presumably because only the strategos was competent (and practice changed after the mid-third century, when other officials acquired the right to issue warrants). They very rarely carried a date, even the day of the month. Apart from the names, that is, they were an open cheque; and it has been guessed that the row of Xs that filled up the last line served to prevent unauthorised additions. It would not be difficult to forge such an order (only a few carried a seal); presumably the messengers who delivered them (only a few carried an address) served to authenticate them. Plaintiffs (almost entirely male) included officials as well as private persons, though the actual charge was not normally specified. The office may have saved time by producing these chits in bulk; sometime two appear side by side on the same sheet, and perhaps many were written seriatim and then cut up for dispatch. It may also have saved stationery by reusing left-overs: many summonses are written across the fibres on longish strips of papyrus – the blank bits, perhaps, at the end of longer rolls, cut off and kept for scrap.[16]

The strategos' proceedings, and especially his financial admin-istration, fell subject to review at the centre. Each nome had its auditor in Alexandria, who reported to the Prefect. The Prefect himself might go through the books and question arrears.[17] At the end of his term, each strategos had to hand over his records, the 'leaving papers', to his successor; there was a fine for late submission.[18] Responsibility con-tinued after death: we find Hierakiaina, the daughter of Hierax, formerly strategos of the Small Diopolite nome in the distant Thebaid, required to confirm that her father had handed in the papers of his office; for-tunately his successor had acknowledged receipt in writing.[19]

Records

A prime concern of the government was to exploit Egypt's resources, human and material; and to this end it documented those resources in detail. In addition to active surveys, it required or received up-to-date information from the population, in writing: census-returns, and declarations of birth and death; claims to privileged status; reports of livestock and baggage-animals; acquisitions of land and houses; declarations of uninundated land; lists of priests and property from the temples. The citizen and his money, the farmer and his fields, the rich and powerful clergy, had the state's eye upon them.

The human resource was the citizen, especially the male citizen, with all his potential as worker and as taxpayer. His very existence can be documented at birth, and at death, and in between at age fourteen, the age of majority and the first payment of poll-tax. Such submissions were not necessarily compulsory, but they allowed the state to update its records, and the citizen to claim his rights, if rights he had – the inherited right to pay a reduced rate of tax, the right which death conveyed to pay tax no more.

The grandest cog in the machine was the census. Other Roman provinces experienced a census from time to time: thus in AD 6, in Judaea, 'there went out a decree from Caesar Augustus, that all the world should be taxed', and Mary and Joseph returned to their official residence at Bethlehem to register.[20] Egypt, exceptionally, maintained a regular cycle: every fourteen years, from perhaps AD 19/20 until 257/8, the Prefect gave orders for the whole population to register itself, household by household. Each return lists those resident, men first, then women:

Official copy.

From Ploution son of Ploution and grandson of Ploution, mother Tapsois, from the City of the Oxyrhynchoi.

'In accordance with the orders given by Maecius Laetus the most illustrious Prefect, I register for the house-by-house census of the past tenth year of our lords Caesars Severus and Antoninus and Geta Caesar [AD 201/2] the quarter share of a house and its porch and fitments which belong to me in the quarter of the North Quay, at which I register –

Me myself Ploution, no trade, no distinguishing marks, aged 48

Dioskoros my slave, no trade, no distinguishing marks, aged [?]8
Women:

Tapsois also called Eudaimonis my daughter living with her husband Apollonios, no trade, no distinguishing marks, aged about 20

Gaiane her full sister, no trade, no distinguishing marks, aged about 15

Aphrodite nicknamed Isidora, bought slave of my daughter Tapsois also called Eudaimonis, by birth from the Oasis, keeping company with her mistress, no trade, no distinguishing marks, aged about 13

Taeros slave belonging to me and my brothers and others, no trade, no distinguishing marks, aged about 35

Taepimachos, another slave belonging to me and my brothers and others, child of the slave Taeros, no trade, no distinguishing marks, aged about 9.

And I swear by the Genius of the Emperors Lucius Septimius Severus Pius Pertinax and Marcus Aurelius Antoninus Pius [*that the information above is the whole truth*].[21]

Archives and Offices

The system rested on a paper mountain. The total documentation must have been enormous. The Prefect Subatianus Aquila, on a tour of Middle Egypt, held court in the convenient location of Arsinoe, the capital of the populous Arsinoite nome (nowadays the Fayûm). There he received 1806 petitions in two and a half days.[22] On other occasions, when the Prefect's office posted answered petitions (the answer written in below the text, to be read by the petitioner), the sequence might run to 500 or more.[23] In the year of a census, the strategoi of the nomes faced the processing of more than a million returns.[24] In a single period of two months the strategos of Oxyrhynchos received at least six letters from other nomes, asking whether anything was known of the whereabouts of missing persons and property. To each one the strategos replied, 'We have absolutely no knowledge,' and it is clear that a detailed search would simply not have been practicable.[25]

In all this, secretaries and filing-clerks (all male, of course) played a major role. They did not leave statues or wall-reliefs, like pharaonic scribes. They functioned behind the scenes, ready to write, copy, or proof-read, equipped with reed-pens, pen-knives, sponges (for deletion), black ink and red ink (red for corrections).[26] Without them the offices and archives would have ceased to function.

All must have been fluent writers; some came close to being calligraphers. By the third century AD we find examples of 'chancery script', a style of handwriting distinguished by its assertive elaboration and rhythmic mannerism: the ensemble is upright and elongated; small letters (α and ο) float high in the line, contrasting with others, like ι, which rise high above and sink far below; everywhere loops and flourishes demonstrate the scribe's mastery of his pen.[27] Some striking examples appear in letters from the Prefect, and it is usually guessed that the style developed in the central secretariat (some have seen the influence of Latin script, which would have been familiar to Roman officials) – a grandiose script to distinguish the communications of the grandees in Alexandria. If so, it did not remain a monopoly. Local officials could have it imitated in their own documents. We find a strategos replying to a letter from the Prefect in a script which the Prefect's own office might have used (though his secretary was careless enough to omit part of the imperial titles).[28] Local individuals could imitate it, themselves or their secretaries, in private contracts and letters.

Incoming documents might be filed, that is pasted one after another to form a roll, each item numbered in the top margin: the file-reference would be in the form 'roll 10 sheet 19'.[29] These files, called 'stuck-together rolls', especially suited long runs of standard forms – census returns, reports of unwatered land and the like; a single roll could run to 400 items and more, and a length of at least 23 feet.[30] Such files were not too unwieldy when tightly rolled – a 30-foot roll would have a diameter of about 3 inches, the cross-section (as W. A. Johnson comments) of a wine-bottle,[31] but it will have required a brisk wrist to check item 300, and any repeated process of scrolling through put a strain on the pasted joins. Nor was the initial pasting quite straightforward. Since there was no standard size of sheet, individual documents might be of different heights. Normally the clerk stuck them up with their lower edges aligned, leaving the top on occasion to wander up and down. That may suggest that these files were stored upright in bins, lower edge flat down, rather than heaped horizontally on shelves. The more tidy-minded trimmed off any projections at the top, even though this might take away bits of writing as well.[32] For extra elegance, the whole file could then be recopied onto a new roll: so for example incoming letters to the strategos Phokion, in AD 161, were glued together within a month of arrival and then copied with a note of their original file-numbers.[33] Private individuals would not normally need to handle so much paper, but they could still stick together a small selection; or there was always the paper-clip, or rather the equivalent now called a 'treasury tag', a piece of papyrus string tied through a hole in the top left corner.[34]

The files needed to be housed, and a series of archives provided for this. At the centre, in Alexandria, the Chief Justice (*archidikastês*) presided over an office which could register private transactions and give them public status, documents deposited in the Nanaion and the Archive of Hadrian. Closer to the citizen were the archives of nome-capitals like Oxyrhynchos: originally a single Public Record Office, then subdivided into a Public Archive, for official documents, census returns and the like, and a Property Archive, which held documentation for sales and purchases of houses and land. It was the business of the second archive to maintain a summary running record of each individual's holdings (*diastrôma*): one sheet to each name, the sheets filed (or pasted into a roll) in alphabetical order, one packet or roll for each location.[35] Thus the state knew who owned what (and was responsible for the taxes on it); and the citizen could check whether the seller of a property was in fact its legal owner.

Breakdown and Reform

The machine was designed to run the country, and run it at a profit. There were, however, factors which might undermine it.

One was incompetence. Officials needed basic skills; yet some of them were amateurs, and even professionals might be underqualified. At higher levels, official business often presupposed technical sophistication and experience, as emerges from surviving manuals: the regulations of the Office of the Idios Logos (115 paragraphs), the technical vocabulary of land-surveying, required serious study.[36] Nor was knowledge enough in itself; the machine needed continuous systematic maintenance. Thus archives had to be kept up to date, yet one in

Oxyrhynchos fell so far behind that the Prefect himself had to order reform. His detailed statement illustrates how much depended on the property registers, and how defective they were, despite the intervention of a whole series of prefects:

> Marcus Mettius Rufus, Prefect of Egypt, says: Klaudios Areios the strategos of the Oxyrhynchite nome has informed me that neither private nor public business is being transacted properly because of the fact that for many years the summary records (*diastrômata*) in the Property Archive have not been kept in the way required, although it has often been decided by the prefects before me that they should receive the necessary upgrading – which is not really possible, unless copies were made from the beginning. Therefore I order all the property-owners, within six months, to register their own property with the Property Archive, and lenders whatever mortgages they have, and the others whatever claims they have. In making this registration, they must state from where the possession of each property has come down to them. Wives also must add a note to the substance of their husbands, if under some local law they have a lien on the property, and similarly children to the substance of their parents, in cases where the usufruct has been secured to the parents by public transactions but the ownership reserved to the children after their death, so that those who make contracts with them may not be trapped through ignorance. And I instruct also writers of contracts and notaries not to complete anything without written authorisation from the Archive, in the knowledge that such proceedings are useless and they themselves will suffer the appropriate penalty as contravening these orders . . .[37]

In everyday record-keeping, mistakes were easily made, to the confusion of the state and the distress of the citizen, who complained that administrative 'wandering' had left him off a list or miswritten his mother's name or confused Belles, son of Dionysios (rich, ripe for liturgy), with Belles, son of Patermouthis (poor and unsuitable), from the same village.[38] At the lowest level, we find (not at Oxyrhynchos) a village scribe who could write only with difficulty. A surviving sheet shows him practising his formal signature – 'I Petaus have submitted this document' – a dozen attempts, and the last as wobbly as the first.[39]

To this the system of compulsory state service ('liturgies') must have contributed. Liturgists served short terms (most often one year), often unwillingly, motivated mainly by the threat of financial penalties. Besides the offices imposed by the central government, there were village liturgies and city liturgies. Besides the liturgists themselves, there were nominators who proposed the names, and guarantors who must under-write the liturgists' performance and financial liability.[40] No wonder that potential liturgists mobilised all possible excuses, and even vol-unteered to surrender their property rather than undertake the burden. The heaviest weight fell on the elite of the nome-capitals, those who (once town councils were set up c. AD 200) provided the town-coun-cillors.[41] Their government might seek to make them tax-collectors, record-keepers, state bankers, supervisors of the granaries and much else; their city was at the same time seeking incumbents for its honorific offices, Clerk of the Market, Town Clerk, High Priest, gymnasiarch and the rest. The minutes of the town council illustrate the pressures: 'Ptolemaios son of Damarion, Chief Priest, said "I entreat you, I cannot serve. I am a man of moderate means, I live in my father's house ..." The Mayor replied, "Ptolemaios still requires to be pressed by you [councillors], for he too shrinks from so great an office ..." The coun-cillors responded, "Upright, faithful Ptolemaios!"'[42]

Records could also suffer physical damage. Fire was one hazard. Only one archive building has been recovered by excavation, at Thmouis in the Nile Delta; the building burned down, and among the ruins were found charred rolls of papyrus (paradoxically, preserved despite the damp conditions precisely because of their charred condition). Since the rolls were heaped in the middle of the floor, the excavators thought of a deliberate burning, perhaps indeed by the brigands called Boukoloi who mounted a rebellion in AD 172.[43]

The long-drawn-out case of the Arsinoite archives reveals other hazards. The authorities first took note when the Prefect Mettius Rufus (again) noticed, during the assizes, that a document from that nome lacked its beginning. Successive enquiries revealed rolls wholly or partly destroyed by age; rolls eaten away at the top 'because the location is hot'; rolls without beginnings and rolls consumed by worms. It was explained that the archive building often collapsed because of its age, and that, during the renovation of the theatre, the archives often had to be moved 'from place to unsuitable place, lying one on top of another in disorder because of their number, given that the nome is very large, with consultation taking place daily and this sort of material being easily destroyed'.[44] The government planned efficient solutions: missing documents to be replaced from Alexandrian archives; existing damaged rolls to be pasted together; a new archive-house to be constructed in place of the ruinous building – all at the cost of those archive-keepers guilty of negligence. On the other side, the archive-keepers and their successors and their clerk, and later the heirs of all these parties, fought doggedly, among themselves and against the authorities, to deny responsibility and avoid the financial penalties. The case dragged on for at least thirty-five years, and required the intervention of at least seven prefects.[45]

Third-century Crisis

Accidents apart, the machine itself has an inbuilt weakness: it needs a push to function, and its natural tendency is to run down. Egyptian history over a long period shows cycles of renewal and decline: central authority weakens, the tax-yield declines, hard-pressed peasants desert their land, the yield declines further; now the government must grant an amnesty, or promise reform, or try to reorganise. So it was again in the second half of the third century, a period of civil war, foreign invasion and short-lived emperors. The last census of the old system was held in AD 257. Its lapsing signified the weakness of government, just as its revival under Diocletian would signal his determination to reinvigorate the imperial structure.

We get an insight into problems and policies from the general overhaul of the system which seems to centre round the short reign of the Emperor Philip the Arabian, who replaced the 19-year-old Gordian III (died of his wounds, or of his own soldiers, after defeat by the Persians) in 244 and lasted until 249, when he was killed and succeeded by the rebellious Decius. It fell to Philip to celebrate the millennium, the thousandth anniversary of the foundation of Rome: an expensive business, no doubt, as were the failed war on the Persian frontier and renewed fighting on the Danube. According to the dyspeptic historian Zosimos, the burden of taxation in the eastern provinces, and the harsh rule of the Emperor's brother Priscus, provoked a revolt in Syria.[46]

The reforms in Egypt may have had as their prime object an increase of revenue, though coloured in part by the characteristic claim to be redressing grievances. Somehow in charge were a pair of high-ranking Romans, an extraordinary dual authority, running in parallel with the normal machinery. Their proclamation, sent to all nomes and originally signed in Latin, set the tone: 'On the authority of Claudius Marcellus the most perfect *rationalis* and of Marcius Salutaris the most excellent *procurator* of the Emperors. The divine providence of our lords the Emperors has lightened the burden of all their Egyptians, worn down as they are by the limitless liturgies. Attached below is a list of which liturgies it has fixed to be abolished and which to remain and how we have determined, from which it will be clear to all that those who before were providing such services to no purpose and as it were only in show, but in reality given over to extortion, are now at least restored without impediment to their own farming. Display! Latin. Oxyrhynchite.'

The schedule which follows deals with only three offices before the papyrus breaks off. The first two are cogs of central importance to the machine, offices normally held by town councillors, the local aristocracy. Recently they had supplied five state bankers, and five keepers of the public records; traditionally both colleges had two members, but clearly the state had been seeking extra financial guarantees by spreading the responsibility. The reform reduced the number to two again, but spread the burden in a different way – one of the record-keepers, and one of the keepers of the property register, would henceforth be ordinary citizens. The possible prestige, and the undoubted burden, has moved beyond the charmed circle. At the same time, the machinery of appointment changed: out went the old *amphodogrammateus* ('secretary of the quarter'), in came the new *phylarchos* ('leader of the tribe') – himself not a town councillor (and therefore perhaps keener to keep councillors up to the mark).[47]

The same authority organised a general survey of land and its cultivation, which was published, and invited those whose holdings were falsely reported to inform them. Even in the Great Oasis, out in the Libyan Desert, officials submitted to them a list of the artesian wells on which local agriculture depended. They also organised the sale of superfluous state land, with the clear intention of bringing it back into cultivation. At about the same time, and perhaps under the same plan, there were changes at the base of the pyramid. In the village administration, the 'village secretary' gave way to a pair of 'village rulers' (comarchs). In the all-important administration of the granaries, *sitologoi* ('corn-collectors') disappeared, and *dekaprôtoi* ('ten chiefs') replaced them.[48]

Even in the day-to-day business of summonses a change is apparent. From *c*.250 AD onwards, the title of the issuing authority was specified (no longer a silence implying the strategos – his power, it seems, was being dispersed); the head watchman gives way to the comarchs; instead of 'send' there was the more peremptory 'send up forthwith'; often the chit ended with the formal endorsement 'I signed'. All designed, one might guess, to be more explicit, and more effective, and closer to the formulae used in other nomes.[49]

This looks like a unified programme: land, tax, liturgies presented a unified problem, for without full cultivation and efficient administration the land would not satisfy local needs and imperial requirements. Local sentiment certainly felt that things had gone downhill since the Emperor Septimius Severus; and there are signs that corn was in short supply – in March 246 the government required Oxyrhynchites to register all private stocks within twenty-four hours, 'so that the city can have its supplies and also the public necessities can be fulfilled'; in October 248 the Mayor is referring to prevailing 'straitened circumstances'.[50] It may be that a financial crisis of the imperial government coincided with (and aggravated) a crisis of agriculture in Egypt. The 'reforms', however, may have shifted the burden rather than reducing it. Certainly the citizens of Arsinoe did their own best to spread the net for liturgists by including villagers. That had been forbidden by Severus, but now (claimed their lawyer) things were different – 'since Severus we have had this new programme, which the Divine Genius of the Emperor Decius will rectify'.[51] Philip the Arabian had recently succumbed to Decius at the battle of Verona; all ills could be ascribed to the defeated regime, and it fell to the victor to reform the reforms.

But the crisis would not go away. The Oxyrhynchites would witness more piecemeal changes in the system, and more special authorities created to deal with dangers civil and military. When at last, in AD 284, the Emperor Diocletian took a firm hold on the Empire, another programme of change began. Egypt (soon to be divided into smaller provinces) joined the world: its special currency and more gradually its special dating-system gave way to the Roman norm. Latin became the language of the higher administration, and Virgil joined Homer among the set-books – linguistic unity, it seems, was to cement a fragmenting Empire. At the same time, the familiar cogs were replaced in the familiar machine: dekaprotoi turned back into sitologoi in the grain-collection, the phylarch turned into the *systatês* in the liturgical nominations, the *rationalis* reappeared, land-registers were revised and derelict land disposed of. The same problems elicited a similar profession of benevolence. 'Our most provident Emperors,' writes the Prefect Aristius Optatus (16 March 297),

> ... having learned that it has come about that the levies of the public taxes are being made in chance fashion, so that some persons get off lightly while others are overburdened, have deigned in the interest of their provincials to root out this most evil and ruinous practice and to give a salutary decision with which the taxes must conform ... Accordingly, since in this too they have experienced the greatest beneficence, let the provincials take care to make their tax-payments with all speed in accordance with the divine decision and absolutely not wait for the tax-collector to exercise compulsion. For it is fitting that each person discharge with the utmost enthusiasm everything that is due to their loyalty, and if anyone should be seen doing otherwise after such concessions he will risk punishment ... The collectors of every kind of tax are also reminded to be on their guard, with all their strength, for if anyone should be seen transgressing, he will risk his head.[52]

In a world dominated by the military, such an appeal to the civilian population (or rather, to the civilian elite that could read Greek) may seem a surprising tribute to tradition. Yet the rhetoric has become more transparent. From the governed, imperial benevolence required the quid pro quo of prompt payment. For the administrators, the punishment for underperforming was no longer financial but capital. 'Risk his head' looked forward to a more brutal age: only fear would keep the machine running.

CHAPTER 11

SURVIVING

• • • •

Egyptians certainly needed no reminder how much of their existence lay beyond human control. Agriculture, and therefore food-supply, depended on a single undependable fact, the height of the Nile's annual flood. The Nile is a god, and his caprice is final. More generally, they faced the enduring problems of being provident in an uncertain world – how to find food, earn a living, buy a house, beat inflation, invest without risk, travel without accident, survive the neighbours. But antiquity has no agony aunts, and no investment advisers. For problem-solving one might have to look to higher powers.

Even small matters might need divine decision. Nike, for example, faced a financial question: should she buy from Tasarapion her slave Sarapion alias Gaion?[1] She turned therefore to the city's grandest deity, Zeus-Helios-Sarapis, who combined in one image of bearded bene-volence the Hellenic antecedents of Zeus, the glory of the Sun (Ra of the Egyptians) and the adaptation of Osiris that the early Greek kings of Egypt had contrived as a symbol of unity. His great temple on the central square, and the various smaller shrines,[2] received petitioners – and no doubt their offerings. You handed in two slips of papyrus, with two versions of the same question, one positive ('Should I . . .?'), one negative ('Should I not . . .?'), and asked the god to 'give back' or 'bring out' the right one.[3] The god chose, perhaps by nodding to left or to right, and the priest handed back the chosen slip. The god's expertise, and that of the 'co-resident' gods who shared his shrine, extended to every aspect of life. 'Do I get the chance to marry?', asked Menander.[4] 'Arsinoe asks you whether I am going to marry Dorion on 11th.'[5] But marriage also had problems: 'Is it better for my son Phanias and his wife not now to come to an agreement with her father, but to oppose him and not to put anything in writing?'[6] Health too: Neilammon asked, 'Do you permit me to use Herminos, the doctor of Hermopolis, to treat my eyes, and is this to my advantage?'[7] The writing may be quite literate, sometimes perhaps that of a temple scribe who writes to dictation. Coarse script and vulgar spelling may point to the petitioner himself: so in the slip which says simply 'If he's coming to me in the month Tybi, you will give me this' – the work of a man so preoccupied with his worries that he forgets to give his own name, and the god's, and that of the important visitor.[8]

Others preferred Thonis, the Egyptian falcon-god, after whom many Oxyrhynchites were named (one citizen carried his image on his signet-ring).[9] Businessmen too need to consult him. A trader asked: 'If you do not want me to trust myself to Diogenes ... in Alexandria because of my contract which is still in the air and I'm afraid for the cargo, give me this.'[10] A group of financiers asked (the god is not named): 'Lord, if it is advantageous for us to approach the Prefect with a higher tender for the $2\frac{1}{2}$ per cent tax and it will be knocked down to us, bring us this chit.'[11] Time passed, and in Christian Egypt the gods gave way to God, but the system continued on the same lines. 'God of our protector St Philoxenos, if you command that we should bring Anoup into your hospital, show your power and let this slip come out.'[12]

The god could advise; it was a question of reaching him. Normally he lived in his sanctuary, where like an earthly ruler he would consider written requests. At festivals he might emerge, the cult-statue carried in procession through the town, and signal his decisions by the motions of his image or its carriage. These practices were common enough to be prohibited by the government. In AD 198/9, a high official, probably (to judge from the peremptory tone) the Prefect himself, issued a circular to local administrators, with the professed purpose of saving fools from those who exploit their foolishness:

Having come across many who think themselves deceived by kinds of divination, I have thought it necessary, with the idea of no risk attaching to their foolishness, to issue a clear prohibition, here and now, to everyone, that they should keep themselves from such dangerous meddling. Therefore, neither by way of oracles, that is by written documents given as if in the divine presence, nor by way of images carried in procession or other such charlatanry, let any one claim to know things beyond the human and put on offer the obscurity of the future, nor let him make himself available to those who enquire about this or give them answers of any kind. If anyone is caught adhering to this claim, let him be convinced that he will be handed over to the supreme penalty.

Each one of you must take measures to display a copy of this letter publicly, on a white board, in clear and legible letters, in the nome-capitals and village by village; and in general he must exert himself, and if he finds someone acting contrary to this prohibition, he must send him in bonds for my decision. Note that you too will not escape the danger, if I should learn of some such persons being again over-looked in the districts under you, indeed you will be liable to the same punishment as those who are being protected, given that each of them, even if he dares to contravene this prohibition, is just one, whereas the man who does not take all measures to restrain them is himself guilty of the danger that they represent to many.

Year 7 of the Emperors Caesars Lucius Septimius Severus Pius Pertinax Arabicus Adiabenicus Parthicus Maximus and Marcus Aurelius Antoninus Augusti . . .[13]

The politically knowing may have found this ukase surprising. The viceroy of the day, Aemilius Saturninus, had been appointed by the Emperor Septimius Severus, who with his family was about to visit Egypt. He was to remain in favour, recalled to Rome and promoted to Prefect of the Imperial Guard, until his co-commander had him murdered. Yet the Emperor Severus himself was notoriously expert in magic and divination. Indeed, he was said in his younger days to have chosen his wife for her horoscope, and to have stood trial for treason after consulting prophets or astrologers about the future of the Emperor Commodus (he was acquitted, a sign of Commodus' growing unpopularity).[14] Perhaps the regime distinguished between vulgar superstition, with which impostors misled its poor subjects, and the science of astrology, in which the ruler placed his faith. The poor subjects, naturally, continued with their superstition.

Doctors and Diseases

Some of these oracle-questions related to health: not directly to cures, but to the choice of a doctor, a difficult and potentially dangerous matter.

Doctors had their detractors. The archetype of Roman conservatism, Cato the Censor, had regarded medicine as a Greek conspiracy to murder foreigners, and even in the first century AD the encyclopedically know-ledgeable Pliny quoted as a common epitaph, 'He died of a crowd of doctors.'[15] But the imperial government generally took a more benevo-lent view, and at least from the second century AD a series of enactments assured the medical profession a privileged status. Cities might employ a fixed number of doctors and teachers, who would enjoy tax-exemption and freedom from various legal and municipal duties.[16] Oxyrhynchos duly appointed 'public physicians', whose duty it was to visit the victims of accident and assault and report their condition to the author-ities.[17] One doctor kept a surgery in the Western Stoa, at the point where, in AD 316, some of the old columns needed new bases.[18] A 'surgery' might be part of the doctor's house. In a letter marked 'Deliver to the surgery', Eudaimon wrote to his mother and grandmothers:

> Heraklammon really upset us when he came, as he said, 'Our sister Kyra has fallen ill,' but we give thanks to the divine providence that helps us everywhere and in everything that she too has recovered. Let her know that the linens of our sister Kyrilla have been cut [down from the loom] and if I find a friend coming your way I'll send them and the purple hooded cape and the shoes. We have received from Helen the embroideress the goods and I found only 4 books in the saddle-bag, whereas you wrote, 'We have sent you 5.' We have received all the other things too, except only the pot of grease. So our brother Theodoros should hurry up and check . . . he provided a pot of ointments instead of the grease. Hurry up also to send me the bronze tablet, so that I can make other instruments, not the same ones, and the heater similarly and the cups . . . [PS] Send also three pounds of ointments . . .[19]

Eudaimon, it seems, was a doctor practising away from home; he needed his (medical) books, and his basic kit. 'Grease' (generally pork fat) was used on axles, and by Roman soldiers for cooking, but it served also as the medium of many ointments. The 'heater' was a metal container for hot water, to be applied to poultices or painful aches. The 'cups' served (as they would do until the nineteenth century) to bleed the patient: the heated vessel is applied to the relevant part and the vacuum draws out the blood. This Oxyrhynchite doctor was on his travels; in reverse Oxyrhynchite patients sought out doctors in other cities – eye-specialists in Hermopolis, close by, but also as far away as Alexandria, where the Harley Street of Egypt could be found.[20]

Doctors might train locally, or in the medical schools of a grander city. Certainly the rubbish-tips of Oxyrhynchos contain every kind of medical book, from technical treatises to basic prescriptions.[21] Medics or medical students were reading works of (or attributed to) Hippocrates, the father of medicine.[22] Some began their medical education from a low enough level, witness the Hippocratic Oath copied laboriously (with misspellings) on the back of an old document,[23] and the portentous *Introduction to Medicine for Young Doctors*, this copied clumsily on the back of an old Homer (it began with definitions of parts of the body, which continued on the front, so that the student of Homer could turn the roll upside down and continue with 'The head consists of the face, the temples and the crown. . .').[24]

The minimalist doctor could espouse the Method, a holistic school which traced all diseases to two conditions (over-loose, over-taut) of the whole body, and treated them with simple therapies of bracing and relaxing, of a kind that the student could master in six months at most. One such treatise discusses principles and prescribes for ear-ache.[25] The fully trained doctor would have mastered the catechism in pathology: how should one treat those with elephantiasis? What is the cause of apoplexy? How does apoplexy differ from similar ailments? How should one treat apoplectics? What is arthritis of the hip? What are its symptoms? What is the treatment?[26] Some specialist even read a detailed commentary on the classic *Poisonous Bites* of Nicander (a notoriously difficult poem, one thousand lines of toxicology in verse); another hand then scribbled medical recipes on the back.[27]

Materials for medicines were widely available. One pharmacist from Oxyrhynchos declared his stock of minerals: alum, blacking, ruddle, copper ore (450 loaves), ochre, salt.[28] The pharmacopoeia listed ingredients of all kinds, their properties, preparation and use – 'Samian Earth', white clay, fig-shoots, the bile of the sea-scorpion.[29] There were external remedies, such as soft plasters.[30] There were medicines for all occasions: 'To stop a nose-bleed: mix powdered frankincense with leek-juice and smear the juice inside. To cause sneezing: grind fresh white hellebore and blow it into the nostrils' – this same handbook prescribed for wounds, discharges, sores and polyps in the nose, but also for liver-problems, dropsy, even leprosy, and for the common quartan fever:

'Hemlock, 3 drachms; henbane, 3 dr.; opium, 2 dr.; castor, 1 dr.; black hellebore, 1 dr. Pound until smooth, mould each separately with water, and make pastilles the size of an Egyptian bean, then dry them in the shade and give them to the patient to drink fasting, having crushed them in half a cup of sweet wine, having washed the patient two hours before taking the medicine and put a hot-water bottle at his feet. Cover him with blankets.'[31] Even literary circles catch cold: in one sheet of notes, the first hand copied out an erotic epigram, another listed more epigrams for a potential anthology, round and about the contribution of yet another, coarser writer, a recipe for cough-mixture: 'Saffron, 3 obols. Tragacanth, 1 drachm. Pine-cones, 1 drachm. One egg. Honey, 3 obols.'[32]

It would of course be better to avoid infection altogether, and for that you needed magic or prayer. Pagans (and indeed Christians, despite the fulminations of their priests) wore amulets. 'The amulet against tonsillitis, which is to be inscribed on the gold plate, send it to Sarmates, writing it on a tablet word for word': Sarmates had the plate, but he needed the magic formula.[33] Christians could appeal to divine mercy. So a later writer (hamfisted and a poor speller) duly copied out recipes for a purge, and then for strangury and for wounds; but in between, introduced by the Christ-monogram: '☧ Certain men met us in the desert and said to the Lord, "Jesus, what cure is there for the sick?" And he says to them, "I have given oil and poured our myrrh for them that believe in the name of the Father and the Holy Ghost and the Son".' '☧ The angels of the Lord went up to mid-heaven, suffering in their eyes and holding a sponge. The Lord says to them, "Why did you come, you that are holy and all-pure?" [They reply:] "We came up to receive healing, Jehovah Sabaoth, for you are powerful and strong."'[34] Here medicine is reinforced by mysticism. In the story, the Lord healed the angels; so in life the Lord might be reminded to heal the human sufferer.

Illness was a fact of life: all the more so in a society in which the average life expectancy at birth could be estimated at 22–25 years.[35] Parents sickened, and children did the necessary business. So Apia's father, who owned his own apartment (bedroom, dining room, balcony) in her house, 'fell ill and is in an unstable condition'; since she did not wish to inherit (presumably his liabilities exceeded his assets), she notified the authorities in advance.[36] 'When my aforementioned mother Techosis was struck down by illness, I did my modest best to nurse her and look after her and never stopped fulfilling the duties proper from children to parents. And so when a few days ago she passed away intestate with me her daughter as her legal heir, I again provided for her funeral and carried out what was proper on her death ...'[37] Small children were especially at risk: 'Isidora to Hermias. Do everything you can, put off everything, come tomorrow. The child is sick, it's become thin, it doesn't eat, it's six days. I'm afraid it may die while you're not here. I tell you, if it dies when you aren't here, keep away, you'll find me hanging.'[38]

Illnesses might be ill defined but none the less disabling. Tryphon the weaver was released from military service, 'suffering from cataracts and poor sight'.[39] Two elders of the village of Nemerai fell ill, and substitutes had to be nominated.[40] The Mayor sought to resign: 'The Mayor said: "I have an illness, and cough from my lungs." The councillors said: "Noble Mayor, do not stop working on our behalf, work in a way worthy of times past!"'[41] Some illnesses disabled completely. An unknown sufferer wrote: 'For the moment I haven't been able to write to anyone because I'm picking up from illness and a great shivering-fit and I could hardly write even this, being in agony.'[42] An unknown Christian wrote: 'I pray to our good Saviour and his beloved Son that they may all help our body, our soul, our spirit. This I write to you being ill, in a terrible state, really unable to get up from my bed, because I am in a really terrible state ...'[43]

In a hot, dusty climate eyes could be especially troublesome: hence the oracle question quoted above.[44] Titianos suffered as a complication of other illnesses:

Titianos to his lady sister, greetings. Since I found someone who was coming up in your direction I was encouraged to write to you what has happened to me. I was gripped for a long while by illness so that I couldn't even stagger. When my illness eased, my eye suppurated and I had trachomas and I suffered terribly and in other parts of my body as well so that it nearly came to surgery, but thank God! My father is still ill, for whose sake I stayed there though I was ill myself, and for his sake I am still here ... Everybody at home fell ill, my mother and all the slaves, so that we don't even have any help, but for everything we pray to God unceasingly ...[45]

Periodically, there would be an epidemic or a pandemic. 'Plague', like 'famine', makes a regular appearance among the eschatological horrors of prophetic and magical books.[46] Some plagues, like the one which came and went Empire-wide for over twenty years from AD 165, made their mark on history. If a plague lasted, it could cause extensive depopulation and (if that depressed agriculture) a general rise in prices.[47] Great cities attracted it: it was believed that around AD 250 half the population of Alexandria died of plague. Local outbreaks could wipe out smaller communities. 'They died of the condition', noted an anxious correspondent. 'If any of those with us in the village falls ill, they do not get up again.'[48] 'There are greater evils ... they are ill with the ailment, so that Sarmates, the one of the school, fell ill and died in seven days from the ailment.'[49] News of them spread rapidly. Pausanias, who had been in Alexandria arranging the transfer of his son or grandson from an infantry legion to a cavalry squadron, wrote to his brother at Oxyrhynchos: 'The gods willing, I shall try to get to you for the festival of the Amesysia. Take pains, Brother, about the mortgage document, so as to get it set up according to custom. Please, Brother, write to me about your health, because I heard at Antinoopolis that with you there has been a plague ...'[50]

Families and individuals succumbed, with strange symptoms. Ptoleminos wrote to Sinthonis 'his sister' (the term of endearment which may mean 'sister' or 'wife'): 'Above everything we pray to God that we may find you well. I want you to know that Achilleus is very ill and has been treated so many times for his feet and right up to now is ill and perhaps a bit more than before, and for this reason I couldn't talk to him. I too became very sick, even to the point of death, but thanks be to God I'm all right.'[51] Sometimes the diagnosis was uncertain but the upshot decisive. A father and a mother died 'of some shivery illness', and Aurelios Pekysis alias Chaeremon became an orphan, for whom his aunt must arrange a guardian.[52]

Assault and Accident

Beyond natural causes, people suffered the usual quota of casual damage. When people described themselves, many had a scar to report. But more serious things could occur, in the street, on the road, in a vineyard, even at a festival.

Thermouthion wrote to Asklepiades the strategos:

There is a little maidservant of mine, a slave born in my house, whose name is Peina, that I loved and cared for like a little daughter, in the hope that when she grew up I should have her to support me in my old age, since I am a woman helpless and alone. As she was crossing the city on the 19th of last month for lessons in singing and other things, with a certain Eucharion, freedwoman of Longinos, escorting her, who at the hour of departure from my house brought in Peina with her right arm bound up, and when I enquired of her the reason, she reported to me that this girl had been knocked down by a certain slave, Polydeukes, who was accompanying a donkey, so that as a result of this her whole arm had been crushed and the most parts of it mutilated and the rest gaping open. And at that time, as I did not have anyone in charge of the strategos' office, I did <not> file a petition about this, thinking that the injury was a passing one, but since it is incurable and I cannot bear my maidservant's pain, because *she* is in danger of her life while *I* am possessed with despair for her life — the facts are clear and you too will be angry when you see them — well, of necessity, I have taken refuge with you as my protector and ask to be helped and to obtain your good will ...'[53]

Judas wrote to his father Joses and wife Maria (it was a Jewish family): 'Make every effort, my lady sister, send me your brother, since I have fallen into sickness as the result of my horse falling [of falling from my horse?]. For when I want to turn onto my other side, I cannot by myself, unless two other people turn me over, and even down to a cup of water I have no one to give me one. So help me, my lady sister... It's in this kind of crisis that a man's true friends are discovered. So please come yourself as well and help me, since I really am in a strange land and ill ... And if you have need of cash, get it from Isaac the cripple, who lives very near you.'[54]

Fatal accidents especially needed reporting: 'To Hierax, strategos, from Leonidas, alias Serenos, officially known as the son of his mother Tauris, from the village of Senepta. Late yesterday the sixth, while a festival was taking place at Senepta, and the castanet-players were performing according to custom at the house of my son-in-law Ploution ... his slave Epaphroditos, aged about 8 years, wishing to lean over from the roof-terrace of the said house and see the castanet-players, fell and was killed. I therefore submit this report and ask you, if you please, to detach one of your assistants to Senepta so that the body of

Epaphroditos can receive the proper laying-out and burial.'[55] 'To Theon, strategos, from Gaios Papirios Maximos. Yesterday the 26th the irrigator of my vineyard near the village of Chysis . . . in my absence, climbed up onto a palm-tree in the vineyard to pollinate it and fell and died, there being nobody there. And today, when I got to the vineyard, I found him stretched out by the palm tree and mutilated by dogs. So I submit the report, asking for the appropriate procedures to take place so that his body can receive burial.'[56]

Accident is one thing. Assault also played its part. Heras to Papontos: '. . . I found that Sabina had struck Syra and I enquired of Syra how she came to be struck and learned from them all that because the things which Syra had in her possession were not immediately released to Sabina she struck Syra with the balcony key which she was holding and Syra is confined to bed up to the present day. Sabina has made herself scarce since the tenth and I heard that she is in the Herakleopolite nome. Harpochras will tell you what he heard in the city about her doings.'[57]

In such incidents, the city's public physicians were sent to examine the victim. Their case-files make gruesome reading. Thus, on 22 February 316, one doctor went out to examine the security-guard Mouis at his hamlet. 'I saw him confined to bed with a cut on the front part of the head, with the bone laid bare, and with two wounds on the crown with the bone laid bare, and below these wounds . . . on the right part of the head and on the left temple . . . swelling, and a swelling with bruising on the [. . .] of the left ear, and a swelling with bruising on the right shoulder-blade and the shoulder, and a blow with swelling on the biggest finger of the right hand, and a swelling with bruising on the wrist of the right hand, and a wound on the left thigh . . . and a wound above the knee, and two wounds on the right thigh from end to end and a wound on the whole of the left side. So I make this report.' A month or so later, two other doctors went to visit Apollonios, an aide of the provincial governor. 'We went there and saw him confined to bed, suffering from unresolved feverish symptoms.' The aide clearly needed a sick-note; Mouis had been comprehensively beaten up.[58]

The same doctor, Heron, it seems, served for twenty or more years, and he and his colleagues witnessed a variety of cases. 'We saw him on a bunk in the public office with gashes on the right side of his head. . . and a swelling on the right side of his forehead and a contusion with a skin wound on his left forearm and a slight contusion on the right forearm.'[59] 'Sent by your Grace, as a result of documents handed in to you by Aurelios Dioskoros, son of Dorotheos, from the said city, so as to submit a written report on the condition of his daughter as he complained [?] resulting from the collapse of the house, so we went to his house and saw that the child has grazes down her hips with bruises and on the right knee a wound. So we report.'[60] 'I was sent by you today which is Pachôn 9 [4 May], as a result of documents handed in to you by Aur. Isidoros . . . to examine his condition and report to you in writing. So I examined the aforementioned Isidoros, who has a wound on his left buttock . . .'[61] A distinguished buttock, for Isidoros held the rank of a cavalry officer with the title 'excellency'.

These hazards apart, individual citizens suffered the usual degrees of depression. The liturgist Gerontios was downcast, because he had had no letters from his brother, and does not know 'how things stand at home or with us or in the city'.[62] The student Theon was downhearted about the incident in the theatre, and about the pretensions of his tutor, and all this leads him to neglect his health.[63] Authority acknowledged the condition; *taedium vitae* was a recognised cause of death in the Roman military. At Oxyrhynchos, Hierax took his own way out: 'To Isidoros, strategos, from Dionysos, son of Apollodoros, son of Dionysios, of the city of Oxyrhynchos, public physician. Today I was assigned by you through your assistant Herakleides the task of inspecting the dead hanged body of Hierax and to report to you whatever condition I find it in. So having inspected it in the presence of the said assistant, in the house of Epagathos . . . in the Plaza Quarter, I found it hanged by a noose. Therefore I report.'[64]

In a world of illnesses, accidents and casual violence, human aid might not be enough. People naturally turned for knowledge and succour to higher powers – the gods in their temples, the stars in the heaven, the dark forces beneath the earth.

Astrologers

'I sent the astrologer (the one with one eye) to call you, and he said he wasn't finding you. At the lighting of the lamps I arrived and when I heard from Serenilla what you have done to her I was pained that you acted in a way which isn't you. So receive her kindly up there this side of the festival. I would have been there already, but on the 25th, at the very rising of the Dog Star, I got bitten by a mad dog, and even now I'm in a terrible way. . .'[65] The rising of the Dog Star signals the rising of the Nile, and much else, and perhaps the 'festival' celebrated that. 'Bitten by a mad dog' may be a social excuse, but even excuses have to be plausible. The rabid writer knew, it seems, more than one astrologer.

Astrologers form an Empire-wide fraternity, not always welcome. The Emperor Augustus had legislated against consulting them (AD 11); again and again they were expelled from Rome – always forbidden and always retained, notes Tacitus acidly.[66] Philosophers, and later the Christian Church, campaigned against this presumptuous reading of the heavens. From the government's point of view, some aspects were potentially treasonable – notably, seeking occult knowledge of the current Emperor's lifespan.

However, astrologers continued to practise. They had the market on their side, as well as their claims to secret lore and technical expertise. The Greeks had named the planets and the signs of the zodiac (and we still use the Roman forms of those names), but fundamental parts of their astronomy had reached them from Mesopotamia – notably the zodiac itself. Astrology too, the use of astronomical data to predict human destinies, had its roots in the same area, as indeed Greeks and Romans acknowledged by using 'Chaldaean' and 'Babylonian' as synonyms of 'astrologer'. If you consulted such a practitioner, you enjoyed in one package the science of the West and the wisdom of the East.

Horoscopes represented the bread and butter of the trade, calculated for all pockets. The minimum form gave the position of the planets at the hour of birth. 'Nativity of Ptolemaios. Year 20 of Severus and Antoninus, Pachôn 22 [17 May AD 212], 3rd hour of the day. Ascendant, Jupiter in Cancer. Sun and Mercury in Taurus, Venus in Aries, Mars and Saturn in Leo, Moon in Sagittarius.'[67] This stands on a neat piece of new papyrus; many others use recycled. The positions given do not always work out astronomically. Of course, some astrologers might be less competent than others. One horoscope got copied twice – once in heavy capitals with several misspellings (taken down by the customer?), then in quick professional cursive, then a third writer has corrected three of the zodiacal positions.[68] Very rarely the professional went to town, and provided full details of the planetary position by degrees and minutes, terms and decan.[69] But for the most part, the client was content with the basic information. Only once does a comment follow: 'There are dangers. Be on your guard for 40 days, because of Mars.'[70] Normally, you would need another consultation to learn what your birth-signs had in store for you.

For information, and for its interpretation, the astrologer had his books, and the rubbish-dumps of Oxyrhynchos have preserved some samples. At one end of the range, there are astral omens on the grand scale: the stars reveal the destinies of kings and countries. 'If the Dog Star rises when Mars is in Gemini, some men will rebel in Egypt or in the country of the Syrians, and the King of Egypt will go with his army and destroy them.'[71] '. . . there will be disorder and war and it shall go badly with the rich, their arrogance will be destroyed and their goods will be confiscated and given to others . . . the beggars shall be exalted and the rich shall be humbled, there will be hunger and weakness and fever [?] in many places . . .'[72] On a lesser scale, one might try to predict the height of the Nile flood, the determinant of the year's economic success.[73]

Already, your zodiacal sign determines your character. Were you born under Aries? Expect to be brilliant, distinguished, commanding, just, a hater of wickedness, free, a leader, bold in thought, boastful, great-souled, unstable, capricious, haughty, absent-minded, full of threats, quick to change your mind. Gemini, by contrast, produces men who are learned, scribes, educationists, artists, lovers of the arts, administrators, takers-on of responsibilities. They are also interpreters, merchants, arbiters of good and evil, wise, inquisitive, initiates in mysteries.[74] If you wanted more precision, another manual divides the year into weeks of five days each; each week (six weeks to each sign) had its presiding Egyptian deity, who determined fates. The lucky, born between April 11 and 15, under the vulture-headed Nebu, might make their living by song and dance. Later in the year you would do less well, since your god 'causes long old age, until a man be bent by old age; he produces hunchbacks or makes men bent by sickness, he causes dwarfs to be born and monstrosities shaped like a beetle and people with no eyes and like a beast and hardly able to speak and deaf and toothless . . .'[75]

More refined spirits might consult the stars in verse. Oxyrhynchites have in use at least four copies of Anubio's manual of astrology.[76] Anubio was a local boy who won a world reputation (named among the disciples of Simon Magus). Born probably at Thebes, in the first century AD, he was named from the Egyptian god of the dead, jackal-headed Anubis, but transmitted his art in Greek and in elegiac verse. As usual, the configuration of the heavenly bodies at your birth fixed your destinies, for better for worse. 'If Jupiter is in the sign of Saturn, and Venus is too, and deadly Mars is in aspect to both Venus and the Moon, and Saturn off by himself is in aspect to the Moon ... he will be the worst of men and sleep with his mother or his stepmother. But if it is a woman who is born with this birth-chart, she will go to the bed of her father or stepfather.'[77] 'When Venus aspects the Moon in right square, she produces men who achieve success and are loveable, honoured by their wives, charming to all their friends – better still if Jupiter is in aspect to Venus.'[78]

Rolling the Dice

Astrology is science, of a kind. From a different standpoint, life was a gamble, and those who wanted to know their future must appeal to a quite different kind of power. Along the West Stoa, near a shrine dedicated to the Homeric hero Achilles, stood another temple: a temple to *Tyche*, 'Luck', a Greek deity dignified by a public apparatus of aristocratic priests and regular offerings.[79] Luck was everywhere; each individual, each city, had its own Luck. Even the Emperor needed Luck; citizens held processions in honour of it,[80] and swore a solemn oath by it, in submitting forms to the bureaucracy, 'that the above information is true'.

Luck maintained an honoured place in the literary classics. Oxyrhynchites who went to their theatre to see revivals of Euripides could hear a classic expression of pessimism, 'Everything turns out unexpectedly'. On comic days, they could see the goddess Luck on stage, in Menander's comedy *Shield*, explaining how she is mistress of all and directs the plot. Luck took physical form in statuary: the Luck of the city, crowned with walls and towers; Luck as the helmsman of life, rudder in hand; Luck as the ruler of the world, her foot on a globe. Even Alexandria, the capital, had its shrine of Luck, and she duly appeared on its coins. Individuals followed suit. They had signet-rings that showed Luck the helmsman;[81] they headed wills and marriage-contracts with the pious hope 'Good Luck!'

In Greek and Egyptian tradition alike any chance event may signify. The philosopher Theophrastus had satirised the Superstitious Man, who if he sees a weasel cross the road will stop until someone else passes the spot, or he himself has thrown three stones over the road. The poet Theocritus had shown his lovesick goatherd playing 'she loves me, she loves me not' with seed pods – and if his right eye twitches, he will see his beloved.[82] And among the papyri there are systematic handbooks of twitches: 'If your left knee jumps, it means changes and trouble from women.'[83] The richer can look to their stables: 'If a horse bites off its tail, it means death to the family.'[84] The accidents of weather too had meaning. If lightning struck a statue, its human neighbour needed to avert the omen. 'If the statue falls over completely, it means destruction for his entire family: so the poor man must purify the statue, and sacrifice to Zeus of Thunder and Herakles and Saviour Luck to the extent of his ability, and appropriate [?] the former portent; but the portent of the fallen statue he should expiate and avert by sacrifice to the same gods.'[85]

You could also take the initiative. You could roll dice, and to see what your throw signified, you (or your local expert) could check the manual. One resource was a mythical magician, Astrampsychos, popular in all ages; the rubbish-dumps of Egypt have remains of ten copies, and medieval manuscripts survive. The pagan version, with its gods, mutated into a Christian version adorned with saints.[86] The principle remained the same. Astrampsychus provides 92 questions, numbered, and 1030 answers, in numbered sections of ten each. Choose your question; take a random number (you can cast lots) between 1 and 10, and add it to the number of your question. The combined number indicates one of the oracular gods, and that god gives the number of the relevant decade of answers. Within the decade, your random number pinpoints the right answer. This convincingly devious procedure opened up a panorama of anxieties. Some belonged to everyday life. Shall I open a factory? Is my property to be sold at auction? Am I to get a legacy? Others suggested high politics, or serious drama. Shall I become an ambassador? Am I to become a town councillor? Will my flight be undetected? Am I to be separated from my wife? Have I been poisoned?

A more literary authority was Homer, who to the Greeks represented the Bible and Shakespeare all in one: familiar to all who have schooling as the foundation of education. A thousand years on from its composition, schoolboys still pored over the classic of classics: 'Homer is a god, not a man,' they copied out ten times to practise their writing. One could pick a line at random, and that line would forecast one's future. It is a tradition that continues with Virgil, and with the Bible. More scientifically, one could use the *Scimitar* or *Homer-oracle*. That had a wide presence. One copy survives as part of a general Handbook of Magic, another on the back of an epic account of the Underworld.[87] A third, found at Oxyrhynchos, suggests the amateur: pocket format, sloppy abbreviated script.[88] All three carry the same text, 216 lines of Homer, chosen one by one, each indexed with three numbers between 1 and 6: beginning with line 1.1.1 and ending with line 6.6.6.

The Oxyrhynchos handbook carries the user-instructions. 'First you must know the days on which to use the oracle. Second you must pray and say the invocation to the god and pray within yourself for what you want. Third you must take a dice and throw it three times and after throwing consult the oracle according to the number produced by your three throws.' The 'days' are limited. You should not use the oracle on the 3rd, 5th, 9th, 10th, 18th, 25th or 29th of the month; some other days only in the morning, or evening. When the right time comes, utter the invocation, which addresses Apollo, the Greek god of prophecy, in verses adapted from (of course) Homer:

> Hear, Lord, that art in Lycia's fertile land
> Or yet in Troy, that hearst in ev'ry place
> His voice who suffers, as I suffer now:
> Tell me this true, that I may come to know
> What most I wish and is my heart's desire.

Then throw the dice, and the *Scimitar* will tell you your destiny. Of course, the answers leave room for interpretation: 1 and 1 and 2 produces 'Courage now, Diomedes, fight against the Trojans'; 1 and 2 and 5, 'I do not know; no one yet knew his own child'; 1 and 3 and 4, 'Hateful to me are his gifts, and I value him at nothing'. It is always useful to have some flexibility in fate.

Magicians

There were remoter resources. Dreams come from somewhere outside, from the world beyond human reasoning, and in an uncertain world they may carry privileged information. The Emperor Constantine the Great, says his biographer, had 10,000 dreams in his lifetime, and remembered every one. That explains, it could be said, how he came to be master of the world. The ill-disposed managed to give their enemies insomnia, for the sleepless lose their access to higher authority. Of course, dreams need interpreting. The handbook of Artemidorus of Daldis, who collected dreams and their outcomes in the mid-second century AD, remained widely influential and survives to this day.

How to wrestle with the unknown? This was the province of the magician, who claimed to have means to persuade, or compel, the unseen powers. Here too dreams played a large part. By this means an enemy might send you a false dream; a lover might put his own image in the mind of the woman he desires; the anxious might solicit the prophetic dream which would reveal the future. A sheet of horoscopes ends with the basic recipe: 'Asking for a dream: write this name on a slip of papyrus . . .' – 'this name' is the divine Name to be invoked. The dream might give a symbolic answer: 'To see a true dream. Go to bed, after eating holy food, and say "By Neith by Neieth, if I will succeed in a certain thing, show me water; if not, fire."'[89] Or the daimon himself might appear: if you wished a visit from Bes, the ithyphallic dwarf who wards off evil, wrap a black cloth round your neck and recite this spell to a lamp, 'I invoke you, the headless god, the one who has his sight on his feet, the one who lightens and thunders: it is you whose mouth pours on fire for ever; it is you who command Necessity. I invoke you . . . Iao Sabaoth Adonai Charbathiao . . .'[90]

Erotic magic played a large part. You aimed to drive the beloved out of her house and into your arms. One odd sheet gives the general formula for involving Hekate, the Greek goddess of witches (fill in the blanks for individual use): 'Night is Hekate, and let Hekate be my messenger and go and stand by the head of —— the daughter of —— and deprive her of sleep until she jumps up and comes to me, —— son of ——, loving me and cherishing me and seeking intercourse with me for the duration of her life!'[91] Another spell must be written on a sea-shell: 'We invoke you, the great god, the great ruler in earth and in heaven, fearful King! Oh that I could have uttered your true name . . . Tear her out of her house, burning in her inwards her guts her marrow, so that she is brought to me. Now! Quickly!'[92]

Magic could touch more mundane problems. There were spells against fever and erysipelas and red blotches, spells to promote conception, to soften the anger of an enemy, to achieve victory over an opponent in the law-courts.[93] The medical uses extended to coughs, tumors, migraine, strangury, scorpion stings, swollen testicles, hardening of the breasts and 'the daily shivering fever'. One sheet of papyrus collects five or more spells which will serve to identify a thief.[94] In the manuals of magic, hymns and rituals rub shoulders with folk medicine and party tricks. You learned how to win at dice or in races, how to attract friends and cause discord between enemies, but also how to become invisible and control your shadow, how to summon genies and get foreknowledge in dreams.

Magic in some ways represented a rival church. Later, with Christianity established, it became an anti-church, yet continued to flourish. Accidentally or not, the bulk of our sources date from precisely the period in which the new religion was establishing its position. Was magic part of the pagan revanche, or did it offer a foothold, just as Christianity did, amid the uncertainties of a disintegrating Empire? Magic had the advantage of being a universal church, its rituals compounded from various sources, Babylonian, Egyptian, Greek, Jewish, Christian; in it Seth, Mithras, Apollo and Jehovah coexisted. It answered so many needs, and yet there is a question about its clientele. How many could afford silver amulets? And how many had the leisure for unrequited love (a luxury never mentioned in the private letters)? People conjured for success in business, or to give their enemies insomnia, but not, it seems, to enhance their harvest or hex their neighbour's donkey. One has sometimes the impression of Mayfair magic, the diversion of well-heeled, sex-crazed urbanites.

Yet the manuals do not entirely disdain the domestic. At the end of the 'Homer Oracle' come the household hints. 'To keep bugs out of the house, mix goat bile with water and sprinkle it. To keep fleas out of the house, wet rosebay with salt water, grind it and spread it.' After that, 'Demokritos' Tricks', designed to promote your social standing. How to make bronze look like gold? Mix raw sulphur with chalk and smear it on. How to eat garlic and not stink? Roast beetroots and eat them.[95]

CHAPTER 12

CHRISTIANS AND CHRISTIANITIES

• • • •

We also visited Oxyrhynchos, a city in the Thebaid, whose wonders beggar description. So full is it of monasteries inside that the monks themselves make the walls resound, and it is surrounded outside by other monasteries, so that there is another city outside the city ... There are twelve churches in it, since the city is very large ... The monks were almost more numerous than the laity, residing at the entrances of the city and in the towers of the gates ... There was no hour by day or by night in which they did not carry on divine service; indeed there was no heretic or pagan inhabitant in the city, all the citizens alike were faithful and under religious instruction, so that the Bishop was able to give the people the kiss of peace in the main square ... Who could state the number of monks and virgins, which was innumerable? From the holy Bishop there we had precise information: ten thousand monks under him, and twenty thousand virgins. As for their hospitality and charity, I cannot express it: our cloaks were torn apart as each group pulled us to their side.[1]

The pious tourist who sketched this picture visited Oxyrhynchos at the end of the fourth century AD. The statistics no doubt say more for his enthusiasm than his sense, but by this time, certainly, Oxyrhynchos, the pharaonic seat of Seth, the shrine of the sacred fish and the divine hippopotamus, had become a Christian city in a Christian Egypt. The revolution encompassed the whole country, not just the Greek-speakers of the towns but the Egyptian-speakers of the villages; and it went with another revolution, which provided the Egyptian language for the first time with a simple alphabetic script, based on Greek, and disseminated the new sacred books translated into what became known as Coptic.

Egypt had always been preoccupied with the afterlife. Now it had a new hope of eternity. Part of the history of Egyptian Christianity can be followed at high level, through the surviving works of Church historians: it is a history of persecution and triumph, martyrs and bishops, hermits and monasteries, centred on Alexandria, full of violent incident, voiced by larger-than-life personalities. The other part comes from the documents: they provide the groundling's view of Egyptian Christians before and after their cult became the established Church.

Christianity took four centuries to conquer the Empire. The imperial government resisted. There were mass executions already under Nero, who used the Christians as scapegoats for the great fire of Rome. The Emperor Trajan approved (c. 110–11 AD) a policy by which individuals who confessed to being Christians faced the death penalty. Systematic persecutions followed, under Decius (250–1), under Valerian (259–60), most famously under Diocletian and his co-emperors (303–11). With the fourth century AD, we reach a tipping point. In AD 312–13 the Emperor Constantine and his colleague Licinius issued edicts of toleration. In AD 391 the Emperor Theodosius I decreed the closing of pagan temples and the banning of pagan cults. This triumph was not total and immediate; nostalgic aristocrats looked back to Hellenic cult, trained magicians continued to invoke the dark powers of tradition. But by the fifth century, Egypt, like most parts of the Empire, was a Christian country. An orthodox (heterodox as it seemed to brother Christians elsewhere) church had become one of the central institutions of the province; bishops were commanding figures, churches and monasteries (endowed by the pious with land and treasure) represented a large economic interest.

Alexandria, the capital of power and of culture, played a special part in Egyptian Christianity, through its catechetical school and its powerful array of scholars, heretics and politicians.

Here, in the second century, Origen (his very name derives from Horus, the Egyptian sun-god) applied to the Bible some of those critical techniques that earlier scholars had applied to Homer. Professional and prolific (his staff included more than seven shorthand writers, working in shifts to take down his dictation, and the same number of copyists and 'girls practised in calligraphy'),[2] Origen left commentaries on many books of the Old and New Testament, and his critical Old Testament, which set out in parallel columns the Hebrew text and its various (looser and less loose) translations into Greek. In the Decian persecution, he underwent torture, and died.

Here, in the second and third centuries, the new religion fought battles of self-definition. It faced an external enemy, the Roman state; it faced competitors like the Persian cult of Mithras, which offered a similar menu of revelation, initiation and salvation. Above all, there was the enemy within, alternative Christianities preached by great names like the mystic and ascetic Basilides. These 'gnostics' – the word means 'those who know' the inner truth – generally saw the created world as evil, with redemption only for the souls of the elect, a view all the more appealing to educated Greeks for looking back to Plato. Platonic too, or neo-Platonic, was the gnostic construction of the universe: an unbegotten God from whom emanates a hierarchy of forces – Mind, Reason, Thought, Wisdom, Power. Basilides wrote a commentary on the Gospel in twenty-four books (the standard length of epics like the *Iliad*). He also maintained (or so his enemies said) that the crucifixion was a trick, for Jesus had replaced himself with a look-alike before ascending into heaven. Gnosticism fought and lost, but not immediately: Coptic translations of its books were still being copied in the fourth and fifth centuries. Even then, the orthodox had their own quarrels to settle. In Alexandria again the presbyter Areios (died *c*.336) and the bishop Athanasios (bishop 328, died 373) waged doctrinal war over the relation between the Son and the Father. Athanasios' victory still informs the Creed, when it declares the Father consubstantial with the Son.

Here, in the fourth century, the Alexandrian mob, always partisan and dangerous, rallied to the new religion, now persecuting instead of persecuted. In AD 391, encouraged by the Patriarch Theophilos, they destroyed the famous Temple of Serapis and broke in pieces the famous statue of the god by Bryaxis. In 415, after a quarrel between the Patriarch Cyril and the Prefect Orestes, a posse created a pagan martyr by lynching the mathematician and philosopher Hypatia, the first woman ever to lecture in Alexandria. 'They watch for her to return home from some-where, and throwing her out of her carriage, they drag her to the church known as the Kaisarion, and stripping off her clothes they took her life with pieces of broken pot, and after tearing her apart limb by limb they brought the limbs together at the so-called Kinaron and consumed them with fire.'[3]

The see of Alexandria (founded, it was said, by St Mark) disputed the primacy with Rome and Constantinople, and its patriarchs continued to play hard in the high politics of the Eastern Empire. It was the same Cyril (bishop 412–44) who had his rival Nestorios of Constantinople deposed at the Council of Ephesos (AD 431), asserting the view that Christ's human and divine natures were not separate but combined – the doctrine (later, heresy) of monophysitism. He had the advantage of presiding over the Council, and a crew of Egyptian dockers to help with persuading the opposition.

Alexandria was its own world. But upriver, in the hinterland, another powerful force made itself felt. Peasants on strike and fugitive criminals had always taken refuge in the Western Desert. Now its rock and sand welcomed a new form of escape. St Anthony became the archetypal hermit, when he left his home (AD 270) and espoused the life of the Christian ascetic. Others followed. Hermits came to live in groups and later, with St Pakhom (died c.349), holy men came to live together in monasteries. The monks were a powerful force for the faith, happily untroubled by the doctrinal disputes which flourished in the capital. Shenoute, the famous Abbot of the White Monastery near Thebes (385–464), led roving patrols to hunt out and destroy idols, and many pharaonic monuments still show evidence of having been defaced. For the Egyptian Church, the example and the legend of the Desert Fathers, the 'athletes of God', remained important, as they remain for today's Coptic Church, part and parcel of a specifically Egyptian Christianity and a specifically Coptic culture with its own language and literature, painting and textiles. For the world outside, the invention of the monastery was a decisive moment: monasticism spread throughout the Eastern Empire, and (after a visit by Bishop Athanasios to Rome in AD 340) to western Europe as well.

Patriarchs have their historians, monks have their devout anecdotes. Ordinary people leave their mark through the papyrus documents, the worm's-eye view of Christianity on the march in Egypt, as seen in the lives of its followers and the circulation of its texts. At Oxyrhynchos, according to the pious travelogue already quoted, the bishop boasted of 10,000 monks and 20,000 nuns. Documents provide the sober practicalities. About 300 AD the authorities were stationing night-watchmen at the North Church and the South Church.[4] By the sixth century the city had at least thirty churches – St John the Baptist, St John the Evangelist, the Church of the Martyrs, the Church of the Resurrection, with many others named from local saints and some commemorating their founders.[5]

Christians and Their Books

Books give the clearest lead, the fragmentary biblical texts from the dumps of Oxyrhynchos, which include some of the earliest surviving Christian manuscripts in the world – a scatter of gospels and non-Gospels whose script would, other things being equal, be dated to the later second century AD, produced in a characteristic format that sets them apart from Jewish scripture and pagan literature alike.[6] Indeed, one of Grenfell and Hunt's first finds on the site fell into this category. This single surviving leaf contains what the editors called 'Sayings of our Lord': 'Jesus says: Unless you fast from the world, you will not find the kingdom of God; and unless you keep the Sabbath as Sabbath, you will not see the Father.'

To modern readers this was a sensational novelty; to the Christians of Oxyrhynchos it must have been a familiar text, for fragments of two more copies turned up later. Scholars came to attribute them to a work long lost but known from references, *The Gospel of Thomas*. That was confirmed in 1956, when a complete copy of a Coptic translation was published from the great cache of Christian books (thirteen codices in one large jar) recovered near Nag Hammadi, sixty miles north of Luxor. This 'Gospel' carried an introduction by the apostle Thomas: 'These are the secret words which the living Jesus spoke and Judas called Thomas wrote them and said, "Whoever finds the interpretation of these words, shall not taste death."' The rest of the book collects, one by one, the sayings of Jesus.[7]

The four Gospels that we know did not attain their canonical status without a struggle. The papyri illustrate the competition: as well as *The Gospel of Thomas*, Oxyrhynchites could read *The Gospel of Mary*, *The Acts of Peter* and *The Wisdom of Jesus Christ*.[8] These books would eventually lose out to charges of inauthenticity and indeed of heresy; that is the reality behind the label 'apocryphal' which attaches to them. Some of them indeed belong to the strain of para-Christianity loosely called Gnosticism, which interprets (as in the *Gospel of Thomas*) the 'secret words'. The gnostics lost the battle, and their writings were destroyed with them; only finds of papyri over the last century have restored some of their texts in Greek and Coptic, so that the modern reader can study the scripture of the losers. However, if what was thrown away is a guide to what was read, Oxrhynchites preferred the main line and what were to be canonical books: they read Matthew and John commonly, though Luke and Mark hardly at all. Gnostic texts turn up only in small numbers. Perhaps the manichaean world-view was too depressing, or the neo-Platonic machinery too complicated. Certainly there is a contrast between the plain speech of the Gospels and (say) the cosmic rhetoric of the risen Christ in *The Wisdom of Jesus Christ*, 'He who has ears, let him hear! The master of everything is not called Father, but Fore-father, for the Father is the beginning of what will show itself in the future. But that Fore-father without beginning, who sees himself in himself as in a mirror, appears like himself. His likeness has shown itself as Fore-father, Father-god and face-to-face with the pre-existing unbegotten Father . . .'[9]

Canonical and apocryphal shared a distinctively Christian book-form. To classical Greeks and Romans, 'book' meant 'roll': a book, like the elegant copy of the orator Hyperides, now in the British Library, in which the text is written column by column along the length of a roll of papyrus (in this case, 12 inches tall and at least 10 feet long).[10] The reader receives his Hyperides rolled up, the end inside and the beginning outside. To read, he unrolls with his right hand and rolls up with his left, so that the successive columns pass before his eyes. When he has finished the last column, the roll will have the beginning inside and the end outside; like the tape of a tape-recorder, it needs to be rewound, for the convenience of the next user. Professional books of this kind are written on one side only, the side with the better writing-surface. That is not economical of papyrus, and so a roll of private accounts or government registers may sometimes be turned over and recycled to copy a book, or a book no longer valued may be turned over and reused for accounts. The handsomest books have no truck with economy: blank backs, wide margins, large spaced lettering. Some may even have had the luxury trappings described by Catullus, central rod with ivory knobs, parchment wrapper dyed in purple – but those parts have not survived in the dumps.[11]

Another book-form was waiting in the wings: the *codex*, a collection of individual sheets folded into pages and bound in quires – the book as we would recognise it. The form was familiar in wood (simple tablets, or tablets hollowed and filled with wax), where several tablets might be pierced and hinged together with string – these were the notebooks in which poets composed and schoolboys did their exercises. Parchment too, the prepared sheep or goat-skin, which offered a more durable medium than papyrus, could be made into a codex, and parchment like wood could be washed or scraped clean and reused as a renewable jotter. These were the beginnings, as we hear of them in the first century AD; by the fifth century AD the jotter had conquered the world, and codices in papyrus and newly fashionable parchment were the universal carriers of texts profane and sacred. Between these dates, the form has a chequered history. In imperial Rome, it seems, parchment miniatures of the Classics could be presented as a fashionable Christmas present: 'Massive Livy is fitted into small parchments.'[12] In the less fashionable parts of Egypt, the finds of papyri have combined in a rather different story. It is certain that Christians there adopted this unclassical form for their own texts. It was not exclusive to them; here and there we find a Homer or Demosthenes in codex-form. But the statistics (given of course that the number of Christian texts is much smaller than the number of pagan texts) make the case. If we look at the literary texts surviving on papyrus, we find a startling disparity. For pagan literature, up to *c*. AD 400, codices represent (very approximately) 2 per cent of copies in the second century, 20 per cent in the third, 75 per cent in the fourth. For texts of scripture, over the same period, the codex accounts for more than 90 per cent, and of the exceptions some (it is not clear how many) derive from Jewish rather than Christian circles. The conclusion is clear. Christians favoured the codex throughout; pagan literature adopted it as a norm only from the fourth century AD – the century of the Christian triumph.[13] So the classics followed where the Gospels led.

This conclusion is deduced from the evidence in the ground: no ancient author tells us the fact or the reason for it. Reasons therefore have to be inferred. Some scholars have suggested that humble Christians felt easier with the humble notebook, or that poor Christians saw advantages in using both sides of the papyrus (the saving has been calculated at 26 per cent).[14] Others think the codex appealed to a persecuted sect, since it was compact and easily concealed; or that it suited Scripture, since it was easier to locate your text by riffling pages than by shuffling through rolls; or that it accommodated, once many pages could be fitted between two covers, an extensive coherent corpus (the four Gospels, the Epistles of Paul) – in the end, the Codex Sinaiticus, in large format on fine parchment, sumptuous enough to have been one of the fifty great bibles copied (about AD 331) to the command of the Emperor Constantine, could take the whole Old and New Testament in two volumes.

All these motives have their plausibility, though some are less plausible than others: it is not clear, for example, that Christians were any more scrupulous than pagans in verifying their references. Another school looks to an exemplar, a work composed in a codex which gave the form prestige among all Christians: such perhaps was the Gospel of St Mark, composed in Rome (where parchment note-books were familiar) and carried to Egypt when (in legend, at least) St Mark founded the See of Alexandria. This makes up in romance what it lacks in fact. The larger question – how, in effect, Europe adopted the book in the form still universal today – will never be answered. Most likely, it seems to me, is yet a third approach. Christians emerged from Jewish communities, with a revelation beyond the classics of their pagan neighbours. The scroll was the vehicle of Jewish Law; the roll was the vehicle of pagan lore. By choosing the codex for their sacred books, early Christians set themselves apart from their origins and from their rivals.[15]

That contrariness may show up in another distinctive feature. In Christian texts, certain common and significant words – Jesus, Father and the like – appear in abbreviated form, shortened to their first and last letters, a horizontal rule above to mark them out. 'Our Father, which art in Heaven, Hallowed be thy Name' becomes 'Our $\overline{\text{FR}}$, which art in $\overline{\text{HVN}}$, $\overline{\text{HD}}$ be thy $\overline{\text{NE}}$'. There is a system: not always consistent, and sometimes more extensive than others, not always fully understood by the copyists who use it. But similarity and contrast again suggest deliberate innovation. Pagan books do not use abbreviations; pagan documents regularly do (by cutting off the end of the word, STR^a for STRATEGOS), and pagan scholars developed their own special system to shorten the immense bulk of their learned works (special short-hand signs for commonly occurring syllables, M' for MEN). The head-and-tail system has no parallel in general use. On the Jewish side, there is one possible parallel – the writing of the divine name as JHVH, the tetragrammaton, which transfers even to the Greek translation of Scripture, where 'the oldest and best manuscripts' (so says Origen) maintained the old Hebrew characters for this central concept (later and worse manuscripts corrupted them more and more, until JHVH ended in an ignominious PIPI). The Christian system showed Jewish roots in identifying a divine name by the shape of its writing, but extended it to a whole rosary of theologically important items (and here, perhaps, it does look sideways to the pagan world, where lawyers, for example, overlined important words in their brief with a view to picking them out in court). It set itself apart (again) from pagan literature, by abbreviating at all and by abbreviating in this unfamiliar fashion.[16]

The pagan reader, then, would have found an early Christian book distinctive in format and in conventions. In the earlier days, at least, the script was often relatively informal, a reformed version of the cursive characters normally used to copy documents. Enlarged initial letters, and the use of numerals ('16') instead of numbers ('sixteen'), might add to that impression, by contrast with the calligraphic formality of copies of the Classics. But that cannot be pushed too far. Homers too were copied in reformed documentary scripts, since no doubt such copies cost less than glossier productions. Conversely, Christian texts could come in luxury form, at least by the mid fourth century: witness the splendid miniature codex, on parchment, of *The Wisdom of Solomon*, once owned by a devout Oxyrhynchite.[17]

Christians and their Persecutors

The readers of such texts were Christians. How much their Christianity showed in their daily doings, how far pagan neighbours could identify them as a coherent sect, is more difficult to judge. Private letters could be revealing; but most letters focus on business, with no appeal to faith, except in the conventional prescript 'I pray for your health'. 'I pray to the gods' is clearly pagan; 'I pray to god' might be Christian, but not exclusively – there were pagan monotheists. Language too might be shared, since Christian and pagan discourses easily overlapped in the style and sentiment inculcated by a classical education. 'I pray that concord and mutual affection remain with you,' writes Ammonios to Apollonios, 'so that you may not be subject to hostile talk and not be in a situation like us. Experience leads me to exhort you to keep the peace and not to give others opportunities to attack you.' Much the same sentiments occur in letters in which the Emperor Constantine rebuked feuding Christians. If this letter from Oxyrhynchos is Christian, its likely date (the turn of the first and second centuries AD) makes it the earliest known document of Christianity.[18]

The expansion of the new faith attracted the attention, sometimes hostile, of the imperial government. The Decian 'persecution' of AD 250–1 was probably not directed specifically at Christians; it was an attempt to conciliate the traditional protecting deities of the Empire by an act of universal conformity. The process was systematic, like that of the census: the head of each household must present himself, perform the required ritual, and obtain a certificate signed by the appropriate officials. The ritual involved the pouring of libations, the offering of animal sacrifice, and the tasting of the sacrificial meat (a kind of pagan eucharist). No conscientious Christian could go through with this.

The edict was promulgated soon after Decius' accession, perhaps late in AD 249. Enforcement must have presented a substantial administrative problem. Egyptian officialdom organised a simultaneous operation in towns and villages, and then set a deadline. All surviving certificates (nearly fifty of them) are dated in June/July 250. At Oxyrhynchos Aurelios Gaion duly presented himself for certification:

> To those chosen to preside over the sacrifices in the city of the Oxyrhynchites, from Aurelios Gaion, son of Ammonios, mother Taeus. Being always accustomed to offer sacrifice and libations and worship to the gods, in accordance with the orders given by the imperial decree, now too in your presence I have offered sacrifice and libations and tasted the sacrificial offerings, along with my wife Taos and Ammonios and Ammonianos my sons and my daughter Thekla through me and I request that you should give me your signature. Year 1 of Imperator Caesar Gaius Messius Quintus Traianus Decius Pius Felix Augustus, Epeiph 3 [27 June AD 250]. I Aurelios Gaion have submitted it. I Aurelios Sarapion alias Chairemon wrote for him since he is illiterate.[19]

A full certificate would carry the signatures of two witnesses, and of the supervising officials.[20]

Some ten years later, officials correspond (and the letter is duly docketed) about Christians: from the scanty remains, it might be guessed that the property of such people was to be listed and then confiscated to the treasury.[21] This coincides with the persecution ordered by Valerian and Gallienus, and no doubt formed part of it. But even before the formal edicts, action was possible; and Christians, it seems, could be identified. On 28 February AD 256, the Mayor of Oxyrhynchos issued an order to the headmen and peace-officers of the nearby village of Mermertha: 'Send up forthwith Petosarapis son of Horos, Christian, or you come up yourselves. Year 3 of Valerianus and Gallienus Augusti, Phamenôth 3.'[22] Many such 'orders to arrest' survive, small slips of papyrus sent by magistrates to officials and policemen. This one has some distinctive features. It is the only one issued by a mayor, and one of only three to carry a precise date: accident, or exceptional situation? Some such orders identify the suspect by his trade or profession; here we have 'Christian'. Many such orders identify an individual whose petition has led to the arrest; this element is missing. One might guess, therefore, that this is a move by the authorities, and that 'Christian' represents the charge. But however that may be, Petosorapis is a striking figure: a villager, with a good pagan name ('He who belongs to Osiris'), now identifiable as a Christian.

Or rather, as spelled, not 'Christian' but 'Chres<t>ian'. Greek *christos*, with *i*, means 'annointed'; Greek *chrêstos*, with *ê*, means 'good'. In contemporary pronunciation, as in Modern Greek, *i* and *ê* were uttered as the same sound, a long *ee*. How far early Christians understood the distinction, we cannot say. Non-Christians perhaps neither knew nor cared. The spelling with *ê* turns up already in the Roman librarian and biographer Suetonius, writing early in the second century and looking back to the reign of Claudius, who in a famous passage mentions Jews continually rioting in Rome 'provoked by Chrestus'.[23] It persists, at a time and place when the Christians are a larger and closer phenomenon, in the letter quoted above; a more vulgar pronunciation drops the *t*, to give *Chresian*, as in fact in the warrant for Petosorapis and perhaps in an athlete's letter to his mother, 'I sent you two talents via Sotas the Chresian[?].'[24] Yet the conflation of 'good' and 'annointed' does not just reflect the contemptuous ignorance of the outsider, since the spelling persists to a time when Christianity is the norm: 'I was deeply saddened, and we are very deeply saddened, because you have dared to do such a thing to Atheatis, although she is a Chrestian, because although she is a laywoman she has never been found doing worldly things.'[25]

In the meantime, churches were built and their functionaries appointed, identifiable targets to a hostile government. In February AD 303 began the most famous of persecutions, mother of many martyrs whose names still appear among the saints of the Coptic Church. It was an epoch so marked that the first year of Diocletian's reign (284/5) served as the beginning of an era, later called the Era of the Martyrs, from which horoscopes often date the birth of their subject and gravestones the death of those who lie beneath. A year later, on 5 February 304, the clerk (*anagnôstês*) of a church near Oxyrhynchos was making an official report, in triplicate, of its destitution:

> In the consulship of our lords Emperors Diocletian for the ninth time and Maximian for the 8th time, Augusti. To the Aurelioi Neilos, alias Ammonios, (ex)gymnasiarch and councillor, prytanis in office, and Sarmates and Matrinos, both (ex)gymnnasiarchs and councillors, *syndikoi*, all of the Glorious and Most Glorious City of the Oxyrhynchites, Aurelios Ammonios son of Kopreus, reader of the one-time church of the village of Chysis. You having imposed on me, in accordance with written instructions from Aurelios Athanasios, the *procurator privatae*, as ordered by the most illustrious *magister privatae* Neratios Apollonides, with regard to handing over all the items in the said one-time church, and me having claimed that the said church had neither gold nor plate nor money nor clothing nor beasts nor slaves nor lands nor property whether from donations or again from bequests, except only for the bronze stuff which was found and handed over to the curator to be conveyed downriver to the most illustrious Alexandria in accordance with the written instructions of our most illustrious prefect Clodius Culcianus, I swear by the Genius of our lords Emperors Diocletian and Maximian Augusti and Constantius and Maximian the most noble Caesars that this is so and that I have falsified nothing or may I be liable to the imperial oath. [Date.] I, Aurelios Ammonios, swore the oath as above. I, Aurelios Serenos, wrote for him since he is illiterate.[26]

Illiterate, although his title *anagnôstês* means literally 'reader'.

Martyrs there certainly were. Some were martyred at Oxyrhynchos itself: Elias the eunuch, Isaac of Tiphre, Epiuse. Some were to be commemorated there, in churches named after them. Some survived through the written narratives of their suffering, circulated and elaborated for the edification of the pious: 'Year 23 of Diocletian [AD 306/7]. Dioskoros from the Upper Kynopolite nome, town councillor, was arrested and brought into court before the Prefect Culcianus. Culcianus said: Dioskoros, we have heard that you are a very intelligent and educated man. Make sacrifice and obey the orders of our Lords the Emperors. Dioskoros said: I do not sacrifice to gods like these, nor do I obey anyone except only God . . .'[27]

Yet ordinary Oxyrhynchite Christians had their own resources. The government devised a variety of measures to disadvantage Christians, among them the requirement that litigants should offer sacrifice before entering the court, thus excluding the conscientious from their rights at law. Kopres found himself in this situation:

Kopres to his sister, Sarapias, very many greetings. Before all else I pray for the good health of you all before the Lord God. I want you to know that we arrived on the 11th. It became known to us that those who present themselves in court are being made to sacrifice. I made a power-of-attorney in favour of my brother. So far we have accomplished nothing. We instructed an advocate on the 12th [?], so that the case about the land could be brought in on the 14th. If we accomplish anything, I'll write to you. I've sent you nothing, since I found Theodoros himself setting out. I'll send them to you by another hand soon. Write to us about the health of you all and how Maximina has been and Asena. If it's possible let him [her?] come with your mother so that his [her?] leucoma can be treated – I myself have seen others treated. I pray for your health. My best wishes to all our friends by name. [Address:] Deliver to my sister, from Kopres. 99 . . .[28]

Kopres did not take his case to court himself, but transferred it to his 'brother'. Why? Perhaps he disliked the requirement to offer sacrifice. Why? Perhaps because he was a Christian. And indeed he was a Christian; he is too discreet to say so, but after the address he indicates the fact in code: '99' = 'Amen'. We do not know whether the code was proof against the persecutors, but clearly the evasion was. The regime might cut off Christians from the law; but business was business, and one had only to find an obliging 'brother' for things to go ahead.

The code that Kopres used depends on a simple convention, which goes back to archaic Greece: each letter of the original Greek alphabet (including three letters which later dropped out of use) serves also as a numeral. Thus:

α	1	ι	10	ρ	100
β	2	κ	20	σ	200
γ	3	λ	30	τ	300
δ	4	μ	40	υ	400
ε	5	ν	50	φ	500
ϛ	6	ξ	60	χ	600
ζ	7	ο	70	ψ	700
η	8	π	80	ω	800
θ	9	ϙ	90	⌇	900

On this basis, any word will have a numerical value, the sum of the letter-numbers that compose it. *Amên* = alpha + mu + eta + nu = 1 + 40 + 8 + 50 = 99. These number-games ranged widely in the Greek and Roman world, as they do among modern occultists (normally under the Hebrew designation *Gematria*). Any word is a number, any number a word. If two different words or phrases share the same number (*isopsephy*), the equation reveals an inner connection between the two terms. A cynical pederast discovered the equation *cash = sex*; cynical dissidents adorned the walls of Rome with the equation *Nero = killed his own mother* (as indeed that Emperor did). At least one Oxyrhynchite kept a list of such things, which includes both the pious and the political: *Isis = the great hope*; *Similis* (the Prefect then in office) = *the good climate*. Christians in turn would use the same method to produce their own equations: *Paul = wisdom, Easter = the good life*. '99' for 'Amen' is a simple product of this system, and any Christian would understand. An obscurer product required more explanation, and still attracts debate, the 'Number of the Beast' – '666', according to tradition, but '616' according to our earliest copy of Revelation (also discovered at Oxyrhynchos).[29]

Diocletian's persecution petered out. Yet the situation must have remained dangerous, at least until 324, when Egypt came under the control of the sympathetic Emperor Constantine. Even so, ordinary lives could retain a Christian commitment. A contract of 316, and other business papers, were found tied up with a copy of the beginning of the First Epistle to the Romans – an odd sheet, written in crude, old-fashioned capitals, like a schoolboy's exercise or perhaps a home-made amulet.[30] A brisk note, undated, written on a piece cut from a recycled petition, shows Old Testament apocrypha (the *Book of Jubilees* or *Little Genesis*, apocryphal and one of the Books of Ezra) circulating from hand to hand: 'To my dearest lady sister, greetings in the Lord. Lend me the Ezra, since I lent you the Little Genesis. Farewell in God from us.'[31] The note, most unusually, names neither writer nor recipient: the informality of close friends? Or the discretion of the persecuted?

By AD 320 Oxyrhynchite Christians are being publicly recorded for their civil duty. In a list of those paying the city poll-tax, Aniketes 'bandy-legs' is followed by Apphous deacon of the church; Besarion the reader stands next to Nikias 'the amazing', a professional athlete to judge from his title.[32] In 321 Constantine himself prohibited working on 'the venerable day of the sun'. This is the beginning of Sunday as holiday; and by 2 October 325 the logistes of Oxyrhynchos was already observing it – his court sat on a Saturday and dragged on into the evening, when he ruled 'The case will be postponed until after the Lord's Day.'[33]

New Faith, Old Problems

Private devotion continued. So Didymos wrote to his friend Athanasios, full of misspellings, the final appeal tucked into the margin where the papyrus ran out: 'In the name of your God in heaven, so may you find brides for your male children, before all else, with me as your debtor for this great favour, apply yourself to the church! The price of the donkey and the other three gold pieces, spend from this and finish the church! Isiaias the stone-mason has already found the stones. So he came to an agreement [?] with the fellow. Buy [for?] two gold pieces, and they are enough. Finish the columns! Make the fishing-boat bring them from Tampemou before the river falls. I ask you not to neglect this request of mine: you are doing it for my soul and for yours.'[34]

It was a new heaven but not necessarily a new earth. The facts and fears of ordinary life remained immutable. Traditional observance survived the change in divine governance. Christian Oxyrhynchites celebrated the Festival of the Nile, just as their pagan predecessors had done. A little amulet-book of the sixth century AD still contains, cheek by jowel with the Creed and Psalm 132 ('Behold, how good and how pleasant it is for brethren to dwell together in unity'), an invocation of the Nile, 'King of rivers, Nile, rich in rains, auspicious in name . . .'[35] Traditional forms survived too: letters of condolence will now refer to the one God, yet the topics of consolation remain the same, without mention of that ultimate consolation that Christians might hope for, the prospect of the life everlasting. Only in the sixth century AD do we find a distinctively Christian comforter, who knows his Bible much better than grammar and spelling: 'Let us praise God that he gave and he took away. Pray that the Lord give them rest and allow you to see them in the paradise where the souls of men are judged. For they have gone to the bosom of Abraham and Isaac and Jacob.'[36]

Tradition recommended appealing to an oracle for help with life's uncertainties. Pagans had put their problems to Sarapis or Thoeris. Christians now put similar questions to the one true God – 'God, ruler of all, holy, truly merciful, creator, father of our lord and saviour Jesus Christ, reveal to me your truth, whether you wish me to go to Chiout or whether I find you with me aiding and benevolent. So be it! 99.' Even the method was the same: 'God of our protector St Philoxenos, if you tell us to put Anoup into your hospital, show your power and let this slip come out' – the petitioner handed in one slip for Yes and one for No, and whichever was returned gave the answer.[37] The general handbook for the perplexed, the *Sortes Astrampsychi*, continued to circulate, with an introductory prayer and some Christian touches to the questions, much as it had in pagan times.

For personal protection one might wear an amulet, a good-luck charm, metal or papyrus, inscribed with a spell, strung round the neck or tucked into the top fold of the tunic (the nearest that Greek dress came to a pocket).[38] Pagan Oxyrhynchos yields a charm against fever, on silver, and an order for a charm against tonsillitis, on gold; a folded slip of papyrus was intended to provide all-purpose protection – 'A EE HHH IIII OOOOO YYYYY ΩΩΩΩΩΩΩ. The nourisher of the whole world overcomes all things. Lord Sarapis, deliver Artemidora.'[39] Here the seven Greek vowels represent the building-blocks of the universe, and the supplicant invokes them in arithmetic crescendo. Fever also threatens Christians, who respond with protective prayers: 'Save and protect Aria from the one-day ague and the daily ague and the nightly ague and the light fever ... Do this benevolently, according to your will, first and according to her faith, because she is a servant of the living god and so that your name may be glorified for ever. The father of Jesus, the son, the mother of Christ, the holy spirit. Abrasax.' Aria's charm still carries a border of magical vowels; and its last word is not Christ but Abrasax, the magical name of the old year-god (A+B+R+A+S+A+X = 365), not foreign to Christian gnostics (therefore heretics) like Basilides but still an exotic intruder among the orthodox, depicted in armour with the head of a cock and the feet of a snake.[40]

Biblical texts carried special powers. When St John Chrysostom, writing in the fourth century AD, comes to explain the phylacteries of the Pharisees, mentioned by St Matthew, he remarks that, in the same way, 'many women nowadays have gospels tied round their necks'.[41] That would hardly be practicable with a full-sized copy; the practice goes some way to explain the miniature texts of Scripture we find among the rubbish. The Old Testament already provided suitable material; Psalm 90, 'Lord, Thou hast been our dwelling place in all generations', was a favourite.[42] The Gospels themselves might serve, or extracts at least, witness a parchment headed 'Healing Gospel according to St Matthew', where some verses are copied as a series of small crosses on a single piece of parchment (to be folded up into a tiny packet).[43] Another mini-booklet, of the third/fourth century AD, contains part (originally the whole?) of *The Epistle of Jude*, reduced to a miniature page 2 inches wide and just over 1 inch high, again a format for easy carrying.[44] What special power attached to this text in particular, we do not know – unless the special convenience of being the shortest book of the New Testament. Certainly it was a do-it-yourself affair, roughly made and copied by an amateur hand. Belief overlapped business, as witness the prayer copied in ornate capitals, 'Save me now and in the time to come through our Lord and Saviour Jesus Christ, through whom the glory and the power for ever and ever, amen' – on the back the note 'Prayer' and then (in cursive) '2136 drachmas. 5 and a half pounds.'[45]

Magic was often multicultural. The desperate hedged their bets by invoking, side by side, all the powers, whether Jewish or Christian or Egyptian or Babylonian. 'The door, Aphrodite, phrodite, rodite, odite, dite, ite, te, Oror, Phorphor, Iao, Sabaoth, Adonai, Artemisian Scorpion: deliver this house from every evil crawler and thing, quickly quickly. St Phokas is here.'[46] Some Christians certainly (those who had the resources) moved in a wider world, between old Hellenism and new faith, between inherited Greek, Latin which showed a new popularity in the fourth century (perhaps the regime promoted it as a token of imperial unity), and the renascent language of the country now given new authority through Coptic translations of Scripture.[47] Chance finds from different parts of Egypt illustrate the mixture. A wooden school-book from the Great Oasis contains copies (by three different hands) of a table of fractions, a verb conjugation, a paraphrase of the beginning of the *Iliad* (all traditional materials of Greek education), plus a text of Psalm 46 in Coptic.[48] The strange codex now in Barcelona contains traditional pagan material, a Latin declamation (in verse) and a Latin classic (Cicero's *Catilinarian Orations* 1–2), but also Christian texts in both languages – an acrostic hymn in Latin, four liturgical prayers and another acrostic hymn in Greek; the Latin at least contains so many mistakes as to suggest an amateur writing out a half-understood text.[49] Yet another, now in the Bodmer Library at Coligny near Geneva, looks like an educational anthology: two extracts from the Old Testament, the apocryphal tale of *Susanna and the Elders* and the opening of *Daniel* (ending in mid-sentence), all in an ambitious literary script; then a heavy, irregular hand adds an alphabet of moral maxims; then a chancery hand contributes the beginning of Thucydides Book VI – a reader, it seems, which combined sacred Jewish stories with the classic history of the Hellenic past.[50]

Greek origins, Roman domination, the renaissance of the native language – the Church of the Egyptian Greeks grew up under many different influences. In the end, Coptic would displace Greek, and it is a Coptic Church that survives the centuries of Muslim rule. At Oxyrhynchos, the rubbish-dumps register a cultural change. In the fifth century, the pagan classics appear much more rarely. In the sixth century they show a certain revival. With the seventh century they virtually disappear. Even the Greek church had regarded them with suspicion; in the end, it seems, piety, poverty and the Arab conquest put an end to the Hellenic education which had for so long underlined the separateness of the Egyptian Greeks. However, more basic and ancient traditions survive all changes of regime and religion. The Festival of the Nile, or the reliance on charms and amulets, passes without difficulty from a pagan to a Christian society. Fifteen hundred years later, E. W. Lane draws his picture of Islamic Egypt: he describes the public festival which celebrates the rise of the Nile, and the written charms (now with words from the Koran) which profess to drive bugs out of the house.

EPILOGUE

'Of middle height, honey-coloured, long-faced, slightly squinting, with a scar on the right wrist': so Tryphon the weaver described himself. We know a lot about him and his fortunes – the sober manoeuvres of work and money, the soap-opera of his wives and children. We know it from his family papers, forty-odd documents which represent one of the first finds made by Grenfell and Hunt when they discovered, in the rubbish-mounds of Oxyrhynchos, a unique dustbin of vanished lives.

This Tryphon was born in AD 8/9, the 38th year of Augustus, the first Roman Emperor and the first Roman ruler of Egypt, the son of Dionysios and Thamounis also known as Thamounion (the diminutive form). Four years later we have a snapshot of his extended family, all, it seems, resident in the same house. It comprised (only the males are listed) the patriarch, Tryphon the elder, weaver, aged 65; then his sons, Didymos, weaver, aged 38, Dionysios, weaver, aged 33, Thoonis, weaver, aged 22. Then the sons of Dionysios: Tryphon our hero, aged 4, and Thoonis, aged one.[1]

The younger Tryphon reappears in the paper record in his early teens, having reached the age of 14, the beginning of his life as a taxpayer; in AD 23 he duly paid poll-tax, pig-tax and dyke-tax from his home in the Hippodrome quarter of the city.[2] As a weaver, he needed also to pay the special tax on weavers.[3] By AD 36 his father must be dead, for Tryphon appeared as his mother's legal guardian.[4] By AD 52, when he was 44, he qualified for an exemption, perhaps exemption from payment of poll-tax, the most fundamental of all, and this because of his medical condition, for which he had undergone an examination which involved travelling 250 miles to the capital Alexandria: he was now certified (in duplicate) to be 'affected by cataract and little-sighted'.[5] In AD 66 he apprenticed (to a weaver) his son Thoonis, who was then under 14, i.e. born when Tryphon was 44 or more.[6] That is the last we hear of him.

The family were professionals in a profession, weaving, for which

Egypt and especially Oxyrhynchos were famous. Tryphon's grandfather and father and two uncles were weavers; Tryphon himself and his younger brother Onnophris, Tryphon's sons Apion and Thoonis. They inherited their craft, but some of them (Onnophris and Thoonis) served apprenticeships outside the family, which will have refreshed their skills and extended their circle.[7] Tryphon's impaired vision did not end his career, at least as overseer. Two years after his medical, we find him buying another loom, 'four feet wide, with two cross-pieces and two uprights', at a cost of 20 drachmas.[8] Tryphon was a careful man, who paid his taxes (sometimes in arrears), and paid them through a bank. He lent and borrowed money in relatively small sums; the transactions were carefully documented (even the loan of 16 drachmas to his mother),[9] and the loans were duly repaid. Some borrowings, it seems, served to top up his capital, which he then invested in house-property.[10] A sober life, which would not appeal to everyone. His younger brother, another Thoonis, so their mother informed the authorities on 7 January AD 44, had 'withdrawn to foreign parts' (i.e. left his registered domicile in Oxyrhynchos). Thoonis is described as 'having no trade' – the playboy, it seems, among so many artisans, and footloose as well.[11]

A provident artisan must be in need of a wife, and by the age of 25 or so Tryphon was duly married, to a woman called Demetrous. Here, however, providence let him down. Demetrous left him, in circumstances which led him to denounce her to the nearest authority, the strategos Alexandros. 'I married Demetrous daughter of Herakleides, and I for my part provided for her suitably, even beyond my means. But she took a hostile attitude to our marriage and in the end went off, and they took away our property of which a detailed list follows below. Therefore I ask that she should be brought before you so that she can get her deserts and give me back our property. As for my other claims against her, I stick to them and shall stick to them. Goodbye! List of items stolen: a [. . .] worth 40 drachmas . . .'[12]

Tryphon was not deterred by this experience. He was now living, in an 'unwritten marriage', with a woman called Saraeus. On 22 May AD 37 they formalised this by a nuptial agreement, under which Saraeus lent Tryphon 40 drachmas in cash and 32 drachmas in goods (a pair of gold earrings and a milk-white tunic), a kind of provisional dowry which would be returned if the pair separated and especially if they separated when Saraeus was pregnant.[13] In fact she was pregnant. Only six weeks later Demetrous reappeared, with her mother, as Tryphon complained to the strategos: 'At a rather late hour on the tenth of the present month Epeiph of the 1st year of Gaius Caesar Augustus [4 July AD 37], these women, Thenamounis . . . and her daughter Demetrous, who have absolutely no grievance with me or with my wife Saraeus, confronted her without any reason and attacked her although she was pregnant . . . blows. . . miscarriage . . .'[14]

Saraeus bore him two sons and a daughter, but even then the family had its problems. The elder son, Apion, born perhaps on 3 January 46 (if the horoscope belongs to him) became the object of a court case. A certain Pesouris had picked up a foundling, as often happened, and needed a wet-nurse to rear him; that wet-nurse was Saraeus (it seems that they needed the money). One of the two nurslings died. Saraeus maintained that it was the foundling, Pesouris claimed that it was Apion, and consequently that the surviving child belonged to him. And so, on 29 March AD 49, the case came before the strategos of the Oxyrhynchite, whose official journal recorded the hearing; and he decided, without resorting to Solomon's tactic, 'since the child seems from his looks to be Saraeus's', in favour of Tryphon.[15] However, Pesouris persisted, indeed in such a way that Tryphon, or so he claimed, was impeded in his normal business. There was nothing for it but to go to the top: and so within a year Tryphon was setting out his case to the Prefect himself: Pesouris (now by his Greek name Syros) 'refused to abide by the verdict but also slows me down in my work as an artisan; therefore I turn to you, our saviour, so that I can obtain justice'.[16] Apparently Tryphon won, though that did not end their difficulties. On 7 November 50 he reports to the authorities that a group of women had attacked them and inflicted several blows on them, so that Saraeus, pregnant again, was confined to her bed in critical condition.[17] Apion survived: in AD 56, by now ten years old, he is found paying tax as an apprentice weaver.[18] Ten years later, his younger brother Thoonis was also apprenticed as a weaver. The family firm was back in action.

Tryphon and his family lived, as all Oxyrhynchites did, in three overlapping worlds.

The oldest was the Egyptian world: partly physical, for no one in Egypt can ignore the geographical constraints of the Nile valley and the all-determining influence of the annual flood, but partly also cultural – the local gods, the ancient wisdom. They dated years by the Roman Emperor in power, but months generally went by their old Egyptian names; business documents adopted the Julian calendar, recently imported by the Romans, but Tryphon's astrologer and his colleagues, despite their reliance on Greek science, continued to use the old Egyptian calendar, which they judged more authentic when it came to exploring the secrets of the stars. Tryphon himself carried a Greek name, derived from Tryphe, the goddess of luxury, but his two brothers had Egyptian names: Onnophris (a title of the resurrected Osiris) and Thoonis (in honour of the falcon god). Such people might despise the 'rustic Egyptians', the native fellahin of the surrounding villages. But they would continue to worship Thoeris, the hippopotamus, and to seek divine guidance through oracles in the Egyptian tradition. The Nile dominated; the festivities that celebrated its rising, and the hymns which accompanied them, formed a continuous tradition that survived all changes of regime and religion, from the pharaohs to the Roman emperors to the Ottoman sultans, from paganism to Christianity to Islam.

Then there is the Greek world, to which Tryphon owed his name and the Hippodrome near which he was born. Greek was the language in which he thought and did business; also the language in which he was illiterate. Greek remained the language of government even at the court of the Roman conquerors. His market town called itself the City of the Sharp-nosed Fish. 'City' is *polis*, the proud Hellenic term for a city-state; 'sharp-nosed' is the Greek name for the Egyptian fish which had been sacred long before the arrival of the Greeks. In this town he held rank, classified as a 'metropolite', the lower of the two classes of citizen who were privileged to pay a reduced rate of poll-tax. It shared Greek customs, like that of exposing unwanted babies, which Pesouris and his kind could own at will. It boasted Greek institutions, like the Gymnasium and the Theatre, and called its magistrates by Greek titles. Among Tryphon's fellow citizens were and would be those who had deeper roots in the Hellenic inheritance: the schoolboys translating Homer, the distressed seeking enlightenment in the Homer Oracle, the collectors of classical poetry and the amateur composers of classicising verses.

Finally there is the Roman world. The Romans had taken Egypt some forty years before Tryphon's birth. Tryphon's documents were dated by the Roman Emperor and it was to the Roman Prefect that he appealed against Pesouris. Here and there the culture of the victors makes itself felt: the city will build itself a Capitol, a Temple of Caesar, and several public baths. Egypt had some experience of belonging to a larger empire, but this was a very large empire with a very absent sovereign. Citizens of Oxyrhynchos flocked to celebrate the rare imperial visit; otherwise they continued to pray for the Emperor and his Eternal Victory, though many of those victories were won two thousand miles away, on the Rhine or the Danube. Taxes were paid, to feed the city of Rome; oxen were requisitioned, to support Roman wars with Persia. Rome commanded the deletion of Geta from the record, and Oxyrhynchite clerks hastened to obey.

Not that the Roman rulers changed fundamentally the administrative system they found; indeed, they would have had nothing with which to replace it, since the Roman republic had not developed full-scale bureaucratic structures. In fact, it was the converse: as the Roman Empire developed, under increasing despotism and the needs of total war, it too adopted an elaborate hierarchical bureaucracy of which Egypt and the other kingdoms of the Near East had provided early exemplars. Egypt remained nominally outside the system, with its own coinage and its own dating, until Diocletian began the push to integration which sought to corset the sagging Empire in enforced uniformity.

But even before that Egypt had come closer to Rome. Egyptians (at least Greek Egyptians) became Roman citizens in AD 212, and that encouraged the likes of Lollianos to appeal unto Caesar. Alexandrian aristocrats no longer appeared as 'pagan martyrs' at open war with Roman emperors. In the same year 212 an 'Egyptian' became, for the first time, a member of the Roman senate. For most people, nonetheless, Rome remained a distant vision, yet its Emperor was everywhere – pictured as Pharaoh on the wall of the new temples that he commissioned; pictured as Hellenic monarch on coins and in patriotic portraits and in the busts carried in procession. An absent god, but a god; much as a Siberian peasant might acknowledge the benevolent authority of the Little Father in St Petersburg.

The Oxyrhynchos of Tryphon survived and flourished. In the third century AD a new ambition and independence made it the Glorious and Most Glorious City which hosted the games of AD 273. It continued to survive and flourish well into the Middle Ages, though the world changed around it. The Roman Empire gave way to the Christian Empire of Byzantium, then to the Islamic Empire of the Caliphate and the regimes that followed. The Hellenic inheritance lost ground, practically and culturally. In the new Christian world, the Church adopted Coptic, the late form of the native Egyptian language, as the vehicle of Scripture and liturgy; in the new Islamic province, Arabic soon took over as the language of government. Egypt itself remained untouched: the fields and the peasants, flood and harvest, the eternal problems of scratching a living and (of concern to pagan, Christian and Islamic magic alike) keeping bugs out of the house.

At some stage the Glorious and Most Glorious City dwindled into a village. When Napoleon's surveyors arrived, they found a site made picturesque only by palm trees, one lone ancient column, and a series of mounds. These mounds preserved, as it turned out, the entire history of the city: not through ruined buildings, but through its intact salvage. When Grenfell and Hunt began to dig el-Behnesa, in 1897, they found a time-capsule of a very special kind. Pompeii preserves a snapshot of Roman life, as it was on one catastrophic day, the buildings and the bodies of those who lived there. Oxyrhynchos offers the converse: not bodies or buildings, but the paper-trail (a trail of paper thrown away by its owners) of a whole culture.

Oxyrhynchos exists again today as a waste-paper city, a virtual landscape which we can repopulate with living and speaking people. The theatre has vanished, but we still have some of the prompt-copies that its actors used. The baths have vanished, but we can reconstruct their dynasty of cloakroom attendants. The market has vanished, but we know its porridge-stall and its imported cow-pats and the harrassed officials who collected the tax on brothels. Long-dead citizens, of whom we have no portrait and no tombstone, communicate from their documents. For some we have enough for a soap-opera: Tryphon the weaver and his wives, Lollianos the school-master and his war with the town council, the public duties and private poetry of Sarapion-Apollonianos and his clan. For others, there is a single glimpse: Senthonis with her pillow-case full of dates, Serenos whose wife sent him 'letters that could shake a stone', the reluctant Mayor who has an illness and coughs from his lungs.

Egypt had always been concerned with immortality, and some at least of its Greeks adopted mummification, a practical way of securing an existence after death both in this world and in the next. Christianity, as it spread through the country, seemed to offer something simpler and better: the life everlasting, and then the resurrection of the body. The citizens of the Sharp-nosed Fish will have shared this concern for their own survival. In the event, their memory does survive – survives, by a strange irony, precisely through the written material that they threw away. Tryphon and countless others lived and died without ever knowing that they were destined to such accidental immortality.

BIBLIOGRAPHY

(I) PUBLICATIONS OF PAPYRUS TEXTS

The principal relevant publication is the series *The Oxyrhynchus Papyri*, vols. I–LXX, London 1898–2006. **Documents published there are referred to simply by volume and item-number**, for example '42.3052' = *The Oxyrhynchus Papyri*, vol. XLII, no. 3052.

Other publications of papyri are quoted by the standard abbreviations, 'P.Amh.' = *The Amherst Papyri*, P.Wisc. = *The Wisconsin Papyri* and the like. For a key to these abbreviations, see John F. Oates and others, *Checklist of editions of Greek, Latin, Demotic and Coptic papyri, ostraca and tablets*, fifth edition, Bulletin of the American Society of Papyrologists, Supplement 9, 2001; a continually updated version can be found at http://scriptorium.lib.duke.edu/papyrus/texts/clist.html. Readers may find it easier to access the online version by link from (for example) the website of the Association internationale de papyrologues or the American Society of Papyrologists.

Sometimes the text or interpretation of the document has been corrected since the first publication: in such cases I add a reference of the type 'BL 7', the relevant volume or volumes in the series *Berichtigungsliste der griechischen Papyrusurkunden aus Ägypten*, vols. I–XI (I Berlin/Leipzig 1922; II Heidelberg 1933; III–XI Leiden 1958–2002).

Sometimes the text of a papyrus can be found more conveniently in an anthology. Such anthologies are quoted by abbreviated title, see section (ii).

(II) ANTHOLOGIES OF PAPYRUS TEXTS

In these, the number indicates the number of the item, not of the page: e.g. NPP 39 = New Papyrological Primer text no. 39.

GDRK   E. Heitsch, *Die griechischen Dichterfragmente der römischen Kaiserzeit* (vol. I, 2nd edn, Göttingen 1963).

GLP   D. L. Page, *Select Papyri III: Literary Papyri, Poetry* (Loeb series) (London and Cambridge, MA 1942).

Hengstl   J. Hengstl, *Griechische Papyri aus Ägypten als Zeugnisse des öffentlichen und privaten Lebens* (Darmstadt 1978).

M.Chr.   L. Mitteis and U. Wilcken, *Grundzüge und Chrestomathie der Papyrus-*

kunde, vol. II, *Juristischer Teil*, part 2, *Chrestomathie* (Leipzig/Berlin 1912).

MZ   Livia Migliardi Zingale, *Vita privata e vita pubblica nei papiri d'Egitto* (Turin 1992).

Naldini   Mario Naldini, *Il cristianesimo in Egitto: lettere private nei papiri dei secoli II–IV*, Nuova edizione ampliata e aggiornata (Fiesole 1998).

NPP   P. W. Pestman, *The New Papyrological Primer* (2nd edn, Leiden 1994).

Rowlandson   Jane Rowlandson, ed., *Women and Society in Greek and Roman Egypt* (Cambridge 1998).

SP   A. S. Hunt and C. C. Edgar, *Select Papyri*, vols. I–II (Loeb series) (London and Cambridge 1932, 1934).

Tibiletti   Giuseppe Tibiletti, *Le lettere private nei papiri greci del III e IV secolo d. C.* (Milan 1979).

W.Chr.   L. Mitteis and U. Wilcken, *Grundzüge und Chrestomathie der Papyruskunde*, vol. I, *Historischer Teil*, part 2, *Chrestomathie* (Leipzig/Berlin 1912).

(III) CLASSICAL AUTHORS

In citing ancient Greek and Latin writers I have used the standard forms of their names and works, for which see for example Liddell-Scott-Jones, *Greek Lexicon* (9th edn) and *The Oxford Latin Dictionary*.

(IV) JOURNALS CITED BY ABBREVIATED TITLE

Aeg.   *Aegyptus*

AJP   *American Journal of Philology*

APF   *Archiv für Papyrusforschung*

CdÉ   *Chronique d'Égypte*

JEA   *Journal of Egyptian Archaeology*

JJP   *Journal of Juristic Papyrology*

JRS   *Journal of Roman Studies*

ZPE   *Zeitschrift für Papyrologie und Epigraphik*

(V) BOOKS AND ARTICLES CITED

Adams (2003)   J. N. Adams, *Bilingualism and the Latin Language* (Cambridge).

Alston (2002)   Richard Alston, *The City in Roman and Byzantine Egypt* (London and New York).

ANRW   H. Temporini, ed., *Aufstieg und Niedergang der römischen Welt* (Berlin and New York).

ArchRep   Egypt Exploration Fund, Archaeological Reports (London 1891–1909).

Aurigemma (1960)   S. Aurigemma, *L'Italia in Africa I* (Rome).

Bagnall (1985)   Roger S. Bagnall, *Currency and Inflation in Fourth Century Egypt*. BASP Supplement 5 (Chico, CA).

Bagnall (1992)   R. S. Bagnall, 'An Owner of Literary Papyri', *Classical Philology* 87: 137–40.

Bagnall (1993)   R. S. Bagnall, *Egypt in Late Antiquity* (Princeton).

Bagnall (1995)   Roger S. Bagnall, *Reading Papyri, Writing Ancient History* (London).

Bagnall and Frier (1994)   Roger S. Bagnall and Bruce W. Frier, *The Demography of Roman Egypt* (Cambridge).

Bagnall and Rathbone (2004)   Roger S. Bagnall and Dominic W. Rathbone, *Egypt from Alexander to the Copts* (London).

Baikie (1924)   James Baikie, *A Century of Excavation in the Land of the Pharaohs* (London).

Battaglia (1989)   Emanuela Battaglia, '*Artos*': *Il lessico della panificazione nei papiri greci* (Milan).

Bauman (1967)   Richard A. Bauman, *The Crimen Maiestatis in the Roman Republic and Augustan Principate* (Johannesburg).

Beard (1991)   M. Beard and others, *Literacy in the Roman World* (Ann Arbor).

Bergamasco (1995)   Marco Bergamasco, 'Le didaskalikai nella ricerca attuale', *Aeg.* 75: 95–167.

Bernand (1960)   A. and E. Bernand, *Les Inscriptions grecques et latines du Colosse de Memnon* (Cairo).

Bianchi (1983)   A. Bianchi, 'Aspetti della politica economico-fiscale di Filippo l'Arabo', *Aeg.* 63: 185–98.

Bing (2002)   P. Bing, 'Medeios of Olynthos, Son of Lampon, and the Iamatika of Posidippus', *ZPE* 140: 297–300.

Bingen (1956)   J. Bingen, 'Les Papyrus de la Fondation Égyptologique Reine Élisabeth XIV: Declaration pour l'épicrisis', *CdÉ* 31: 109–17.

Bingen (1970)   J. Bingen, 'Note sur l'éphébie en Égypte romaine', *CdÉ* 45: 356.

Biscottini (1966)   M. V. Biscottini, 'L'archivio di Tryphon, tessitore di Oxyrhynchos', *Aeg.* 46: 60–90 and 186–292.

BL   see above, section (I).

Bogaert (1994)   R. Bogaert, *Trapezitica Aegyptiaca* (Florence).

Bogaert (1995)   R. Bogaert, 'Liste géographique des banques et des banquiers de l'Égypte romaine, 30ᵃ–284', *ZPE* 109: 151–7.

Bonneau (1964)   D. Bonneau, *La Crue du Nil, divinité Égyptienne* (Paris).

Bonneau (1971)   D. Bonneau, *Le Fisc et le Nil* (Paris).

Bonneau (1993)   D. Bonneau, *Le Régime administratif de l'eau du Nil dans l'Égypte grecque, romaine et byzantine* (Leiden).

Bowman (1971)   A. K. Bowman, *The Town Councils of Roman Egypt* (American Studies in Papyrology 11) (Toronto).

Bowman (1996)   Alan K. Bowman, *Egypt after the Pharaohs* (2nd edn, London).

Bowman and Rogan (1999)   A. K. Bowman and E. Rogan (eds), *Agriculture in Egypt* (Oxford).

Bowman and Woolf (1994)   A. K. Bowman and G. Woolf (eds), *Literacy and Power* (Cambridge).

Bowman et al. (2007)   A. K. Bowman et al. (eds), *Oxyrhynchus: a City and its Texts* (London).

Brennan (1998)   T. Corey Brennan, 'The poets Julia Balbilla and Damo at the colossus of Memnon', *Classical World* 91.5: 215–34.

Brosius (2003)   M. Brosius (ed.), *Ancient Archives* (Oxford).

Burkhalter (1990)   F. Burkhalter, 'Archives locales et archives centrales en Égypte romaine', *Chiron* 20: 191–215.

Cameron (1965)   A. Cameron, 'Wandering Poets', *Historia* 14: 470–509.

Caminos (1954)   R. Caminos, *Late-Egyptian Miscellanies* (Oxford).

Casanova (1984)   Gerardo Casanova, 'La peste nella documentazione greca d'Egitto', *Atti del XVII Congresso Internazionale di Papirologia* 3: 949–56 (Naples).

Casson (1995)   L. Casson, *Ships and Seamanship in the Ancient World* (reprint with addenda and corrigenda) (Baltimore and London).

Cavallo (1965)   G. Cavallo, 'La scrittura del P. Berol. 11532: contributo allo studio dello stile di cancelleria nei papiri greci di età Romana', *Aeg.* 45: 216–49.

Chadwick (1993)   Henry Chadwick, *The Early Church* (2nd edn, London).

Chalon (1964)   G. Chalon, *L'Édit de Tiberius Julius Alexander* (Olten and Lausanne).

Chapa (1998)   J. Chapa, *Letters of condolence on Greek papyri* (*Papyrologica Florentina* 29) (Florence).

Chouliara-Raiou (1989)   Hélène Chouliara-Raiou, *L'Abeille et le miel en Égypte d'après les papyrus grecs* (Ioannina).

Chouliara-Raiou (2003)   Hélène Chouliara-Raiou, *Hê halieia stên Aigypto hypo to phôs tôn hellênikôn papyrôn* (Ioannina).

Cockle (1981)   H. M. Cockle, 'Pottery Manufacture in Roman Egypt: a New Papyrus', *JRS* 71: 87–97.

Cockle (1984)   W. E. H. Cockle, 'State archives in Graeco-roman Egypt', *JEA* 70: 106–22.

Cohen (1931)   D. Cohen, 'La Papyrologie dans les Pays-Bas', *CdÉ* 6: 408.

Crawford (1973)   Dorothy Crawford, 'Garlic-Growing and Agricultural Specialisation in Graeco-Roman Egypt', *CdÉ* 48: 350–63.

Cribiore (1995)   R. Cribiore, 'A Hymn to the Nile', *ZPE* 106: 97–106.

Cribiore (1996)   R. Cribiore, *Writing, Teachers, and Students in Graeco-Roman Egypt* (Atlanta).

Cribiore (2001)   R. Cribiore, *Gymnastics of the Mind: Greek Education in Hellenistic and Roman Egypt* (Princeton).

Cubberley (1985)   A. L. Cubberley, 'Bread-baking in Roman Italy', in Wilkins et al. (1985) 55–68.

Cugusi (1992)   P. Cugusi, *Corpus Epistolarum Latinarum* (Florence).

Curl (2005)   James Stevens Curl, *The Egyptian Revival* (3rd edn, London).

Daris (2003)   Sergio Daris, ed., *Dizionario dei nomi geografici e topografici dell'Egitto greco-romano. Supplemento 3* (Pisa).

Dietz (1986)   K. Dietz, 'Ein neuer Meilenstein aus dem Jahre 201 n.Chr. aus Kösching', *Das archäologische Jahr in Bayern* 1985: 110–11.

Doxiadis (1995)   E. Doxiadis, *The Mysterious Fayum Portraits* (London).

Eliott (1993)   J. K. Elliott, *The Apocryphal New Testament* (Oxford).

Empereur (1998)   J.-Y. Empereur, *Alexandria Rediscovered* (London).

Fichman (1971)   I. F. Fichman, 'Die Bevölkerungszahl von Oxyrhynchos in byzantinischer Zeit', *APF* 21: 111–20.

Frankfurter (1998)   David Frankfurter, *Religion in Roman Egypt* (Princeton).

Frisch (1986)   Peter Frisch, *Zehn agonistische Papyri* (Opladen).

Funghi and Messeri (1992a)   M. S. Funghi and G. Messeri Savorelli, 'Note papirologiche e paleografiche', *Tyche* 7: 75–88.

Funghi and Messeri (1992b)   M. S. Funghi and G. Messeri Savorelli, 'Lo "Scriba di Pindaro" e le Biblioteche di Ossirinco', *Studi classici e orientali* 42: 43–62.

Gamble (1995)   H. Gamble, *Books and Readers in the Early Church* (New Haven and London).

Gamer-Wallert (1970)   Ingrid Gamer-Wallert, *Fische und Fischkulte im Alten Ägypten* (Wiesbaden).

Garbrecht (1996)   G. Garbrecht, 'Historical Water Storage for Irrigation in the Fayum Depression (Egypt)', *Irrigation and Drainage Systems*, vol. 10, no. 1: 47–76.

Gardiner (1961)   Sir Alan Gardiner, *Egypt of the Pharaohs* (Oxford).

GLH   C. H. Roberts, *Greek Literary Hands 350 BC–AD 400* (Oxford 1955).

GMAW²   E. G. Turner, *Greek Manuscripts of the Ancient World* (2nd edn, London 1987).

Goddio (1998)   F. Goddio, *Alexandria. The Submerged Royal Quarter* (London).

Goodman (1997)   Martin Goodman, *The Roman World 44 BC–AD 180* (London).

Gordon (1983)   Arthur E. Gordon, *Illustrated Introduction to Latin Epigraphy* (Berkeley).

Gullini (1956)   G. Gullini, *I mosaici di Palestrina* (Rome).

Habermann (2000)   W. Habermann, *Zur Wasserversorgung einer Metropole im kaiserzeitlichen Ägypten* (Munich).

Haensch (1994)   R. Haensch, 'Die Bearbeitungsweisen von Petitionen in der Provinz Aegyptus', *ZPE* 100: 487–546.

Hardy (1952)   Edward R. Hardy, *Christian Egypt: Church and People* (New York).

Harris (1989)   W. V. Harris, *Ancient Literacy* (Cambridge, MA).

Hawass (2000)   Zahi A. Hawass, *The Valley of the Golden Mummies* (London).

Heinen (1991)   H. Heinen, 'Herrscherkult im römischen Ägypten und damnatio memoriae Getas', *Mitteilungen des deutschen archäologischen Instituts (Römische Abteilung)* 98: 263–98.

Hendriks et al. (1981)   I. H. M. Hendriks, P. J. Parsons, K. A. Worp, 'Papyri from the Groningen Collection I', *ZPE* 41: 71–83.

Henrichs (1973)   A. Henrichs, 'Zwei Orakelfragen', *ZPE* 11: 115–19.

Hombert and Préaux (1952)   Marcel Hombert and Claire Préaux, *Recherches sur le recensement dans l'Égypte romaine* (Leiden).

Husselman (1951)   Elinor M. Husselman, 'Two Customs House Receipts from Egypt', *Transactions of the American Philological Association* 82: 164–7.

Husson (1983)   Geneviève Husson, OIKIA. *Le Vocabulaire de la maison privée en Égypte d'après les papyrus grecs* (Paris).

James (1982)   T. G. H. James (ed.), *Excavating in Egypt* (London).

Johnson (1936)   Allan Chester Johnson, *Roman Egypt to the reign of Diocletian* (An Economic Survey of Ancient Rome, ed. Tenney Frank, vol. 2) (Baltimore).

Johnson (2000)   W. A. Johnson, 'Towards a Sociology of Reading in Classical Antiquity', *AJP* 121: 593–627.

Johnson (2004)   William A. Johnson, *Bookrolls and Scribes in Oxyrhynchus* (Toronto).

Kaiser (1994)   F. Kaiser, *Recueil des inscriptions grecques et latines (non funéraires) d'Alexandrie impériale* (Cairo).

Kaster (1988)   Robert A. Kaster, *Guardians of Language: the Grammarian and Society in Late Antiquity* (Berkeley).

Kennedy (2004)   Hugh Kennedy, *The Court of the Caliphs* (London).

Keyes (1935)   C. W. Keyes, 'The Greek Letter of Introduction', *AJP* 56: 28–44.

Kienast (1996)   D. Kienast, *Römische Kaisertabelle* (2nd edn, Darmstadt).

Koenen (1968)   L. Koenen, 'Die Prophezeiungen des "Töpfers"', *ZPE* 2: 178–209.

Koskenniemi (1956)   H. Koskenniemi, *Studien zur Idee und Phraseologie des griechischen Briefes bis 400 n. Chr* (Helsinki).

Krüger (1990)   J. Krüger, *Oxyrhynchos in der Kaiserzeit. Studien zur Topographie und Literaturrezeption* (Bern, Frankfurt, New York and Paris).

Kuhlmann (1994)   P. A. Kuhlmann, *Die Giessener literarischen Papyri und die Caracalla-Erlasse* (Giessen).

Laks and Most (1997)   A. Laks and G. W. Most, eds, *Studies on the Derveni Papyrus* (Oxford).

Lama (1991)   M. Lama, 'Aspetti di tecnica libraria ad Ossirinco: copie letterarie su rotoli documentari', *Aeg.* 71: 55–120.

Lane (1836)   E. W. Lane, *An Account of the Manners and Customs of the Modern Egyptians* (London).

Lauffer (1971)   Siegfried Lauffer, *Diokletians Preisedikt* (Berlin).

Lehnus (2007)   L. Lehnus, 'Bernard Pyne Grenfell and Arthur Surridge Hunt,' in M. Capasso (ed.), *Hermae: Scholars and Scholarship in Papyrology* (Pisa).

Lembke (2004)   K. Lembke, *Ägyptens späte Blüte* (Mainz).

Lewis (1974)   N. Lewis, *Papyrus in Classical Antiquity* (Oxford).

Lewis (1983)   Naphtali Lewis, *Life in Egypt under Roman Rule* (Oxford).

Lewis (1997)   N. Lewis, *The Compulsory Public Services of Roman Egypt* (2nd edn, Florence).

Lührmann (2000)   D. Lührmann, *Fragmente apokryph gewordener Evangelien* (Marburg).

Łukaszewicz (1986)   A. Łukaszewicz, *Les édifices publiques dans les villes de l'Égypte romaine: Problèmes administratifs et financiers* (Warsaw).

Łukaszewicz (1992)   A. Łukaszewicz, 'Antoninus the κόρυφος (Note on P.Oxy. XLVI 3298.2)', *JJP* 22: 43–6.

Łukaszewicz (1994)   Adam Łukaszewicz, 'ΟΝΗΣΙΣ ΑΠΟ ΒΙΒΛΙΩΝ', *JJP* 24: 97–103.

Maehler (1983)   Herwig Maehler, 'Häuser und ihre Bewohner im Fayûm in der Kaiserzeit', in Günter Grimm et al., (eds), *Das römisch-byzantinische Ägypten* (Mainz 1983), 119–37.

Malherbe (1988)   A. J. Malherbe, *Ancient epistolary theorists* (Atlanta).

Maltomini (1995)   F. Maltomini, 'P.Lond. 121 (= PGM VII), 1–221: Homer-omanteion', *ZPE* 106: 107–22.

Meyboom (1995)   P. G. P. Meyboom, *The Nile Mosaic of Palestrina* (Leiden).

Meyer-Termeer (1978)   A. Meyer-Termeer, *Die Haftung der Schiffer im grie-chischen und römischen Recht* (Zutphen).

Millar (1977)   Fergus Millar, *The Emperor in the Roman World* (London).

Milne (1908)   J. G. Milne, 'Relics of Graeco-Egyptian Schools', *Journal of Hellenic Studies* 28: 121–32.

Montserrat (1996)   Dominic Montserrat, *Sex and Society in Graeco-Roman Egypt* (London and New York).

Montserrat (2007)   D. Montserrat, 'The Digs at Oxyrhynchus and their Journ-alistic Coverage', in Bowman et al. (2007).

Morgan (1998)   Teresa Morgan, *Literate Education in the Hellenistic and Roman Worlds* (Cambridge).

M-P³   [list of all literary papyri recovered in Egypt by author and genre] http://promethee.philo.ulg.ac.be/cedopal/index.htm

Musurillo (1954)   H. Musurillo, *The Acts of the Pagan Martyrs* (Oxford).

Musurillo (1962)   H. Musurillo, *Acta Alexandrinorum* (Leipzig).

Neugebauer and van Hoesen (1959)   O. Neugebauer and H. B. van Hoesen, *Greek Horoscopes* (Philadelphia).

OGIS   W. Dittenberger (ed.), *Orientis Graecae Inscriptiones Selectae*, 2 vols. (Leipzig 1903, 1905).

Ohly (1928)   K. Ohly, *Stichometrische Untersuchungen* (Leipzig).

Osley (1980)   A. S. Osley, *Scribes and Sources* (London).

Otranto (2000)   R. Otranto, *Antiche liste di libri su papiro* (Rome).

Papini (1990)   Lucia Papini, 'Struttura e prassi delle domande oracolari su papiro', *Analecta Papyrologica* 2: 11–20.

Parássoglou (1979)   G. M. Parássoglou, 'ΔΕΞΙΑ ΧΕΙΡ ΚΑΙ ΓΟΝΥ', *Scrittura e Civiltà* 3: 5–21.

Parsons (1967)   P. J. Parsons, 'Philippus Arabs and Egypt', *JRS* 57: 134–41.

Pearson and Goehring (1986)   Birger A. Pearson and James E. Goehring (eds), *The Roots of Egyptian Christianity* (Philadelphia).

Perpillou-Thomas (1992)   F. Perpillou-Thomas, 'Une bouillie de céréales: l'athèra', *Aeg.* 72: 103–10.

PGM   K. Preisendanz, ed., *Papyri Graecae Magicae*, 2 vols., rev. A. Henrichs (Stuttgart 1973–4).

Poll (1996)   I. J. Poll, 'Ladefähigkeit und Grösse der Nilschiffe', *APF* 42/1: 127–38.

Potter (1990)   D. S. Potter, *Prophecy and History* (Oxford).

Potter (2004)   David S. Potter, *The Roman Empire at Bay* (London and New York).

Quirke (2004)   Stephen Quirke, *Egyptian Literature 1800 BC: Questions and Read-ings* (London).

Rathbone (1986)   D. W. Rathbone, 'The Dates of the Recognition in Egypt of the Emperors from Caracalla to Diocletianus', *ZPE* 62: 101–29.

Rathbone (1990)   D. W. Rathbone, 'Village, Land and Population in Graeco-Roman Egypt', *Proceedings of the Cambridge Philological Society* (n.s.) 36: 103–42.

Rathbone (1991)   Dominic Rathbone, *Economic Rationalism and Rural Society in Third-century AD Egypt* (Cambridge).

Rea (1971)   John R. Rea, 'Notes on some IIId and IVth century documents', *CdE* 46: 142–57.

Rea (1989)   J. R. Rea, 'On κηρυκίνη', *ZPE* 79: 201–6.

Rea (1993)   J. R. Rea, 'A Student's Letter to his Father: P.Oxy. XVIII 2190 Revised', *ZPE* 99: 75–88.

Reinhart (1998)   Peter Reinhart, *Crust and Crumb* (Berkeley).

Riggs (2005)   Christina Riggs, *The Beautiful Burial in Roman Egypt* (Oxford).

Roberts (1979)   C. H. Roberts, *Manuscript, Society and Belief in Early Christian Egypt* (London).

Roberts and Skeat (1983)   C. H. Roberts and T. C. Skeat, *The Birth of the Codex* (Oxford).

Roca-Puig (1965)   R. Roca-Puig, *Himne a la Verge Maria* (2nd edn, Barcelona).

Roca-Puig (1977)   R. Roca-Puig, *Cicero. Catilinàries (I et II in Cat.). Papyri Barcinonenses* (Barcelona).

Roca-Puig (1994)   R. Roca-Puig, *Anàfora de Barcelona: i altres pregàries (Missa del segle IV)*, (3rd edn, Barcelona).

Roca-Puig (2000)   R. Roca-Puig, *Alcestis. Hexàmetres Llatins* (2nd edn, Barcelona).

Saenger (1997)   Paul Saenger, *Space between Words: the Origins of Silent Reading* (Stanford).

Sauneron (1952)   S. Sauneron, 'Les querelles impériales vues à travers les scènes du Temple d'Esné', *Bulletin de l'Institut français d'archéologie orientale* 51: 115–21.

Sauneron (1975)   S. Sauneron, *Le Temple d'Esna* 6.1 (Cairo).

Shipley (2000)   Graham Shipley, *The Greek World after Alexander* (London and New York).

Sijpesteijn (1969)   P. J. Sijpesteijn, 'A New Document Concerning Hadrian's Visit to Egypt', *Historia* 18: 109–18.

Sijpesteijn (1979)   P. J. Sijpesteijn, 'A Scribe at Work', *Bulletin of the American Society of Papyrologists* 16: 277–80.

Skeat (1978)   T. C. Skeat, 'A Table of Isopsephisms', *ZPE* 31: 45–54.

Skeat (1982)   T. C. Skeat, 'The Length of the Standard Papyrus Roll and the Cost-Advantage of the Codex', *ZPE* 45: 169–75.

Skeat (1997)   T. C. Skeat, 'The Oldest Manuscript of the Four Gospels', *New Testament Studies* 43: 1–34.

SM   Robert W. Daniel and Franco Maltomini (eds), *Supplementum Magicum* I–II (Opladen 1990, 1992).

SNG von Auloc   (Hans von Aulock), *Sylloge Nummorum Graecorum, Deutschland*: Sammlung von Aulock (Berlin 1957–81).

Stanton (1984)   G. R. Stanton, 'The Proposed Earliest Christian Letter on Papyrus', *ZPE* 54: 49–63.

Stanton (2004)   G. R. Stanton, *Jesus and Gospel* (Cambridge).

Steinby (1994)   E. M. Steinby, *Lexicon Topographicum Urbis Romae* I (Rome).

Stewart (2001)   Randall Stewart, *Sortes Astrampsychi* II (Stuttgart (Teubner)).

Tacoma (2006)   Laurens E. Tacoma, *Fragile Hierarchies. The Urban Élites of Third-century Roman Egypt* (Leiden and Boston).

Taubenschlag (1955)   Raphael Taubenschlag, *The Law of Greco-Roman Egypt* (Warsaw).

Thiede (1995)   C. P. Thiede, 'Papyrus Magdalen Greek 17 (Gregory-Aland Π^{64}): a Reappraisal', *ZPE* 105: 13–20.

Thomas (1975)   J. D. Thomas, 'The Introduction of Dekaprotoi and Comarchs into Egypt in the Third Century AD', *ZPE* 19: 111–17.

Thompson (1985)   Dorothy Thompson, 'Food for Ptolemaic Temple-workers', in Wilkins et al. (1985) 316–25.

Trapp (2003)   M. Trapp, *Greek and Latin Letters* (Cambridge).

Turner (1952)   E. G. Turner, 'Roman Oxyrhynchus', *JEA* 38: 78–93.

Turner (1974)   E. G. Turner, 'A Commander-in-chief's Order from Saqqara', *JEA* 60: 239–42.

Turner (1977)   E. G. Turner, *The Typology of the Early Codex* (Philadelphia).

Vandoni (1964)   Mariangela Vandoni, *Feste pubbliche e private nei documenti greci* (Milan).

van Haelst (1976)   Joseph van Haelst, *Catalogue des papyrus littéraires juifs et chrétiens* (Paris).

van Minnen (1986)   P. van Minnen, 'The Volume of the Oxyrhynchite Textile Trade', *Münstersche Beiträge zur antiken Handelsgeschichte* 5: 88–95.

van Rossum-Steenbeek (1998)   M. van Rossum-Steenbeek, *Greek Readers' Digests?* (Leiden).

Wallace (1938)   Sherman LeRoy Wallace, *Taxation in Egypt* (Princeton).

Whitehorne (1977)   J. Whitehorne, 'P.Oxy. XLIII 3119: A Document of Valerian's Persecution?', *ZPE* 24: 187–96.

Whitehorne (1984)   John E. G. Whitehorne, 'Tryphon's Second Marriage (P.Oxy. II 267)', *Atti del XVII Congresso Internazionale di Papirologia* 3: 1267–74 (Naples).

Whitehorne (1988)   J. E. G. Whitehorne, 'Recent Research on the Strategi of Roman Egypt (to 1985)', in *ANRW* 2.10.1.598–617.

Whitehorne (1995)   John Whitehorne, 'The Pagan Cults of Roman Oxyrhynchus', in *ANRW* 2.18.5.3050–91.

Wifstrand (1933)   A. Wifstrand, 'Ein metrischer Kolophon in einem Homerpapyrus', *Hermes* 68: 468–72.

Wilkins et al. (1985)   J. Wilkins et al. (eds), *Food in Antiquity* (Exeter).

Willcocks (1935)   Sir William Willcocks, *Sixty Years in the East* (Edinburgh and London).

Wilson (1988)   Hilary Wilson, *Egyptian Food and Drink* (Princes Risborough).

Wittfogel (1963)   Karl A. Wittfogel, *Oriental Despotism* (New Haven and London).

Wolff (1978)   Hans Julius Wolff, *Das Recht der griechischen Papyri Ägyptens*, II (Munich).

Youtie (1971a)   H. C. Youtie, 'βραδέως γράφων: Between Literacy and Illiteracy', *Greek, Roman and Byzantine Studies* 12: 239–261 (= id., *Scriptiunculae* 2.629–51, Amsterdam 1973).

Youtie (1971b)   H. C. Youtie, ''Αγράμματος: An Aspect of Greek Society in Egypt', *Harvard Studies in Classical Philology* 75: 161–76 (= id., *Scriptiunculae* 2.611–27, Amsterdam 1973).

Youtie (1975)   H. C. Youtie, 'ΥΠΟΓΡΑΦΕΥΣ: The Social Impact of Illiteracy in Graeco-Roman Egypt', *ZPE* 17: 201–21 (= id., *Scriptiunculae Posteriores* 1.179–99, Bonn 1981).

Youtie (1983)   L. C. Youtie, 'Lost Examples of ΕΞΟΠΤΟΣ', *ZPE* 50: 59–60.

Ziebarth (1913)   E. Ziebarth, *Aus der antiken Schule* (Bonn).

NOTES

CHAPTER 1: EXCAVATING EGYPT

Bibliography. On the origins of the Egypt Exploration Society see James (1982). For Egyptomania see Curl (2005).

1 *The Spectator* no. 1 (1 March 1711), quoted by Baikie (1924) 9.
2 Robert Southey, *Letters from England* (1807), Letter 71 (ed. Jack Simmons, London 1951, 449); Maria Edgeworth, *The Absentee* (1812), ch. ii (quoted on the website Egyptomania.org, © 2005 Noreen Doyle).
3 Quoted by James (1982) 14.
4 Gardiner (1961) 16.
5 *A Thousand Miles up the Nile*, 1891 edition, 353.

CHAPTER 2: A WEALTH OF GARBAGE

Bibliography. Grenfell and Hunt wrote their own accounts in the *Archaeological Reports*, *Egypt Exploration Fund*. For an outline of their campaigns see E. G. Turner, 'The Graeco-Roman Branch', in James (1982). For further documents and press reactions see Montserrat (2007). I am greatly indebted to these two essays, and to the Egypt Exploration Society for permission to quote relevant documents. For Grenfell and Hunt themselves see Lehnus (2007).

Sections of this chapter have already appeared in *TLS* (29 May 1998) and in *Omnibus*. I am grateful for permission to repeat them in revised form.

1 Kennedy (2004) 153.
2 Montserrat (2007).
3 Montserrat (2007).
4 *ArchRep* (1902/3) 6.
5 Montserrat (2007).
6 James (1982) 168.
7 Montserrat (2007).
8 Monserrat (2007).
9 James (1982) 168f.
10 *ArchRep* (1904/5) 13.
11 Bagnall and Rathbone (2004) 161. Bowman et al. (2007).
12 *The Shorter Poems, 1807–1820, by William Wordsworth*, ed. Carl H. Ketcham (Ithaca and London 1989) 286, lines 49–54.

13 SB 1.5124.
14 P.Lond.Lit. 28.
15 Montserrat (2007).
16 Ronald Firbank, *Vainglory* (1915) ch. 2.
17 Quoted in Cohen (1931) 408.
18 1.119.
19 Montserrat (2007).
20 *The Oxyrhynchus Papyri* vol. L p. vi.
21 2.299.3.
22 12.1488.24.
23 50.3530.

CHAPTER 3 : EGYPTIAN GREEKS

Bibliography. For a brilliant overview of Greek Egypt see Bowman (1996). For Egypt in the Hellenistic world see Shipley (2000). For a well-illustrated survey of Egypt in the Roman period see Lembke (2004). For an archaeological guide see Bagnall and Rathbone (2004). For structures of Egyptian life: Bagnall (1993).

1   Herodas 1.26–32.
2   Turner (1974).
3   Empereur (1998). Goddio (1998).
4   Theocritus 14.59.
5   Bing (2002).
6   14.1681.
7   Plutarch, *Moralia* 380B (*de Iside et Osiride* 72).
8   Doxiadis (1995) ill. 13–14 and p. 187. In general: Riggs (2005).
9   For these portraits and many more: Doxiadis (1995).
10 Lewis (1974).
11 Below, pp. 159–60.
12 Laks and Most (1997).
13 Theocritus 15.48.
14 Horace, *Odes* 1.37.
15 42.3061.
16 See chapter 5, n. 24.
17 Below, pp. 76–80.

CHAPTER 4: 'GLORIOUS AND MOST GLORIOUS CITY'

Bibliography. We have many details about the topography of Oxyrhynchos, but it has proved very difficult to construct a reliable map of the city from these and from the archaeological reports. See Turner (1952); Łukaszewicz (1986); Krüger (1990); Alston (2002); Daris (2003) 86–115; Bagnall and Rathbone (2004) 158–61. This chapter aims to depict the city in the late third century AD, but takes details also from earlier and later documents.

1 For the Games, see the documents collected by Frisch (1986).

2 Pausanias, in a hurry to take his son from Alexandria to Koptos, went by river: 14.1666 (SP 1.149; Tibiletti 3; MZ 93).

3 60.4087–8.

4 42.3052.

5 43.3111.12, 45.3250.22, P.Oxy.Hels. 37.6.

6 'Tomis': 10.1259.12; 22.2341.18; 51.3638.12; P.Gen. 2.116. 'Our river': 22.2341. Hydrography: Garbrecht (1996). Harbour: Krüger (1990) 107.

7 Plutarch, *de Iside et Osiride* 380B–C.

8 W.Chr. 474 [= 1.43 verso] v 1; PSI 8.955 (vi AD).

9 Gates: W.Chr. 474. Population (a difficult question): *c.*15,000 Alston (2002) 331–3; 20,000–25,000 Rathbone (1990) 120–1; 30,000 Fichman (1971) 114–16. Buildings: Krüger (1990) 101–9.

10 50.3555.

11 14.1773.40, 1678.28.

12 Krüger (1990) 82–8.

13 64.4441.

14 Krüger (1990) 101; Whitehorne (1995) 3078–9.

15 Wall: 2.242.14. Side-gate and sack-maker: 51.3642. Pylon and statue: 43.3094.44 (if this refers to Oxyrhynchos, not to Alexandria).

16 43.3094.43–4.

17 Whitehorne (1995) 3078ff.

18 SB 16.12695 (AD 143). P.Köln 5.228 (AD 176). Below, p. 104.

19 50.3567 (AD 252). On the cult: Whitehorne (1995) 3080–2.

20 P.Wisc. 1.3 (BL 6; 7).

21 W.Chr. 474 iv 14–23 (watchmen), 12 (columns).

22 8.1117 (AD 178) (BL 1; 3).

23 12.1550 (BL 4); 3.579; P.Rein. 2.93–4 (BL 4).

24 P.Köln 1.57, cf. 12.1484.

25 41.2976.

26 P.Heid. 4.334 (cf. P.Köln 6.279), with Rea (1989).

27 Whitehorne (1995).

28 17.2109.

29 45.3265 (P.Coll.Youtie 2.81) (*xystos*). P.Amh. 2.124, 10. 1266.8, 2.390 (wrestling). 12.1450 (open porch and ball-court, perhaps in the Gymnasium).

30 Oil: P.Erl. 18.6 (BL 3). Local poet: 7.1015. Cakes: P.Stras. 5.339.13 (provenance?).

31 P.Giss. 50. 2.300. Cf SB 8.9921 (provenance?), P.Mich. 5.312.13–14.

32 17.2127, 45.3265.

33 PIFAO 3.37 (BL 9).

34 P.Stras. 4.222 (BL 5).

35 64.4441 vi 14 (lane); P.Genova 1.22.10 (the quarter, also connected with the East Stoa). On the baths: Krüger (1990) 110–24.

36 44.3173, 3176.

37 43.3088.

38 W.Chr. 33, see note 51.

39 17.2127.

40 Glass: 45.3265 (P.Coll.Youtie 2.81) (AD 326). Tin: 44.3185. Bronze: P.Laur. 4.155 (BL 8).

41 Lessees: see p. 58. Bathmen: 12.1499–1500.

42 W.Chr. 193, see the revised text and admirable commentary in Habermann (2000).

43 31.2569 (AD 265) (BL 6). P.Oslo 3.111.127, 129 may or may not refer to water-raising. Krüger (1990) 114f. on a canal apparently connected with the Imperial Baths.

44 Krüger (1990) 125f. (Epidauros, Miletos; twice the size of that at Thamugadi).

45 Diaries: 42.3072 (strategos), 45.3248 (exegete?). Sacrifices: 17.2127.

46 Upkeep: P.Coll.Youtie 1.28.13? Security: 7.1050.16, W.Chr. 474 iii 4 and 6 (AD 295).

47 PSI 13.1331 (SB 5.7994).

48 6.937.

49 7.1050. See also 3.519.

50 See GMAW^2 no. 32 and p. 149 n. 63.

51 W.Chr. 33 (3.473; plate GMAW^2 no. 69), if indeed it refers to Oxyrhynchos, see BL 8.235.

52 On density: Alston (2002) 331.

53 64.4438.

54 M.Chr. 182 (2.243) (BL 7).

55 M.Chr. 193 (2.274).

56 24.2406 (assuming that the dimensions given are in royal cubits). Some scholars have thought this so small that they regard the plan as representing a house-tomb or part of a shared house. See Husson (1983) 308–10; Maehler (1983) 136–7.

57 14.1634.

58 3.498 (SP 1.19).

59 14.1648 iii 56.

60 16.1958?

61 47.3366 (P.Coll.Youtie 2.66).

62 6.964.

63 W.Chr. 474 i 20.

64 E.g. 64.4438.

65 See the Demotic law-code translated in 46.3285.32–7.

66 10.1272.

67 1.69 (but this is in a neighbouring village).

68 17.2145; 44.3173, 3176, 50.3566 (the bath of Arrios Apolinarios, later public – if it was actually part of his house); P.Theon. 15.

69 See the documents collected in C.Pap.Gr. 1.

70 44.3200.25 and often.

71 14.1761.

72 M.Chr. 305.24 (3.494) (SP 1.84), AD 156; PSI 12.1263 i 8, AD 166/7.

73 46.3292, datable 259/64, from someone resident in the village of Nesmeimis; cf. 33.2681, BGU 3.935 (undated) (attack on Herakleopolis Magna?).

74 For the discovery, at Bahariya, in 1996, of four tombs containing 105 mummies of the Graeco-Roman period, see Hawass (2000).

75 61.4126.6.

76 1.73.12.

77 50.3568.

78 P.Mert. 1.26 (BL 4; 7).

79 34.2711.

80 PSI 10.1102.

81 12.1413.

82 12.1414.

83 P.Turner 38 (AD 274/5).

84 P.Oxy. vol. 40.

85 40.2940.

86 P.Stras. 7.616.

87 12.1455.

88 43.3115.

89 61.4119.

90 51.3612.

91 P.Coll.Youtie 2.70.

92 14.1646.

93 14.1633.

94 14.1631.1 note.

95 P.Thomas 20.

96 10.1264.

97 12.1544 (assuming that this is the famous Pelusium, not the obscure village in the Fayûm).

98 SB 14.12111.

99 8.1135 (BL 4).

100 P.Flor. 1.63 (BL 3; 6; 7; 8; 9), see the revised text in Rea (1971).

101 P.Giss. 50 (BL 8).

102 Lauffer (1971) 7.75.

103 P.Oslo 3.111.

104 42.3028; 14.1662; P.Erl. 18.

105 42.3048; 33.2664.

106 Jerome, *Chron.* p. 219 Helm.

107 12.1450.

108 P.Coll.Youtie 2.66.

109 P.Oxy. vol. 40 p. 2.

110 Titles: Daris (2003) 91. Street: 1.55. Assizes: 12.1456.

111 43.3135 (date?).

112 Letter of Town Council: Frisch (1986) no. 2 (BGU 4.1073). Application: Frisch (1986) no. 1 (BGU 4.1074).

CHAPTER 5: LORD AND GOD

Bibliography. For the Roman Emperor see Millar (1977). For basic chronology see Kienast (1996). For the history of the Roman Empire see Goodman (1997) and Potter (2004).

1   10.1271 (BL 2.2; 8) (SP 2.304); BGU V (*Gnomon of the Idios Logos*) §§ 64, 68.
2   P.Mert. 2.73 (BL 6; 8). 36.2782 (BL 6; 10).
3   55.3781 (NPP 29).
4   Rathbone (1986).
5   7.1021 (BL 2) (W.Chr. 113; SP 2.235; Hengstl 10).
6   OGIS 669.5–6; Chalon (1964).
7   Dio Cassius 79.15.3; 53.3092.5 note.
8   42.3055 (BL 8).
9   P.Michael. 21 (if rightly read).
10 63.4352 fr. 5 ii 20.
11 SB 6.9617 (BL 8) (NPP 34). On the visit, Sijpesteijn (1969).
12 P.Panop.Beatty 1.112.
13 Bernand (1960) no. 28. On Balbilla's ancestry: Brennan (1998).
14 31.2553 (assuming that the 'city' there mentioned is Oxyrhynchos itself).
15 Poems on Antinoos: 8.1085, 50.3537 verso, 63.4352, perhaps 54.3723 (all but the first probably local poets).
16 Niger still recognised on 5 February 194 (BGU 13.2285); Severus' 'coming to power' celebrated on 13 February (W.Chr. 96 iv 6).
17 42.3019 (BL 8).
18 P.Col. VI (*Apokrimata*) (BL 4; 7; 8; 9).
19 4.705 (BL 1; 2) (W.Chr. 153 and C.Pap.Jud. 2.450; W.Chr. 407).
20 Bowman (1971).
21 Herodian 4.8.8.
22 Kaiser (1994) no. 14. Princes of darkness: Ephesians 6.12.
23 Dio Cassius 77.22.1, Herodian 4.9.3.
24 P.Giss. 40 ii 16ff. (W.Chr. 22, SP 2.215), revised text in Kuhlmann (1994) 215–55.
25 12.1449, P.Oslo 3.94, 61.4125, 10.1265.
26 Dio Cassius 77.2.
27 Dio Cassius 78.12.5–6.
28 Gordon (1983) pl. 73 (compare the bronze dedication ibid. pl. 72).
29 Steinby (1994) 105–6.
30 E.g. SNG von Aulock no. 7688.
31 Dietz (1986).
32 BGU 11.2056 (BL 6; 8).
33 Sauneron (1952) 115f.; plate also in this book, ill. 21. Full publication of reliefs and inscriptions: Sauneron (1975).
34 SB 6.9234 (P.Customs 282) with Husselman (1951).
35 Colours and wax for imperial images in the early fourth century: 55.3791–2.

36 12.1449 (BL 1; 7; 9; 11) (lines 1–17 = SP 2.405).

37 On this tondo (Staatliche Museen zu Berlin, Preussischer Kulturbesitz, Anti-kensammlung 31329) see Heinen (1991). Reproduced here as ill. 20.

38 1.56 (BL 1; 3; 8) (M.Chr. 320; NPP 55 with plate on p. 37). On the date see 47.3346.1 note.

39 Geta's name deleted in 17.2121 and PSI 12.1245; not deleted in PSI 12.1243–4.

40 1.54 (W.Chr. 34).

41 47.3340.

42 Dio Cassius 79.13.2–4, 79.16.7, 79.20.2.

43 49.3475. 'Pseudantoninos' Dio Cassius 79.1.

44 46.3298 introd.

45 31.2551 verso i 20 (for the reading see 46.3299.2 note).

46 46.3299.

47 46.3298. Łukaszewicz (1992) argues that the crucial word means 'corrupter of virgins' rather than 'catamite'; not only was Elagabalus effeminate, see Herodian 5.6.2, Dio Cassius 79.13–16, but he also contracted a scandalous marriage with a Vestal Virgin, Herodian 5.6.2, Dio Cassius 79.9.

48 Dio Cassius 77.9.5.

49 P.Giss. 40, revised text in Kuhlmann (1994).

50 12.1467 (BL 8; 11) (SP 2.305; NPP 65).

51 12.1475.

52 *Digest* 49.1.25.

53 17.2104 (BL 2.2; 3; 6; 7; 8; 9), 43.3106.

54 P.Coll.Youtie 2.66, text reprinted as 47.3366 (BL 7; 9; 11).

55 43.3109.

56 Avidius Cassius: proclamation, P.Amst. 1.27; letter to Alexandrians, SB 10.10295b (BL 6; 8)?; at Oxyrhynchos, SB 6.9550. Reign and death: Dio Cassius 71.27.3.

57 Malalas, *Chron.* 308–9 Dindorf (*The Chronicle of John Malalas*, translated by E. M. Jeffreys and others, Sydney 1986).

58 Diodorus Siculus 1.83.8.

59 Strabo 17.1

60 P.Brem. 1 (C.Pap.Jud. 2.438).

61 4.705 ii (BL 1; 2) (W.Chr. 153 and C.Pap.Jud. 2.450). See p. 66 above.

62 22.2332. Revised text: Koenen (1968).

63 Musurillo (1954); a few additional items in Musurillo (1962). For the items relating to the Jewish community see also C.Pap.Jud. vol. 2.

64 42.3020.

65 25.2435.

66 3.471, Musurillo VII.

67 10.1242, Musurillo VIII.

68 1.33 Musurillo XIB.

69 Defamation of the Emperor: Tacitus, *Ann.* 1.72. Penalties for distributing anonymous libels: *Digest* 47.10.5.9 (Ulpian). See Bauman (1967) 246–65. Death penalty for collecting or reading libels: *Cod. Theod.* 9.34.7 (late 4th cent.).

CHAPTER 6: THE RIVER

Bibliography. For the Nile see Bonneau (1964), (1971), (1993). For shipping see Casson (1995). For fishing see Chouliara-Raiou (2003) (in modern Greek with a summary in French).

1　Bowman and Rogan (1999) 1–2.
2　Seneca, *NQ* 4A.2.10.
3　Plutarch, *Qu. Conv.* 8.5.13 (*Mor.* 725E).
4　Strabo 17.1.3.
5　Pliny, *NH* 5.58.
6　*The Travels of Ibn Battūta*, translated by H. A. R. Gibb, vol. I (Cambridge 1958) 49.
7　Herodotus 2.97.
8　Achilles Tatius 4.12. Cf. Heliodorus 9.4ff.
9　Aurigemma (1960) tav. 84.
10　Pliny, *NH* 36.58; copy illustrated (ill. 24) originally from the Iseum Campense in Rome, now in the Vatican Museum.
11　Nile mosaic: detailed illustrations in Gullini (1956), which also shows which parts of the mosaic are ancient and which later restoration; recent discussion Meyboom (1995).
12　The name Anabasis: e.g. 44.3197.
13　'The Great River', 17.2125.18, 38.2876.10. 'Our river' and 'Tomis river': see ch.4, n.6.
14　22.2341 (BL 4).
15　1.43 verso v 1 (W.Chr. 474 v 1).
16　14.1631.24.
17　12.1409 (BL 2) (SP 2. 225; MZ 44).
18　38.2847 (BL 8).
19　49.3508 (BL 8; 10).
20　49.3475.
21　38.2853 (found at Oxyrhynchos, but probably relating to another nome, see 58.3926).
22　45.3264 (= P.Coll.Youtie 21).
23　41.2985 (BL 8; 10).
24　20.2272.19–21 (BL 4).
25　PSI 13.1333.
26　16.1854 (BL 2.2; 11).
27　59.4004 (BL 11).
28　16.1862.45–8.
29　4.742 (BL 1; 5; 8).
30　59.3993.26–36.
31　31.2569.
32　14.1671 (BL 5).
33　18.2182 (BL 4; 5; 7; 8).
34　59.3989.

35 Willcocks (1935) 98 and 100.

36 3.486.31–5 (M.Chr. 59).

37 Land carried away: e.g. 55.3804.171, eroded 12.1434.19. 'Islands': 12.1445 ii 13. See Bonneau (1971) 66ff.

38 Return of unwatered land: e.g. 65.4488; 'Nile-watered' and 'unwatered': 58.3955.16. Reduction of rent: e.g. 67.4595. Land surveys: Bonneau (1971) 90ff. Related terms: 38.2847. Director of land-surveys: 42.3032, 3046.

39 44.3167 (BL 9).

40 3.425; GLP no. 97; GDRK 3.

41 Lane (1836) ch. XIV.

42 45.3250 (BL 8; 9). On such contracts: Meyer-Termeer (1978); supplement in P.Köln 10.416 introd.

43 On Nile boats: Casson (1995) 340–3; Poll (1996). On ship-owners: Bagnall (1993) 36f.

44 P.Hib. 2.198.110–125 (BL 6; 9).

45 P.Oxy.Hels. 37 (BL 8).

46 *Parasema*: Casson (1995) 344–60; local gods, P.Panop.Beatty 2.209.

47 24.2415 (BL 11).

48 On capacities and dimensions: Poll (1996).

49 Casson (1995) 331–43. 'Broad-bottoms' belonging to the state: 34.2715.9, 51.3636.1, 60.4078. 'Greek boats' e.g. 17.2136, 22.2547. Cargo in 'bedroom-carriers': wood 14.1738, pots P.Oxy.Hels. 37.

50 Strabo 17.1.16.

51 Strabo 17.1.50.

52 P.Mert. 1.19, cf 31.2568.

53 Carrying wine: 1220.12. Ferrying corn: P.Köln 5.229; 31.2568.

54 17.2153.

55 59.3989 (p. 88 above).

56 59.3990.

57 P.Lond. 3.1164(h) (BL 4; 7) (SP 1.38). For the technical terms: Casson (1995) 257f.

58 'Perhaps six years' wages . . .': Bagnall (1993) 36.

59 Oath of Clemens: 59.3975. Seven skippers: PSI 9.1048.

60 31.2568 (BL 8; 11).

61 E.g. 49.3494.

62 4.708 (BL 8) (W.Chr. 432).

63 Sample-carriers: 10.1254; 60.4064.

64 SB 6.9223 (BL 7; 10).

65 10.1299 (BL 3; 6; 11) (Naldini 76).

66 On fishing rights, Wallace (1938) 219–21; Taubenschlag (1955) 664–6.

67 'Seine-fishermen', P.Corn. 46; 'sacred net-fishermen', 64.4440.

68 49.3495 (BL 11).

69 Plutarch, *de Iside et Osiride* 7 (353C), Aelian, *HA* 10.46; Egyptian worship of *oxyrhynchos* and *lepidotos*, already Strabo 17.1.40. Sacred fish in Egypt: Gamer-Wallert (1970).

70 PSI 8.901 (BL 2.2; 3) (SP 2.329).

71 Superintendents: 46.3268. Tax-farmers: 46.3270, P.Leid.Inst. 60.

72 P.Turner 25 (BL 8; 11) (MZ 33).

73 SB 12.11234.

74 SB 18.13150.

75 46.3267, 3269, 3270.

76 'Inundation of the present year': 46.3269.1–2, 3270.9. 'The past inundation': P.Leid.Inst. 60.

77 46.3269, 3270, cf. 3267.5.

78 19.2234 (BL 7; 9; 10).

79 Tertullian, *Apol.* 40.2.

80 22.2332 iii; revised text in Koenen (1968).

81 31.2554.9–18.

82 See Bonneau (1964); Frankfurter (1998) 42–6.

83 P.Wisc. 1.9.2–5 (BL 7) (cf. P.Wash.Univ. 1.4.9).

84 3.519 (BL 1; 5; 8) (W.Chr. 492; SP 2.402; Vandoni 36).

85 7.1050 (BL 1; 8) (Vandoni 39).

86 24.2409 (BL 11).

87 9.1211 (SP 2.403; Vandoni 37).

88 36.2782 (BL 10), above, pp. 61f.

89 43.3148.

90 15.1796 (GLP 124; GDRK 60).

91 Cribiore (1995) (third–fourth century AD, perhaps from the Fayûm).

92 P.Turner 10 (sixth century AD).

93 P.Lond.Lit. 239 (sixth or seventh century AD, provenance unknown).

CHAPTER 7: MARKETS

Bibliography. See Johnson (1936); Bowman (1996) ch. 4; Bagnall (1993) 78–92; Alston (2002) 337–42.

1 List of trades and services: Daris (2003) (Oxyrhynchos); CPR 13 pp. 49ff. (Egypt in general).

2 'Seller of everything': 3.520 (BL 1; 5; 11).

3 Alston (2002) 208–10.

4 46.3300.

5 P.Oslo 3.144 (BL 3; 11).

6 P.Gron. inv. 66, see Hendriks et al. (1981).

7 P.Oxy.Hels. 40 (BL 8) with van Minnen (1986).

8 42.3074.2.

9 7.1037.

10 SB 16.12695, SB 20.14996, P.Köln 5.228; platform 2.237.vii.20 (SP 2.258).

11 12.1455, PSI 6.692 (BL 1; 9), 64.4441 vi 14-15.

12 PSI 14.1417, 43.3145, SB 6.9214.

13 SB 16.12695 (top of another SB 20.14996).

14 P.Köln 5.228 with P.Köln 4.196.

15 P.Oslo 2.49 (BL 2.2; 3).

16 51.3628–36 (fifth century), with Bagnall (1985) 5–6.

17 8.1158 (BL 9).

18 17.2109 (SP 2.356).

19 Wines of Oxyrhynchos: 54.3765.5–7. Lollianos: 47.3366.29–30.

20 54.3740, 3762, 68.4683.

21 12.1432 (BL 5; 6; 8), 44.3189 (BL 7; 9).

22 Perpillou-Thomas (1992); Thompson (1985) 320–3.

23 Pherecrates fr. 113.3 KA.

24 Typically Egyptian: Pliny, *NH* 22.121. Galen: 11. 142 K.

25 24.2423 verso iii 19.

26 SB 10.10567.35–7.

27 65.4480.

28 Diocletian's edict: Lauffer (1971).

29 PSI 8.965; revised text in SB 14.12134 (BL 8), but see Bagnall (1985) 23.

30 51.3624–6; 54.3731 and following; SB 16.12628 and 12648 (BL 9).

31 45.3244.

32 12.1455 (BL 3).

33 1.83 (BL 9) (W.Chr. 430; SP 2.331).

34 40.2892–940.

35 12.1454 (BL 2.2; 8).

36 6.908 (BL 1) (W.Chr. 426).

37 State visits: W.Chr. 415 (the Prefect visits Hermopolis), 63.4387 (AD 401). Catering for troops: 43.3124.

38 42.3048 (BL 11) and other documents cited in the introduction.

39 Battaglia (1989).

40 Athenaeus 3.109ff.

41 4.736.26 (SP 1.186).

42 P.Ryl. 4.629–30, 639.

43 P.Ross.Georg. 2.41; 16.2046 (BL 5; 6; 10; 11).

44 12.1454 (BL 2.2; 8).

45 P.Wisc. 1.5 (BL 6; 11) (MZ 32).

46 Sending wheat to be ground: 4.736 (SP 1.186); 739. Hiring a quern: M.Chr. 165.

47 Millers and head-millers: 14.3169.91, 43.3120.5. Oven-men, see n. 55. Makers of fine bread: SB 16.12695.9. Cake-makers: 33.2672. 'Confectioner to the strategos': 48.3390.3.

48 12.1454; 51.3625.

49 14.1655 (BL 4; 9).

50 16.1890 (BL 8).

51 6.908 (BL 1) (W.Chr. 426).

52 Battaglia (1989) 156.

53 Battaglia (1989) 146–60.

54 Bought from potter: P.Kell. 4.1269. Part of house: e.g. SB 20.14199.

55 8.1142.9f. and 65.4493.24.

56 Reinhart (1998).

57 Cubberley (1985).

58 Wilson (1988) ch. 2.

59 9.1211 (SP 2.403).

60 1.113 (BL 2.2; 11).

61 4.736 (BL 2; 3; 4; 8) (SP 1.186).

62 W.Chr. 415.

63 4.738 (BL 1; 11).

64 54.3738, 3760.

65 67.4582. See in general Chouliara-Raiou (1989).

66 54.3766 (BL 10).

67 P.Köln 5.228.

68 PSI 3.202; 14.1764.

69 1.108 (SP 1.188; Hengstl 81).

70 18.2190.62–3 (revised text SB 22.15708).

71 Crawford (1973).

72 54.3761.

73 Pliny the Elder, *NH* 31.94. The philosopher: Seneca *Ep.* 95.25.

74 54.3749.

75 54.3731, 3733, 3766 (BL 10).

76 45.3265.

77 54.3766.

78 50.3595, cf 3596–7 (BL 8). Discussion: Cockle (1981).

79 50.3596.

80 41.2996.

81 55.3811 (MZ 99).

82 18.2197 (BL 9; 10), cf. 55.3804.151.

83 Great Praetorium: 31.2581 ii 23. 'Well-baked brick': Youtie (1983).

84 General account of the apprenticeship-contracts: Bergamasco (1995).

85 55.3809.

86 67.4596.

87 Holidays: eighteen days, 14.1647; twenty days, 4.725 (SP 1.14; Hengstl 102); three days a month, P.Fouad 1.37 (BL 3; 6).

88 31.2586.

89 31.2586 (BL 6; 8; 10).

90 41.2971.

91 60.4059.

92 41.2958–67.

93 List of banks at Oxyrhynchos: Bogaert (1995) 151–7.

94 'Exchange banks': Bogaert (1994) 95ff.

95 12.1411 (BL 8) (SP 2.230).

96 'Bank transfers': Wolff (1978) 95ff.

97 55.3798.

98 43.3146.8 note (BL 7; 8; 10). See Bagnall (1993) 75–7.

99 Banks did occasionally make transactions in corn, but no doubt only in exceptional circumstances: Bogaert (1994) 397–406.

100 31.2589.

101 31.2591.

CHAPTER 8: FAMILY AND FRIENDS

Bibliography. For the private letter in the Greek and Roman world, and a selection of examples with translation, see Trapp (2003). For ancient theories of letter-writing see Malherbe (1988). For language see Koskenniemi (1956). For selections of papyrus letters see SP 1; Tibiletti. For letters of condolence see Chapa (1998). For letters of introduction see Keyes (1935). For Christian letters see Naldini.

1 42.3067 (Tibiletti 11).

2 Koskenniemi (1956) 172–86.

3 2 Thess. 3.17.

4 Educated hand: 42.3069; semi-literate: P.Oxy.Hels. 45. Very occasionally an educated writer adds accents, punctuation and the like (see e.g. 1.122, 31.2603, 55.3812) – an extra touch of class, for such things are normally reserved for texts of high poetry.

5 56.3860.43–4.

6 For Rio, see Walter Salles' film *Central Station* (1998).

7 61.4127.

8 42.3066 on the back of 42.3054.

9 P.Oxy.Hels. 47.

10 P.Abinn. 21 on the back of P.Abinn. 41.

11 GLH 22; Rathbone (1991) 12f.

12 SB 6.9017.15.

13 P.Flor. 3.367 (SP 1. 147), provenance uncertain (Fayûm?).

14 48.3396.32 and note; 55.3814.31 note.

15 20.2273.32.

16 P.Oslo 3.84.

17 41.2983–4.

18 P.Petaus 84; 43.3095.

19 59.3993.

20 P.Flor. 3.371 (the catalogue on the front: Otranto (2000) no. 12), provenance unknown.

21 PSI 4.299 (SP 1.158, Naldini 8).

22 31.2599 introduction, Koskenniemi (1956) 92.

23 41.2980; 14.1678.28 (Naldini 9), cf. 1773.40 (Naldini 10).

24 34.2719 (BL 6, 7, 8, 10).

25 59.3996 (likely but not certain that Harpokratiaina could not read).

26 SB 18.13867 (BL 10) (Rowlandson 246), provenance unknown.

27 Illegible letters: P.Col.Zen. 2.68, PSI 4.403.

28 3.528 (BL 2.2, 8) (SP 1.125; Hengstl 88), below, pp. 132 f.

29 59.3979. Other good examples: 14.1683 (Naldini 65); 41.2996.

30 41.2980.

31 14.1757.

32 P.Oxy.Hels. 48.

33 47.3356.

34 59.3997.

35 4.743.20–1.

36 42.3086.

37 31.2594.

38 8.1165.

39 1.119 (BL 1; 2.2; 3; 4; 6) (Hengstl 82).

40 P.Bon. 5; latest edition in Cugusi (1992) text 1. Another fragmentary manual of the sixth century AD, from Hermoupolis: BKT 9.94.

41 Ps-Demetrius, *Typoi Epistolikoi*, and Ps-Libanius, *Epistolimaioi Charakteres*: Greek text edited by V. Weichert (1910), English translation in Malherbe (1988).

42 PHamb. 4.254, second century AD?, provenance unknown.

43 1.115 (BL 2.2; 9; 11); Chapa (1998) no. 2.

44 1.116 (BL 1); 1.187, full text now SB 20.15180.

45 PSI 12.1248 (BL 6; 7; 9); revised text Chapa (1998) no. 6.

46 See in general Keyes (1935).

47 P.Mich. 8.468 ii 35–41 (Karanis).

48 2.292 (BL 2.2; 8) (SP 1.106).

49 12.1424 (BL 10; 11). For Heras see 63.4358 introduction.

50 56.3857.

51 See below, pp. 205 f.

52 31.2603.34–5 (Naldini 47).

53 42.3069 (Tibiletti 20).

54 3.528, see note 28.

55 42.3063.

56 36.2783 (BL 8; 9) (Tibiletti 9).

57 Arrival: e.g. P.Köln 1.56. Books: 18.2192.

58 42.3065 (Tibiletti 10).

59 34.2725.

60 42.3070 (BL 8; 11). See Montserrat (1996) 136–9.

61 33.2679.

62 42.3060 (BL 7; 8).

63 42.3059.

64 14.1676 (BL 11).

65 46.3313.

CHAPTER 9: POETS AND PEDANTS

Bibliography. For education and society in Greek Egypt see Cribiore (2001). For education and society in the Graeco-Roman world see Morgan (1998).

1 P.Coll.Youtie vol. 2 pp. 441ff.

2 Lauffer (1971) 7.65–71.

3 Philogelos 61.

4 See pp. 143–4 below.

5 Heliodorus Astrol., *Comm. in Paulum Alexandrinum* p. 84.23.

6 Milne (1908) 121.

7 64.4441 iv 18–20, 47.3366. Note also 2.221 (P.Lond.Lit. 178), a commentary on the *Iliad* signed in the margin by 'Ammonios, son of Ammonios, *grammatikos*'.

8 22.2345.2.

9 22.2338 (BL 7; 8; 11), headed 'List of Naucratites'.

10 Quintilian *Inst.* 1.4.2. See in general Kaster (1988).

11 55.3808.

12 18.2190, see below, pp. 149–50.

13 P.Gen 2.111 (BL 8) (provenance?).

14 18.2186 (BL 7; 8), cf P.Mich. 14.676. P.Flor. 3.382.79 (BL 6). See Bingen (1970) 356.

15 6.930 (W.Chr. 138; SP 1.130).

16 10.1296 (SP 1.137).

17 3.531 (BL 2.2; 4; 10) (W.Chr. 482; Hengstl 83). See Łukaszewicz (1994).

18 SB 3.6262 (BL 2.2) (SP 1.133).

19 P.Oslo 3.156.

20 P.Giss. 80 (SP 1.116).

21 47.3366.

22 Athenaeus 453D.

23 P.Lond.Lit. 253 + *ZPE* 86 (1991): 231–2 = Cribiore (1996) no. 383.

24 Osley (1980) 55.

25 31.2604.

26 P.Köln 2.66.

27 Cribiore (1996) no. 106.

28 Cribiore (1996) no. 134, provenance unknown.

29 42.3004.

30 44.3174 (BL 7).

31 53.3712.

32 Saenger (1997).

33 A balanced view of the long argument about silent reading: Johnson (2000).

34 Cribiore (1996) no. 363.

35 Cribiore (1996) nos. 364, 385, 388.

36 Theon, *Progymnasmata* p. 24 Patillon.

37 Nikolaos of Myra 18.1–6 Felten.

38 62.4321.

39 Van Rossum-Steenbeek (1998) 56f.

40 56.3829.

41 Glosses to *Iliad* 1.1: P.Achm. 2 and Ziebarth (1913) no. 29.

42 O.Bodl. 2.2000, provenance unknown.

43 18.2190, revised text in Rea (1993), reprinted as SB 22.15708.

44 Above, p. 16.

45 Turner (1952) 89–90. Lama (1991).

46 Funghi and Messeri (1992a, 1992b).

47 Bagnall (1992).

48 6.907 (M.Chr. 317; FIRA 3 no. 51), on back of Africanus 3.412.

49 14.1690.

50 11.1386,1392; 11.1365.

51 Statistics: Krüger (1990) 214.

52 42.3010. 29.2891.

53 22.2331.

54 3.413. 27.2458.

55 42.3069, p. 132 above.

56 P.Mil.Vogl. 11 (Otranto (2000) no. 5).

57 P.Mert. 1.19.

58 51.3643.

59 On literacy in general: Harris (1989); Beard (1991); Bowman and Woolf (1994).

60 31.2586.

61 33.2673.

62 1.71 col. i (BL 7).

63 See p. 126.

64 24.2421 i 10? Note P.Kell. 1.66.20–1.

65 See Youtie (1971a, 1971b, 1975).

66 12.1467 (AD 263).

67 50.3537.

68 7.1015.

69 22.2338, see n. 9.

70 63.4352.

71 P. Bodmer XXIX (fourth/fifth centuries AD).

72 *Vitae Philosophorum et Sophistarum* 493.

73 Cameron (1965).

74 P.Lond. inv. 2110, published by Ohly (1928) 88–9 and 127–8 (text reprinted as SB 20.14599).

75 P.Lond.Lit. 11, as corrected by Wifstrand (1933) 468.

76 Parássoglou (1979) 16–18.

77 *Anthologia Palatina* 9.206; 6.63–8.

78 Johnson (2004) 61–5 (more work by Scribe A2 has been published since, see 69.4720, 4734).

79 18.2192 (BL 2.2; 3; 7; 9) (Otranto (2000) no. 11).

80 P.Sorbonne 2272e, Menander *Sikyonios*, colophon, as corrected by Parássoglou (1979).

CHAPTER 10: BUREAUCRATS

Bibliography. For a general overview see Bowman (1996). For archives see Cockle (1984); Burkhalter (1990). For liturgies see Lewis (1997). For city administration see Bowman (1971).

1 For the 'Satire of the trades', see Caminos (1954). Translation quoted by permission from Quirke (2004) 121–6.

2 Wittfogel (1963).

3 17.2116, 51.3615.

4 Whitehorne (1988).

5 59.3973. 60.4063–7. 51.3602–5.

6 Turner (1952) 89–90. See above, pp. 150 f.

7 42.3072–4.

8 22.2348.

9 52.3694.

10 60.4059.

11 59.3973.

12 Fires: 59.3978; 41.2997. Accidental death: 3.475 (BL 8; 9) (W.Chr. 494; SP 2.337; Hengstl 95).

13 42.3074.

14 1.37 (BL 8; 10) (M.Chr. 79; C.Pap.Gr. 1 no. 19; NPP 17; MZ 75). Below, p. 213.

15 31.2576.

16 Recent examples: 61.4114–16 introduction (with bibliography); 65.4485–6. Two together e.g. 65.4486.

17 55.3807 (but see BL 10).

18 1.61 (BL 1; 3; 7; 8).

19 51.3601.

20 Luke 2.1–5.

21 12.1548 (BL 6).

22 P.Yale 1.61 (AD 209?).

23 Haensch (1994) 487.

24 Hombert and Préaux (1952) 40.

25 60.4060.

26 Red ink: Sijpesteijn (1979).

27 Chancery hand: Cavallo (1965); P.Köln 8.351 introduction.

28 45.3243

29 W. Clarysse in Brosius (2003) 344–59; list of examples on the website lhpc.arts.kuleuven.ac.be/archives_folder/tomos.xls

30 P.Oslo 3.98 (Herakleopolis) numbered 392; P.Brux. 1 has at least 107 items and a length of at least 23 feet.

31 Johnson (2004) 150.

32 Top edge uneven, e.g. 46.3276-84; top edge trimmed, 60.4059.

33 60.4060.

34 33.2673, 50.3574.

35 38.2848.

36 'Gnomon of the Idios Logos': 42.3014. Land-surveying: 38.2847.

37 2.237 viii 27–43 (BL 1) (M.Chr. 192; SP 2.219).

38 40.2918.12, 43.3096, 46.3273.

39 P.Petaus 121.

40 Lewis (1997).

41 Bowman (1971).

42 12.1415.22–7.

43 P.Thmouis.

44 P.Fam.Tebt. 15.66–70.

45 Summary of case: P.Fam.Tebt. pp. 97–108.

46 Zosimus 1.20.2.

47 33.2664 (BL 6; 8; 9).

48 Reforms under Philip: Parsons (1967); Thomas (1975); Bianchi (1983).

49 61.4114–16 introduction (with bibliography).

50 Registering corn-stocks: 42.3048 (BL 11). Straitened circumstances: P.Erl. 18 (BL 3; 5; 6).

51 SB 5.7696 (BL 3; 4; 6; 7; 8).

52 P.Cair.Isid. 1 (BL 5; 9).

CHAPTER 11: SURVIVING

Bibliography. See Lewis (1983); Bagnall (1993) chapters 5 and 8.

1 8.1149.

2 12.1449.

3 On procedures: Henrichs (1973); Papini (1990); Frankfurter (1998) 145–97.

4 9.1213.

5 31.2613.

6 8.1148.

7 42.3078 (BL 8).

8 65.4470.

9 3.494.32.

10 P.Köln 4.202.

11 55.3799.

12 8.1150 (sixth century) (PGM P8b).

13 SB 14.12144 (BL 8).

14 Murder of Saturninus: Dio Cassius 76.14.2. Severus: SHA Sev. 3.9, 4.3.

15 Pliny, *NH* 29.11 and 14.

16 Summary of legislation: P.Coll.Youtie vol. 2 pp. 441–4.

17 Doctors in the papyri: CPR vol. 13 pp. 89–100.

18 64.4441 iv 8.

19 59.4001 (BL 11 on lines 30f.).

20 Hermopolis: 42.3078. Alexandria (probably): 31.2601.32.

21 List of texts: M-P^3.

22 PSI 2.116. P.Med.inv. 71.77v (*Aeg.* 52 (1972) 76). 9.1184.

23 31.2547.

24 PSI 12.1275.

25 2.234 + 52.3654 (parts of the same roll, M-P^3 2360.2).

26 P.Mil.Vogl. 1.15.

27 19.2221 + P.Köln 5.206.

28 31.2567.

29 53.3701.

30 P.XVIICongr. 19v.

31 8.1088 (M-P³ 2409).

32 54.3724.

33 42.3068 (BL 7).

34 11.1384 (M-P³ 2410).

35 Bagnall and Frier (1994) 109. See Potter (2004) 584 n. 57 for criticisms of the estimate.

36 1.76.

37 8.1121.9.

38 PSI 3.177 (BL 1; 6).

39 1.39 (W.Chr. 456) (BL 1; 6; 7; 8).

40 P.Leit. 1.

41 12.1414.26 (BL 3; 6; 7; 8).

42 P.Oxy.Hels. 46.15–19.

43 8.1161 (Naldini 60).

44 42.3058.5.

45 PSI 4.299 (BL 2; 6) (SP 1.158; Naldini 8).

46 On 'plague' see e.g. Casanova (1984); Alston (2002) 259, 364–6. *Or. Sib.* 13.10; PGM 1.4.1400.

47 Bagnall and Frier (1994) 173–8.

48 55.3817.

49 PSI 3.211.

50 14.1666 (SP 1.149; Tibiletti 3; MZ 93).

51 55.3816.

52 P.Mert. 1.26.

53 50.3555 (BL 8; 10).

54 46.3314.

55 3.475 (W.Chr. 494; SP 2.337; Hengstl 95).

56 C.Pap.Gr. vol. 2 p. 221.

57 51.3644.

58 64.4441 i. 6.896 ii.

59 44.3195 ii.

60 1.52 (BL 1; 7).

61 54.3729.

62 P.Corn. 52.

63 18.2190 (see above, p. 149).

64 1.51.

65 61.4126.

66 Augustus: Dio Cassius 56.25.5 (AD 11). Tacitus: *Hist.* 1.22.

67 P.Oxy.Astr. 4242.

68 P.Oxy.Astr. 4247.

69 P.Oxy.Astr. 4245.

70 4.804 (Neugebauer and van Hoesen (1959) no. −3).

71 65.4471.

72 31.2554, cf 65.4772.

73 65.4473.

74 65.4476.

75 3.465.

76 P.Oxy. vol. 66 pp. 57ff.

77 66.4504 ii 13ff.

78 66.4505 fr. 1.3–6.

79 64.4441 v 4 attests this shrine. The priest: 3.507.4–6. Offerings: 31.2553.3 (but this perhaps refers to Alexandria, Whitehorne (1995) 3083).

80 P.Mert. 2.73.4.

81 M.Chr. 304.19, P.Wisc. 1.13.15.

82 Theophrastus, *Characters* 16. Theocritus 3.27.

83 From Oxyrhynchos: P.Oslo 3.76 (fragment). Quotation taken from the more complete P.Ryl. 1.28.

84 Unpublished text, quoted by kind permission of the Egypt Exploration Society.

85 6.885.

86 Papyri: 67.4581 and introduction. Collected text: Stewart (2001).

87 P.Lond. 121 (PGM VII); revised text in Maltomini (1995). P.Bon. 1.3, with corrections in SM 77.

88 56.3831.

89 56.3834.12–18.

90 46.3298 verso 41–4, 36.2753 (= SM 85, 90).

91 68.4672.

92 68.4674.

93 56.3834 (SM 79).

94 56.3835 (SM 86).

95 PMG VII 149–54,167–86.

CHAPTER 12: CHRISTIANS AND CHRISTIANITIES

Bibliography. See Hardy (1952); Roberts (1979); Pearson and Goehring (1986); Chadwick (1993).

1 *Historia Monachorum in Aegypto* 5.

2 Eusebius, *HE* 6.23.

3 Socrates, *HE* 7.15.

4 W.Chr. 474 i 10, iii 19 (assuming that these *ekklesiai* were churches).

5 Lists of churches: 11.1357, 67.4618–19.

6 For example, five fragments of St Matthew's gospel from Oxyrhynchos have been judged to date before c. AD 250 (1.2, 34.2683, 64.4403–5). Greek books carry no date; scholars assign them an approximate date on the basis of the script. Such datings must naturally be taken with a pinch of salt. Even so, the much-publicised attempt of the late C. P. Thiede to backdate one particular papyrus of St Matthew to the middle or late first century (Thiede (1995)) has

been universally rejected by such experts as Skeat (1997).

7 Greek texts: Lührmann (2000) 106–131. English translation: Elliott (1993) 123–47.

8 50.3525, 6.849, 8.1081.

9 8.1081 (Lührmann (2000) 96–101).

10 P.Lond.Lit. 132.

11 Catullus 22.6–8.

12 Martial 14.190.

13 See Roberts and Skeat (1983).

14 Skeat (1982).

15 For general discussions, see Stanton (2004); Gamble (1995).

16 Roberts (1979) 26–48; Gamble (1995) 75–8.

17 65.4444.

18 42.3057 (BL 8). Stanton (1984) argues persuasively that nothing in the letter proves a Christian origin.

19 12.1464 (SP 2.318). Most recently: 58.3929. For the general procedure, see e.g. Potter (1990) 261–7.

20 Witnesses: 41.2990.

21 43.3119 (BL 7; 8), mentioning the '7th year' of an unnamed emperor, perhaps Valerian (AD 259/60).

22 42.3035. On such orders see p. 164.

23 Suetonius, *Claud.* 25.4.

24 PSI 14.1412.10 (completer text SB 12.10772) (BL 4; 5; 6; 7). In line 10 Rea (36.2785.2 note) recognised 'Chresian'. Others have suggested 'Chresimou', 'son of Chresimos'.

25 P.Laur. 2.42, fourth/fifth century AD? (BL 7; 8) (Tibiletti 34).

26 33.2673 (BL 8; 9; 10; 11).

27 Passion of St Dioskoros: 50.3529.

28 31.2601 (Naldini 35; NPP 69).

29 Pederast: Strato, *Anthologia Palatina* 12.6. Nero: Suetonius, *Nero* 39.2. List from Oxyrhynchos: 45.3239, see Skeat (1978). Christian equations: Skeat (1978). '616': 66.4499.323.

30 2.209 (van Haelst (1976) 490).

31 63.4365 (BL 11).

32 55.3787.24–5, 56–7 (BL 10 on the date).

33 The day of the Sun: Cod.Just. 3.12.2(3). The Lord's Day: 54.3759.38; see further 48.3407.

34 59.4003, fourth/fifth century AD.

35 Nile festival: 43.3148 (AD 424). The amulet-book (of uncertain provenance): P.Lond.Lit. 239.

36 16.1874 (Chapa (1998) no. 12).

37 Questions to the oracle: 6.925, 8.1150. Above, p. 176.

38 The amulet in the pocket: PGM XXXVI 40.

39 Against fever, SM 2; against tonsillitis, SM 5; 'Deliver Artemidora', SM 7.

40 Abrasax: 6.924.

41 *Commentary on St Matthew*, PG 58.6691.

42 Miniature codices: Turner (1977) 22–3 (on papyrus), 30–1 (more commonly on parchment). Psalm 90: e.g. 17.2065.

43 8.1077 (and pl. i) (van Haelst (1976) 341).

44 34.2684 (van Haelst (1976) 558).

45 The prayer: 3.407 (P.Lond.Lit. 230) (van Haelst (1976) 952).

46 7.1060 (van Haelst (1976) 957).

47 The rise of Latin in Egypt: Adams (2003).

48 Cribiore (1996) 388.

49 Roca-Puig (1965, 1977, 1994, 2000).

50 P.Bodmer XXVII, XLV–XLVI.

EPILOGUE

Sources. Most of Tryphon's papers were published in *The Oxyrhynchus Papyri*, vols. I and II (1898, 1899). The archive is collected and discussed by Biscottini (1966), who also prints full texts of pieces of which Grenfell and Hunt gave only descriptions (these texts were then reprinted in SB 10). An additional text published as 34.2720. For details of the story and further bibliography see Whitehorne (1984); Rowlandson pp. 112–18.

1 B. 1 (2.314 descr.) = SB 10.10220 (BL 7), joined by Vandoni to the end of B. 9 (2.288).

2 B. 7 (2.311 descr.) = SB 10.10223, May/July 23.

3 B. 9 (2.288), years 8–11 of Tiberius = AD 21/2–24/5.

4 B. 14 (2.322 descr.) = SB 10.10236.

5 B. 28 (1.39) (W.Chr. 456).

6 B. 38 (2.275) (W.Chr. 324; SP 1.13).

7 B. 14 (2.322 descr.) = SB 10.10236; 38 (2.275).

8 B. 30 (2.264) (M.Chr. 266).

9 B. 16 (2.319 descr.) = SB 10.10238, 16 December 37.

10 B. 31–2 (2.304 descr. = SB 10.10246; 1.99)? B. 35–6 (2.320 descr.; 2.318 descr. = SB 10.10248–9)?

11 B. 19 (2.251).

12 B 10 (2.282) (BL 8) (M.Chr. 117), AD 30–5.

13 B. 12 (2.267) (M.Chr. 281).

14 B. 17 (2.315 descr.) = SB 10.10239 (BL 7) (Rowlandson 89).

15 B. 23 (1.37) (BL 6; 8; 10) (M.Chr. 79; SP 2.257; NPP 17; C.Pap.Gr. 1.19; MZ 75; Rowlandson 91).

16 B. 24 (1.38) (BL 6) (M.Chr. 58).

17 B.26 (2.324 descr.) = SB 10.10244 (BL 7).

18 B. 33 (2.310 descr.) = SB 10.10247.

INDEX